I WISH I WAS ME

I WISH I WAS ME

The Autobiography

Pete Waterman

Virgin

First published in Great Britain in 2000 by
Virgin Publishing Ltd
Thames Wharf Studios
Rainville Road
London W6 9HA

A catalogue record for this book is available from
the British Library.

ISBN 1 85227 900 1

Typeset by TW Typesetting, Plymouth, Devon

Printed and bound in Great Britain by
Creative Print and Design (Wales), Ebbw Vale

Special thanks must first go to Paul Mathur,
without whom this book would not have been possible,
and also to Steve Jenkins, Melissa Harrison
and Stuart Slater.

Heartfelt thanks to the special women in my life,
Helen Dann and Jane Curtis,
and my loyal and faithful staff and friends,
Mark, Karl, Little Pete, Dan, Paul, Steve, Dan, Al, Tony,
Rene, Brian and Viv.

Dedicated to my wonderful children,
Paul, Pete, Toni and Charlie.

Contents

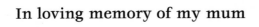

In loving memory of my mum

Introduction

T THE END OF 1999 I sat in the flat above my office in London and watched the builders rip my old recording studios apart. The building had been famous in earlier times, first as a power station and then as the photographic studios where Anthony Armstrong Jones met Princess Margaret. But that notoriety had been trumped by what I'd done there with my partners Mike Stock and Matt Aitken. Over a period of fifteen years we'd become the most successful hitmakers in the history of the record industry, outselling the Beatles and creating, with Kylie Minogue, Jason Donovan, Mel & Kim, Bananarama and many others, the most influential pop empire of modern times.

The records I've been involved with have sold over 500 million copies, and I've chalked up nineteen Number Ones in Britain alone. But four years earlier I'd seen my success almost snatched away from me, to the extent that people wouldn't even return my phone calls. Undeterred, I'd built my company back up and made it more successful than ever with the pop phenomenon that is Steps.

In November 1999 I'd finally ended my relationship with Mike Stock and Matt Aitken after a court case that had gone on for seven years and I'd been tempted, knowing that new studios would cost half a million pounds to build, to retire from the business. But I realised that I could never just walk away. Pop music meant too much to me and I knew that I hadn't even begun to deliver all that I was capable of. I saw the thirty years that had gone before as an apprenticeship and now I knew I'd learned what I needed to start the job properly. I wanted to carry on, to keep striving towards making ever greater records and to keep on living the dream that had been born back in Coventry in the sixties thanks to Motown and the Beatles.

My life has been an extraordinary journey, filled with highs and lows. Although I consider myself the luckiest man in the world, getting where I am has taken hard work and enormous resilience. People come up to me and say, 'I wish I was you', thinking that I've had a life of ease and luxury. I tell them that if that had been the case, I wish I was me too. The reality has been far tougher and the struggles long and hard.

At the end of 1999, as the builders finished gutting one set of studios, they started building a new set right next door. And I knew that it was time to close one chapter of my life and move on to the next.

This is the story of that first chapter and while it's never been easy, it's been one hell of an adventure.

1 The Sun Has Got His Hat On

I WAS BORN ON 15 January 1947, the worst day for weather in British history. The worst day of the worst winter. I was brought up with my dad telling everyone how, the night I was born, he was up on the roof trying to stop the snow falling on my mum. I was a breech birth, dead on arrival, strangled by the umbilical cord, but in 1947 there was always a midwife around, or someone to hatch, match and dispatch. This woman had sent my granddad over the road to the pub to get a bottle of brandy. He brought it back, she shoved a spoonful down my throat, whacked my arse and I promptly burst into life. Courtesy of Martell, I think it was. Starting life with a death certificate would have been a bit weird.

Being born just after the war, my early childhood was pretty bleak in terms of the world I came into. I was born in the corner house on Burlington Road in Stoke Heath, Coventry, where my mum and dad lived with my granddad. Across the road there was a former metal stamping works which had been bombed so it was nothing but craters and rubble. For a kid it was fantastic. Massive old mangled pieces of machinery melted by the heat of the fires and just left there. You can't beat bombs for making great playgrounds.

The unusual thing about the house was that in a long road, ours was the only council house, the rest were private. And behind us there was a council estate. That doesn't mean a lot now, but it did then. It meant that although we were on a council estate it wasn't like being on a council estate, because you were surrounded by mates whose parents had good jobs and were on a pretty good income. I didn't grow up feeling like a council house kid. We had curtains, even if they were cardboard.

My gran and granddad were from Leicester. My grandfather had been caretaker of Rugby School before going on to work for the Duke of Knarborough as his valet and then, as an upholsterer, he opened his own furniture shop in Coventry. My dad's parents were from Stanley in Newcastle. My gran walked down from Newcastle to Coventry in the Depression, so the family had roots stretching from Coventry and Leicester to Newcastle.

My mum's dad was great. A cantankerous old sod, he taught me how to cheat at dominoes. My dad's mum was an incredible, tiny lady. My dad used to take me down on the crossbar of his bike to see her every Sunday morning, to the posh side of the family. That side of the family all owned their own houses, they all had good jobs, and they were all choir singers. My Uncle Albert was a leading light in the Working Men's Choir and all that side of the family was very musical. If there was a family wedding you'd hear 'The Blaydon Races' sung spectacularly.

I was always closer to my mum's side of the family and although they weren't singers, my girl cousins on that side were my musical inspiration. Jean was sixteen in 1956 and into Johnny Ray and Bill Hayley. I used to go with my mum to their house every Tuesday afternoon to watch *Andy Pandy*, because they had a television. While my mum and auntie went over the road for a drink, Jean used to come home at lunchtime and I was subjected to all these rock'n'roll records. I can still remember listening to 'Just Walkin' In The Rain' by Johnny Ray like it was yesterday. It was different to anything I'd heard at home because my dad was a Deanna Durbin fan and it didn't sound anything like that.

We had the worst record player in the world at home. It was a wind-up gramophone with a broken spring so you had to turn the records with your finger. I tell you, I was bloody good at it. We only had three records in the house. One was Deanna Durbin. One was by Benjamin Gigli. And the other, which I remember best of all and I must have played five million times, was on Mayflower Records and it was called

'The Sun Has Got His Hat On'. I loved that record. You'd spin it with your finger and listen through the horn.

Jean had access to this thing that was a kind of stereo, because her dad, my Uncle Ernie, was a classical music fanatic and had a great radiogram for his Wagner records. Well, it wasn't really a stereo, but it had two speakers. Listening to records on it was awe-inspiring. Every Tuesday I'd go there with my mum on the number seven bus and walk across the bombed city centre to listen to Jean play these great records. Coventry was still makeshift, with a wooden Woolworths and seven-odd bombed buildings in every street, but there was a sense even then of it being the first of the brand new cities, of everything starting again.

I was brought up in a dirty, desolate, magical world. And of course there was poverty, but you just accepted it. We never used to have enough money to last the week, so my mum didn't put the electricity on until my dad got off the bus at the end of the street on the way back from work. She cooked his dinner in advance on the open fire, then when she saw him getting off the bus she'd put a bob in the meter and whack the food into the oven as the electricity came on. He never knew we went without electricity all the rest of the time, and I don't think he ever guessed.

I was brought up with my mum protecting my dad, and all of us, from the realities of life. We had no money, but I can't remember wanting for anything. My best mate, Keith Jackson, had fantastic toys though, because his dad had a good job as a toolmaker and I guess that was one of the things that made me aware we were poorer. He had the best train set, and model airplanes and all that. Living where we did gave me my love of trains that's stayed with me all my life. The railway was fifty yards down the road and you'd see coal trains going to the colliery all night. You'd sit in school and watch the trains going past all day. The trains were always there. So for me railways came to have a special aura. I always loved the enormity, the aesthetically pleasing design, the beauty of the carriages. It was more than just collecting the train numbers that appealed to me, although I was a trainspotter from 1955 up until I discovered girls. And as long as I can remember I have never, ever not been interested in trains.

5

Unsurprisingly, when I was young I only wanted to be a railwayman. Recently I've done some research into the Newcastle side of the family and found out that my great grandfather was a train driver on the Great Northern Railway, so maybe it's in the genes. My dad wasn't interested in trains, he worked in the aircraft industry and lived, breathed and slept aeroplanes, but I never got the bug. I found the aircraft industry very impersonal. There seemed to be no job satisfaction, but the world of the railways was completely different.

It was such a great time to be growing up in. Immediately after the war, things were tough, but it was all so exciting. And everything was still forming; the world seemed to be coming together. There was a kind of openness to everything. For instance, when I used to listen to *Workers Playtime* on the radio, there'd be a diverse selection of music. One minute it would be Mantovani, the next it would be Glenn Miller, Anne Shelton or Alma Cogan. Such an incredible range of music in one show, and although it all washed over me at the time, I'm sure deep down it had some effect on me.

Because I was born in 1947, when schools were ludicrously overcrowded, there wasn't the pressure there is today to go to school as soon as you were five. In fact I was seven and a half before I started school. There were 63 kids in my class and, to be honest, the teachers didn't really want another one. If you were quite happy sitting at home and your mother wasn't pushing you to go to school, you didn't go. There was no urgency, no one cared. And that was at the heart of my education. If I didn't turn up I was doing them all a favour. They didn't need another little scruffy urchin from Stoke Heath around. That's why I didn't learn to read and write. I wasn't even allowed a pen until I was 11; at school we were just supposed to write things out in the air with our fingers. That's not going to inspire anyone to learn, is it? If I liked a lesson I turned up, if I didn't I just used to go off and play around by the canal or among the bombed buildings. It was fantastic. Me and my mate Keith used to go off on walks with my granddad for miles and miles every day. The teachers didn't mind; it was one less schoolkid to deal with, and their classes were full to bursting anyway.

I spent a lot of time on my own as a child and this gave me a love of the countryside that's never left me. As much as I liked Coventry and its desolation, I also loved the English countryside in the fifties. I always wanted to own a farm. I didn't want to be a farmer, I just wanted to own a farm. The English countryside at that time was very different from what it is now – in fact contemporary India reminds me of what it was like back then. I loved the pace of life, the higgledy-piggledyness of the place. Those tight, complete communities regulating their own way of life. That contrast between the urban environment and the country was very important to me. That's the thing with the West Midlands: you've got these vital, sprawling industrial cities and just outside them this wonderful countryside.

Every Christmas we used to go to stay with my cousins and we'd travel there on the bus. We used to take the telly with us – and it wasn't a small thing, it was like a shed. We had to change buses, and lug it up a huge hill at the other end. And on top of that we had a turkey in a kit bag. It was like we were emigrating or something, but we were only going away for Christmas.

At that time there was still rationing, and one of the things that was rationed was coal. This gave me my first opportunity to turn adversity to my benefit. People used to have to take their ration books to coal merchants to buy half a ton or a hundredweight, but you had to take your own sack and go to pick it up. We had a coal merchant's in Shakespeare Street about half a mile from our house and when I was ten, me and my mum and my six-year-old sister Kay used to go down there with the pram, fill it with coal and drag it back. Before long I was doing this on my own. I'd adapted the pram chassis so it could get a hundredweight on it and I used to charge the neighbours sixpence to go and fetch their coal. I'd go up and down the street three or four times and make two shillings. Unless they were pensioners – my mum wouldn't let me charge them. It was tough, but I absolutely bloody loved it. I was the wagon train driver fetching the coal for the workers and having adventures in my head; pushing hundredweights of coal in the pouring rain and it was wonderful. I was working for a living.

I soon learned that people were lazy and would always offer you money to run errands. Sixpence here, tuppence there. Doing things that other people didn't want to do was very lucrative, and if you could do three jobs at once, that was even better. So I ended up with some money to spend on my train set or on a new football or whatever. If I wanted to buy anything, I had to finance it myself. There just wasn't any money from my parents for fripperies, they couldn't afford it.

But there were always opportunities to make money yourself. We had a lot of bad winters in the early fifties and there would always be someone who'd offer you threepence to clear the snow from the front of their house. If a neighbour offered me threepence for clearing snow I'd make cartoon characters look slow. I can still shovel like a madman.

There was a wonderful atmosphere when I was growing up, despite the fact that we had no money. We used to play cards or dominoes every single night and people would come round to play, bringing a bottle of beer or two. It was all very sociable. My dad was friendly with a lot of German prisoners of war who stayed on in England afterwards. He spoke fluent German so he befriended them, as well as a load of Russians and Ukrainians who'd also stayed on after the war because of the aircraft industry. They were living in awful hostels and so they were glad to be able to come round and see my dad. We used to have some very strange people round the house. They'd be talking to my dad in German and my granddad would be wandering around shouting at them and calling them Nazis. My dad also ran the local boxing, football and cricket teams, so you'd get all these kids knocking on the door and asking if he was coming out to play. He was a really important figure in the community while my mum was much more into the social side – she'd be down the pub chatting with the neighbours. The combination made for a sociable upbringing, with people coming in and out of the house all the time. The door was always open. In fact my twenty-first birthday present from my mum and dad was the key to the front door – literally. They had to put a lock on the door first so they could buy me a key, though. It was the first time I'd ever seen the door closed.

I didn't have much in the way of toys when I was small, but there were a few things in my bedroom that I always remember. One was a fantastic painting by a German prisoner of war of Donald Duck. Then there were a couple of toys. One was a stuffed giant panda from China made from real panda skin. The other was a rabbit with cellophane ears. Thankfully, I don't imagine they make stuffed pandas with real panda skin any more.

By the age of 11 or 12, I was going to school but not really enjoying it except for three subjects: maths, music and science. The other kids used to pay me to do their maths. They'd give me an apple or a bit of toast. I don't know why I was good at maths when I couldn't read or write. I suppose it was because numbers interested me and if something interested me I ended up being pretty good at it. If it didn't, I just pretended it wasn't there, and turned my mind off. English bored me. 'I before E except after C'. What was that all about? Why can you spell 'to' three different ways? We used to read a book about Fluff The Cat and Nip The Dog and it was like purgatory.

And then there was music. It wasn't a subject that had really appealed to me until I went to senior school. We had a teacher called Cyril, a young guy who was a jazz keyboard player. He was in a jazz band and played on Fridays down at the Mercer's Arms, which was about two streets from me, right by the Coventry football ground. He was a good guy and took time to connect with the kids he was teaching.

Now you've got to realise that at this time in my life I'd be going to bed by 7.30 every night. I'd be tired by half past six and actually ask to go to bed. So it was quite rare to stay up late, something which made my trip one Friday night down to the Mercer's Arms seem even more of an adventure. I couldn't get in, of course, because we were only kids, but we stood outside in the dark and listened to the strains of Dixieland jazz coming from the packed, rowdy local.

The next week I went to the teacher and said, 'I came to listen to you on Friday. I stood out back and listened.'

'What did you think?' he asked.

'Well,' I said, 'I quite liked it.' And I hummed him one of the tunes I'd heard.

'Have you heard that before?' he asked me.

'No,' I said, 'I just remembered it.'

I told him about how I had the knack of hearing a song once and remembering it. He didn't believe me, because you know how full of nonsense kids are, so he played me some songs and asked me what they were. Of course I could tell him, because they were all records I'd heard from my Uncle Ernie. And from then on he'd always ask me to stay behind after the class had finished and he'd play me different kinds of music, asking what I thought of it. Within about four months I was really into music in a big way. I waited every week for him to play me more music. And then I got wise and ended up hanging around after school had finished so he'd let me listen to more records. There I was, in 1958, listening to things like Louis Armstrong, Johnny Dodds, Thelonius Monk, all that. And this wasn't snobbery, it was stuff that I genuinely liked. Cyril told me the whole history of jazz, how all the movements fitted together and where they were all coming from, and without realising it he was giving me an enormous musical education.

At the same time I had my cousin Jean playing me things like 'Singin' The Blues' by Guy Mitchell and 'Just Walkin' In The Rain' by Johnny Ray, and then all the classical and choir stuff and George Formby and Alma Cogan coming from relatives. So suddenly I was exposed to an incredible diversity of music. And you don't think about it, it just slowly becomes a hugely important part of your life. I found I'd just taken on board all these bits and pieces and suddenly I was really into music. Not any sort of music more than any other, at that stage, just into music itself. Because I was dropping in and out of other people's lives there were no constrictions on the sort of stuff I was listening to; I was surrounded by people playing me what they liked. I wasn't interested in learning any instrument, I just wanted to hear music.

One thing I did like was singing. I used to stand up in front of the class during milk break and the teacher would get me to sing. While I was singing I used to pretend to play guitar. So there I was, doing all the movements as I sung, pretending I was Elvis Presley or Lonnie Donegan. I'd invented air guitar and I was still at junior school!

I loved church music then, and I still do. I'm not religious, but I find something incredibly moving about choral music.

If you're not moved by a song like 'Abide With Me' then, frankly, you're dead. I'd joined a choir when I was seven and carried that on right through my childhood. I used to hate choir practice, in fact I hated practising anything, I've always been much more into just getting on with it. Anyway, when I was about eleven we used to have to sing at weddings all the time, but I could see that most people weren't actually particularly religious. They only went to church because that was where they had to go to get married. And most people only knew about three bloody hymns.

One day I was sitting at Friday night choir practice and we were given the three hymns for the following week's wedding. I remember one of them was 'The Lord Is My Shepherd'. That was *always* one of them. And I thought, 'Doesn't anyone realise that "The Lord Is My Shepherd" is a funeral hymn? Doesn't he know it's about dying? Why does he want it sung at a wedding? And wouldn't it be better to have a hymn like "Love Divine All Love Excelling"?'

So I went over and talked to the best man and asked him if he went to church every week. He said he hadn't been since he was baptised. I said, 'I suppose you're going to pick the same three hymns that everyone else does?' and he admitted he was. 'Well,' I said, 'if he's your best mate and you want to impress him, how about letting me pick your three hymns. I'll teach the choir to sing them and then at the wedding I'll make sure they give it loads. They'll be singing like angels and you'll be the hero. It'll light the church up. And at the end of it, if we do a great job, drop me half a crown.'

'OK,' he said, 'you're on.'

So I picked three big, up, giving-it-rice wedding hymns and when the choirmaster came back in I'd circled them in the book, and of course he thought they were the ones the best man had chosen. I think he was a bit surprised that they weren't the usual ones, but he was ready to practise them. When he'd gone I turned to the other lads in the choir and I said, 'Right, there's tuppence in this for each of you who gives this the full volume. I want no pussyfooting about, we're going to make this really good. So you get two bob to split between you and I get sixpence for sorting it all out. Are we in?'

The next Saturday the wedding was fantastic, we sang like angels and the best man was a hero. He came over and congratulated me and handed over five bob. Five bob! That was double what he had said he was going to pay in the first place. My dad was only earning forty bob a week.

I told the vicar I'd picked the hymns and asked him if I could sort out the hymns for all the best men in the future and he agreed. So for a while that's what I did and we started to make a nice bit of money. Then I realised we were in a triangle of about four churches, and if we had bikes with gears I could probably do two weddings an hour on a Saturday morning. We could probably get in four weddings a day! From that day on we became the Flying Choir, going from church to church and planning it all like a military operation. And that was my first experience of what it was like to be an entrepreneur.

From then on school didn't matter because I realised I could make money without having to work like my dad. And I realised too, in a vague way at least, that music could pay, that there was a value to it. I guess the bottom line was that I could spot a pop tune. Sure, back then it was a *church* pop tune, but it was a pop tune all the same. I could spot what the public loved and what gave them emotion. There was no correlation between this and traditional education. It was just instinct.

Because music wasn't something I was being forced to listen to, it was something I could just respond to naturally and something I loved. And because it was beginning to make me some money, by the age of 12 I was building up a brilliant record collection. Each week before choir practice I'd go to the record shop in North Street, round the corner from the church, and listen to records for a couple of hours, and maybe buy a couple. They were about three shillings each. Records had become a major part of my life.

One of the older lads had a portable record player and we used to sit on the common and play Bobby Darin, Elvis Presley, Buddy Holly, all that. The records I had, though, were right across the board. I'd have jazz, folk, classical, pop, rock'n'roll, everything. I didn't have anything of my own to play them on until 1961 when my Christmas present was a Fidelity record player. I bought two records to go with it:

'Midnight In Moscow' by Kenny Ball and his Jazzmen, and 'Walking Back To Happiness' by Helen Shapiro.

By then I'd also started to collect American r'n'b records like 'Shop Around' by The Miracles. I'd got a crystal radio and I used to listen to the American Forces Network and they'd play all these records. There were two record shops in Coventry, Fennell's and Payne's, which stocked all that kind of music and the owners had good ears so they'd get the best records in. I was getting really early Motown stuff, or London America as the label they came out on then was called. I had a mate called Rob who played me things like Gary US Bonds, so I'd buy that stuff as well.

People started asking me to come along to their parties to play my records, for which I'd get paid half a crown. There were no such things as DJs then, but I got paid just to sit in the corner and change the records over. I suddenly found, at the age of 12 or 13, that I could pull all these birds. I was quite enjoying what was happening in my life.

Because of the era I grew up in, I was there at the beginnings of the first general youth culture. The invention of the portable record player and transistor radios meant that you got people hanging out on Sunday afternoons listening to Alan Freeman's *Pick Of The Pops*, playing records and being involved in what was a new, highly social scene. Suddenly the Flying Choir seemed very naive.

People today probably don't realise just how little freedom we had away from the home in the late fifties and how wonderful and new it was all becoming. This was a world where we still had National Service, so people would get to 17 and then disappear for two years. Previously when they came back they were just like their parents, but now they were coming back from Catterick with the record players and records they'd bought, and the afternoons on the common were one great big party. It was a massive social change. In the past music had been confined to the house and because you were respectful to your parents in those days, if your parents said, 'Turn that bloody row off', you turned that bloody row off. Now you could take that bloody row outside and play it with your mates. And if we were doing that then

I assume a large percentage of the young British public must have been doing it too. At the time we weren't aware of just how revolutionary it was, but looking back it's clear that something very important was being set in motion back then.

Everyone wanted to buy a record to play on the common that no one else had, so it became a bit of a competition. I bought *Melody Maker* and *NME* religiously every week and went through the American charts. In fact I cut out and kept every week's American charts for ten years from 1958. I'd buy at least one record out of them every week.

I was lucky that Auntie Elsie lived in a place near Leicester called Claybrook Magna, because it wasn't far from the American Air Force Base. My mum used to go down the pub and lead the singsongs and she'd get friendly with the American GIs who would bring things for me. I'd get *Marvel* and *Mad* comics, Levi's jeans and hand-me-down jackets and all these strange records that they'd got off the jukebox in the camp. The flights were coming in three times a week with all the latest American records, and when the GIs got bored of them they'd give them to me. As a result I'd have them months before they were released in England. Between 1959 and 1961 my whole life changed completely. Even though I was younger than some of the other people, I was accepted because I had the records they liked. My record collection was becoming integral to everything important in my life.

By 1960 school meant nothing to me. The things that were important were the things I did outside school, like playing records or trainspotting. I was supposed to turn up, but if I didn't, no one cared. I had no qualifications. In fact I remember turning up for one exam and walking out after ten minutes. I was a lost case. With the secondary school system at the time, people like us were only going to become fodder for industry anyway. You'd be working towards a choice of two jobs, each one at one of the worst factories in Coventry, places that made Charles Dickens' Britain look healthy. Most of them were casting companies where they couldn't keep any labour because the conditions were just so bad that no one stuck at it for long. These jobs were mindless, in dirty and appalling conditions.

I did have a couple of nice teachers in my last two years at school, particularly the headmaster and deputy head. They showed an interest in me that no one else had. I was in the bottom class and I was pretty much bottom of the bottom class, but they made me a prefect. They said I had great leadership qualities and they needed leadership in the bottom classes as well as the top; that they needed the worst part of the school to be led by someone who understood the problems of that part of the school – that someone was me.

We had Nigerian kids, Asian kids (the first was called Bluey Patel), even an Aborigine called Johnny Haynes, named after the footballer. I got along with these kids particularly well, especially the Asians. I think the people who made me a prefect had seen the way that I'd befriended them and taken them home for tea, all that, while the other kids had been a bit stand-offish, and they'd wanted me to know that they'd noticed. It was quite an honour, so while academically my last couple of years at school meant nothing, socially I'd been given some sort of reward. I used to have to work the school gates and report people who were late, but I did deals with the kids and I was flexible about reporting them. The lateness dropped. I wasn't treating them as my inferior, I was just saying, 'Come on lads, it's OK if you're a few minutes late, but don't take the piss.' Working the gate also meant I got to miss the first half-hour of the first lesson as well. It was a win-win situation all round.

I wasn't quite 15 when I left school at Christmas 1961. I can't remember a single thing I learned in the two years before that. All I remember is flying round singing songs with the choir for half a crown, sitting on the common playing records and going off trainspotting. Most important of all was music, but the railways came a pretty close second.

In 1958 I started to take railways very seriously. They had become a major passion. In between singing, if I hadn't got a wedding on, I was either at Rugby, Coventry, Wolverhampton or Birmingham stations looking at trains. I used to cycle all over the place or somehow get the money to go there.

In 1959, someone told me there was great trainspotting at Leamington Spa so I went there from Coventry. And, as with just about everything else in my life, I didn't do any research or anything, I just went. Now, the problem with this is that if, for instance, there happen to be two stations at Leamington Spa and you're sitting at the wrong one, you can be there for an awfully long time thinking it's rubbish and wondering what everyone else is going on about. The two stations are right next to each other and I could hear all these trains going by, but I couldn't see anything. So I stood on top of a gas mains box and I remember seeing a Great Western Hall Class go through in black mixed traffic lining, with copper chimney and brass safety valve. It was one of the most beautiful things I'd ever seen in my life. I stood watching the trains from the top of that gas box for hours, until a kid came along and pointed out that if I cared to walk through the underpass right next to me it would bring me out on the other station platform. I went over and I was completely smitten – I fell in love with Western Region trains. I used to cycle to Leamington whenever I could because it only took forty minutes. I'd be there all the time, just watching the trains.

Then, one day, my mate Michael, who was a big trainspotter, told me I ought to go to Wolverhampton and Oxley and Snow Hill in Birmingham. So off I went to Birmingham. First time I'd ever been there in my life. I had no idea where I was going. I got a porter to tell me how to walk over to Snow Hill and off I trotted. And to this day I can remember the sight and the smell of what I saw. There were steam engines everywhere, this overwhelming noise and a huge sense of beauty. I got a platform ticket and I spent all day there. I went again the next week and the next one. Then I went off to the sheds round the area where they kept the engines and got thrown out with a thick ear.

Eventually I rolled up in Wolverhampton and it was magic. One of the great moments in my life. It was the most bizarre and wonderful chaos. I remember walking round the wall, over the canal and coming across this extraordinary cauldron of activity. There was so much debris, steam, and the smell of hot oil. It was fantastic, and it changed my life. From then on, every weekend I'd do the rounds of all the sheds, covering most of the West Midlands. How could school ever compete with that?

By 1960 British railways were well into their modernisation programme, so every railway sidings had scrapped engines sitting there. They used to put sacks over the chimneys and just leave them there in rows. I used to sit in these engines for hours with the egg sandwich and Thermos flask provided by my mum and just soak up the atmosphere. Mates of mine were doing the same thing and at school we used to swap the shed plates from the front of the engines. These were the little plates on the front of the engines that told them which shed they were supposed to go back to. They used to change hands at school for a shilling a time, so I started buying a few, especially the local ones. You could clean them up, paint them, and put them on your wall.

One day I met a kid in Wolverhampton who told me about an engine which was just falling to bits. We got some tools and took the number plate off the side of the engine and took it home, and I did it up really nice. I kept on doing that, buying stuff from school mates and building up a bit of a collection. Then one day all these police came to the house to arrest me. They told me they'd arrested my mate Michael, too, and they were doing us for receiving stolen property. I just thought it was all scrap, but they said it was the property of the railways.

When they saw my collection they couldn't believe how beautifully I'd cleaned all the stuff up. A couple of weeks later I got summoned to court at Wolverhampton, but they realised that what I'd done wasn't done out of vandalism, it was out of a genuine love for the trains. They couldn't believe it when I told them how I used to take a rag down to the sidings and spend an afternoon cleaning the old, scrapped engines that were sitting there. The judge was lenient. He fined me five shillings and ordered me to go to the works at Wolverhampton every Saturday and make tea for the people there. I couldn't believe it: this wasn't punishment, this was a reward! They even sent me a ticket to get there!

Because I was there every week there was a job for me there when I left school. Ironically, knocking off all these bits and pieces got me my first job – I didn't even have to go for the interview. But there I was with a job as a labourer on the boilers and it was one of the best jobs I ever had in my life.

It was tough, and often so cold that we used to sit in wheelbarrows of asbestos to keep warm, but the people there were the most wonderful I ever met. I loved the camaraderie, the sense of honour, and the knowledge and passion of the railwaymen. They'd been there since the turn of the century, they'd seen the whole industry grow. They weren't highly paid, but they loved trains. I was among kindred spirits and I found out you're either a railwayman or you're not. You either love them or can't understand what people see in them. The bottom line is that I'm passionate about railways, full stop.

I was there for 14 months, but by then steam was being phased out. There was talk of me moving to Swindon, but I didn't want to move away from home, so I had to leave the job. And I still regret, in every way other than financially, that I didn't follow a railway career. What the job gave me was respect for attention to detail, for complete dedication to something you believed in. And I've never forgotten that.

2 A Hard Day's Night

WHEN I LEFT SCHOOL my life was split in two. There was the church gang and another gang who were into cycle speedway and record collecting. I was kind of floating between the two. Gradually, though, my contact with the church gang began to wane and I started to hang out with people who were older than me. They were a bit more streetwise, although by today's standards they were incredibly well behaved. The church kids would go to the cinema to see *El Cid*; the other gang would go and see *Dr No*. It was a very controlled rebellion. The older kids though, they knew girls, and girls who weren't just mates' sisters. Now, I wasn't particularly interested in girls at first and frankly couldn't be bothered with them. But we started going up to the Locarno club in Coventry and it was different. You couldn't just dance on your own or you would have been thrown out, so you had to learn a bit about chat-up lines. I loved dancing so I had to meet girls if I was going to be able to dance.

I was in one of the chorister's football teams although I wasn't much good at sport. We used to call in at a café called the Café Sinclair, which was the place to be seen at the time. It had red stools, mirrors, the lot. Having a milk shake there was about as outrageous as our choir got. But by then I was bit wiser than the rest of the gang and I had better chat-up lines than they had. So whereas theirs was 'What hymn will you be singing next Sunday?', mine was 'What are you doing later?'

When I met a girl down there called Irene Blake, who'd gone to my school and who now looked like Connie Stevens with all the hair and everything, I wasn't as shy as they were about chatting her up. I got her to go with me to a party and started going out with her. She was fantastic, but suddenly she wanted to see me every night and I didn't have any of my freedom any more. How was I going to be able to go off looking at trains and stuff? She was a great person but she started talking about getting engaged and it did my head in.

Around this time, in 1962, I'd gone into a record shop in North Street and met the EMI rep. He was trying to sell the manager of the store a new record and because he knew I was a big record collector he asked me if I wanted to have a listen and tell him what I thought.

'I've got this record,' he said, 'by a new group called the Beatles. The track's called "Love Me Do" and it's going to be played on Radio Luxembourg.'

It was a white label, Parlophone, with a big, red 'A' on it. I've still got it to this day. It started playing and it was amazing. I instantly realised that it sounded just like a tune by one of my favourites, Leroy Van Dyke, but it was still fantastic. He gave me a copy of the record and I went round playing it to everyone saying, 'You've got to listen to this. The Beatles. Brilliant.'

There used to be a place in Coventry called the Matrix Ballroom, which was a canteen-cum-ballroom for the Matrix Machine Tool Company. Every Saturday night they had a big American act like Little Richard or Gene Vincent. And once a month they had a dinner dance, so they moved the pop night to the Friday night when they'd have lesser acts.

Back then no one could put on anything that went past ten-thirty on a Friday night and besides, there were no buses after eleven. There was no such thing as nightlife since you had to be at work on Saturday morning.

Every ballroom had a policeman in it and a works fireman. These people all had to have tea breaks, so the group would go on, then it would all stop for the tea break. The act would stop dead. The boys would be on one side of the ballroom and the girls the other, and you could only dance with the same girl for three or four dances or you were asked to leave. These were not wild affairs. There was a dance band and then a pop group and it was seven shillings to get in. That was entertainment in the early sixties.

It was 1962 and I was nearly sixteen years old. I'd been brought up in post-war Britain where everything was pretty grey, I was living in Coventry which was the most modern city in Britain, a city built around the ideology of the shopping precinct, but still nothing worked. Everyone was working a 47-hour week and it was bloody bleak. Whichever way you went you were surrounded by rules because it was still such an incredibly rigid, disciplined society. London may have had the teddy boys, but the provinces were regimentally disciplined. Anybody who says it wasn't like that is lying. People might have been shaking a few feathers, but there was no revolution going on.

And then the Beatles played the Coventry Matrix for eight bob. I couldn't believe it, but sure enough, they were booked. I didn't take Irene, I went down there on my own. And it was awesome. You can't overestimate just how important that night was. There I was at the first gig the Beatles played as the Beatles. The night before they'd been the Silver Beetles, but they'd got this gig for sixty quid and it paid for their petrol to get them back from Hamburg. So they played it. And I was there.

They had a blue van with writing all over it, and they had Vox amplifiers, which was already pretty unusual. Then they came onstage and they were wearing jeans and quirky jackets. They had short hair, but it was sort of thick. Back then every group was like the Shadows, walking round the stage in time and everything. The Beatles didn't do that.

I'd met them earlier round the pub after they'd set up, and they were really friendly. I remember talking to George Harrison about his Chet Atkins guitar, which was the guitar everyone wanted. Everybody else had Fenders. And Paul had a funny-looking bass that was the wrong way round. I hadn't been to Liverpool, so I couldn't understand their accents half the time. I thought they were German. But anyway they were really nice to talk to.

There were about a hundred people at the gig. The Beatles hit the stage, went, '1,2,3,4 . . . Well she was just seventeen . . .' and it just blew your head off. No one started their gigs like that with that rush of energy. It was the first time anyone had ever even brought an amplifier on stage with more than ten watts of power. It was loud and exciting and just raw energy, but with these great pop songs. There was none of that onstage choreography, just all these great songs one after the other. I felt punch-drunk watching them. Then, at the point when they were supposed to play the National Anthem like everyone did those days, they did a drum roll and went straight into 'Twist And Shout'. The policeman almost had a heart attack. Suddenly this was a real revolution and I knew that whatever badge it was that these lads were wearing I had to have it, I had to be a part of it.

The next day I was in Woolworths Café and I was telling everyone I knew that they had to go and see the Beatles the following week at the Nuneaton Co-op Hall. So we all went, about forty or fifty of us, and this time there were seven hundred people there. By the end of that night those seven hundred people were going bananas. The next week they were at Leicester Corn Exchange and this time there were thousands there. This was something that was just exploding in the space of a month. In addition all these other groups were coming along, like Herman's Hermits and Billy J Kramer, so I went to the manager of the Locarno and persuaded him to book Kramer and his band the Dakotas. So suddenly I'm tipping people off about which bands to book. I was making my first real connection with the music industry, although my only motivation was to get into the Locarno for free, because it was somewhere I could get a drink. I couldn't drink at the pub over the road from my house because, what with all the drama the night I was born, everyone knew exactly how old I was.

One night I took Irene down to the railway line. The Fyffes banana vans used to be parked in the sidings by my house, so we went to sit in one of them. I was lying on my back looking up at the stars, singing something like 'The Night Has A Thousand Eyes', when suddenly a sound came wafting from across the canal. It was a guy playing a harmonica and he was playing 'Love Me Do' in the dark. It was a defining moment in my life. I suddenly knew that whatever I ended up doing in my life it would be something to do with music.

I got straight up and took Irene home. Then I went back to my house and sat there and realised that anything that could affect me the way that tune had, as it wafted over to me, was something I *had* to be part of. I just knew that there was something magical about it and that nothing else mattered, not even girls.

That Christmas, 1962, I said to my mate Keith, 'We've got to buy some musical instruments and start a group. Get some mates in and write some songs.' Everyone thought I was barmy and no one took it particularly seriously. That's the way I've found things usually are. But the idea was in our heads.

I got laid off from the railway, signed on the dole, spent the money on a Buddy Holly record and my mother gave me a clip round the ear. So I went off and got a job as a gravedigger, which wasn't a complete success. In fact it only lasted two hours. Then I got a job in my local foundry as a clipper, which was even worse and only lasted ten minutes! Finally Keith's dad got me a job at G.E.C., the General Electric Company. It brought in a regular wage, but the job itself was completely unimportant. Every spare moment I had was spent listening to music, buying music, talking about music, whatever I could do to be surrounded by music. When the Beatles album came out I skipped work in the morning so I could buy it and go and learn all the songs by the afternoon. I was completely obsessed with and possessed by music. Even the railways had taken second place.

I went to see loads of bands, including the Rolling Stones, who were just starting. I approached some of the people who put the bands on and asked if I could play records during the tea breaks. Anything to get me involved in the whole thing.

I hated working in the machine shop at the G.E.C., I didn't like all the dirt. So I moved into the telecommunications department or, as it was called then, the telephone division. I liked it there, because it was clean and full of women. The job involved getting the jobs ready for the women to wire. And it was there that I met a girl called Anne who went on to be my first wife. I started to revert to hanging around with my mates at church, thinking about getting a group together. My mum and dad had got involved in the local Working Men's Club and they had a concert room there where you could go and practise. So my mates and me started this band called the Pilgrims and we used to do a regular turn. We were probably the worst thing most people had ever heard, but we were having fun. I was serious about it, but no one else was. I even went out and bought a proper guitar. We did a few original songs and a load of cover versions of songs that no one else had ever heard.

By now I was getting quite involved in the whole music thing. I knew all the people at the record shops, I'd got friendly with the up-and-coming bands and, through a mate who was social secretary at the G.E.C. Apprentices' Club, I even got to book the Rolling Stones for a gig around the time that they put out 'Come On', before they were really famous. I think we paid them £80. And then the next week I got the Who for the Locarno in Coventry for £65. I'd started to get to know the people from the agencies and the people who booked bands. It wasn't making me any money, but it got me in free, sometimes got me some free records or some beers with my mates. I'd begun to create a little scene for myself, but there was no formality to any of it. It was all based around friends of friends, very small time. I was networking, but not consciously. It was more just hanging around.

By 1965 the whole Beatlemania phenomenon had gone barmy. Looking back, the whole thing seemed to take just five minutes to explode. They were putting albums out every few months and it really squashed your life up. You'd be having all these new experiences, doing different things and it had all been and gone in six months – and then you were onto something else. For a while at least I was in a band called Tomorrow's Kind, who actually looked like they might have gone on to be famous. They didn't, of course, but we did pick up a bit of a local following, and we started gigging three or four nights a week, while I was still holding down the day job at the G.E.C. That continued for a couple of years, but I eventually realised that I didn't really have any genuine talent. I could fake it like buggery, but I was never going to be top of the charts.

One night in 1966 we were playing a gig and one of the other bands didn't turn up, so I dashed home and got my records, came back and played them before the band came on. Now no one really did this at the time and the landlord of the pub where we were playing said he really liked it. He offered me ten bob to come back again and play records the following week. This wasn't some sort of complicated system. It was a record player with a microphone next to it going through the PA, but for ten bob, I wasn't about to complain. So by a quirk of fate, just because the other group hadn't turned up, I went from being the lead singer in a not very good band to being the only DJ in Coventry. Just about the only live DJ anywhere for that matter; Jimmy Savile was probably the only person doing it. He wasn't known as a DJ of course, he was just known as an Assistant Ballroom Manager. We'd heard people playing records on the pirate radio stations like Radio London or Radio Caroline North and I'd met Jimmy a couple of times and found what he did quite inspiring. I began to play records more than I played instruments, and, because I'd got to know the right people, I started to get people asking me to play records.

This was the middle of the whole mod thing, with people lobbing deckchairs at the rockers at Margate and everyone doing drugs. I couldn't do drugs, though, because I had to play records. So while everyone else was necking Black Bombers and French Blues and Purple Hearts or whatever, I was sitting at the back with half a pint of beer playing records. However, I started to hang around with people who would later go on to be known as hippies. They weren't hippies then, they were more beatniks, but two years down the line they were going to turn into hippies. They were into all sorts of really strange music, the sort you'd hear on John Peel's *Perfumed Garden* show. Now, I was a Motown DJ. Pop music, that was what I played, so all this weird stuff was coming from a completely new place for me. These guys were hanging round with the likes of Graham Bond, Jeff Beck and Eric Clapton, so I got to meet them too. By this time my marriage was in trouble, so I was spending less and less time at home and more and more time with these guys. I guess they were student types and they were certainly a lot more worldly-wise than I was. They were dropping acid and introducing me to Syd Barrett and Soft Machine, people like that. One day they even turned up with Bob Dylan. And because these people were so far ahead of their time, I was meeting all these incredible people like Fleetwood Mac before they were famous. I came down to London a couple of times, but most of this was going on in the Midlands, round Coventry or Birmingham. And in the midst of it all I'd started to really take the DJing seriously.

Some people I knew had opened a club above a pub, the Bulls Head in Coventry, called Stocks and it was really good, but it was a bit amateur. It was a tiny place, but it was better than the scout hut that they'd just been thrown out of for being too noisy. They played Sam and Dave and had flashing lights, which made it a discotheque. And that was what everyone called a discotheque then. The real ones like Barbarella's in Birmingham didn't start until 1969 or 1970 so this was a very innocent, ramshackle scene.

I opened a 'club' called the Floorboards Club a couple of nights a week, which brought in thirty or forty quid a week. I'd spend twenty of it on records and most of the rest on transport and stuff, but as a club it really took off. It gave me an education in the logistics of running a club, in terms of where you bulk-buy soft drinks cheaply and where to get good doormen, and how important it was to have the right music. And before too long I was DJing at loads of other places as well and I had started to do really good business. Such good business that it even used to affect the attendances at the Mecca club, the biggest in town. I'd built my own decks and my own sound system and by 1968 the whole thing was really taking off.

DJs were beginning to get popular, but because I'd already been doing it for a couple of years, I had a head start on everyone else. And my contacts were paying off. One week I'd be doing a wedding or a twenty-first birthday, the next I'd be doing warm-up DJing for Fleetwood Mac and Joe Cocker's gigs in the Midlands. The bottom line was that I was entertaining people. I played 'Jump Up And Down And Wave Your Knickers In The Air' three times on the run at a Pink Floyd gig one night just to annoy the punters. I'd be playing progressive rock a couple of nights a week and Motown and underground soul stuff the rest, working almost every night of the week all the time.

I wasn't making any money, but I wasn't doing it for the money, I was doing it because it was so exciting and I loved music more than anything else. I was playing all around the Midlands, and I built up a good reputation as someone who knew what was going on and someone whom the promoters could call at short notice and rely on. Not that this was even remotely like the big time. Everything was so amateur then. Things would be run out of the back room of a pub or the front room of a butcher's. It wasn't glamorous. It wasn't professional and, in terms of how the industry works today, it was no big thing. But to me it was a very big thing indeed. It was *everything*. I'd started to be certain about wanting a career in music and I felt like I was getting closer to the source.

Larry Page was a Mecca manager. He managed one of the two Mecca Ballrooms in Coventry, the Orchid, which was near where I lived. And it was rough, by God it was rough. Larry, being a Londoner, knew everyone, and he managed the Kinks as well. So he bought them up to play and I met them. He was incredibly 'in' and doing all the booking himself. He used to put the groups on under moody promoters' names, but it was really him doing the promoting and he was putting all his own groups on. It was fantastic for me because I got to see people like the Kinks, the Troggs and Georgie Fame when they were really raw and before they were famous. Larry was a bit of a wide boy, but he would introduce you to talent. He was a big name in Coventry because he had a foot in the London camp, and he was one of the few people who did have an idea what pop music was all about. He was a great sounding-board. He must have been 25, 30 at the time, very flash, very astute, but he'd always have time to talk to you. And that was important, because we were still pushing, still learning. Putting 500 kids in a pub which should have held 150, probably inciting violence with the volume and ferocity of the music.

I was never into the fashion side of it all. I have never seen the correlation between the music and the fashion. Sure I wore the clothes, but I wasn't a fashion victim. Maybe that's one of the reasons I've done what I've done for so long. The only thing that matters to me is if the music's any good or not. And it was the same back then. If the music was good, I'd play it. At the time that probably held me back whereas if I'd been trendier, I might have made it bigger quicker. But then again I wouldn't have spent the time building up the knowledge that I had and got into so much different music. I even got into the Beach Boys when I was eighteen, certainly way before John Lennon got into it.

Now there's a first. What the hell was a boy from Coventry doing listening to surf music? There aren't many beaches in Coventry. You couldn't 'hang ten' down the Trent. And to be honest, it was the music that attracted me much more than the imagery of America. British films had far more fascination for me than Hollywood. I grew up watching George Formby and Gracie Fields and that was the iconography that appealed. But the Beach Boys didn't half write some good songs. I loved a lot of American music, but an awful lot of it was rubbish as well. I didn't fall in love with the American Dream, I fell in love with great music.

The usual way to get into the record industry back then was to become a rep, taking the records round to try and sell them to the shops. The whole industry was still based around London. I'd managed to get involved without becoming a rep and without living in London. I was a DJ without going down the expected route of becoming manager of one of the dance halls. The industry was still in its infancy and it was frighteningly amateur, but it still had some unwritten rules. I'd broken most of them, and I'd gone through doors that no one else had been through. I'd even built most of the doors by bringing enthusiasm and hard work to a business that, I have to reiterate, was a world away in terms of naivety from the record industry people know today. I'd not done any of this with any focussed plan in mind, but without knowing it I'd moved everything in my life towards the next step.

And I'd put the connections in place over a period of four or five years. Now I was ready to make them work. And the first casualty of that was my marriage.

3 The Year Of Decision

PRETTY MUCH AS soon as I'd married Anne, in 1970, I'd started DJing six nights a week. To be fair, it was as much because I needed to work those six nights as because it was a job offered to me. I'd rented a flat, which was quite expensive what with buying furniture and everything, so I had to supplement my income from my day job. Without the DJing I couldn't have afforded to be married. And of course working all that time meant that the marriage suffered. It was never going to work out. I'd been at the G.E.C. for four years and the job just wasn't paying enough.

Musically, the time was marvellous for me, but personally things were very traumatic. Despite the way the DJing was taking off, I felt completely unfulfilled. Sure, things were going well for me musically, but I just couldn't reconcile myself to the responsibilities and expectations that came from being a married man. I was very set in my ways, always have been, and I found it all a heavy burden. I'd be working with Joe Cocker one night, then coming back and having to worry how the rent was going to be paid at the end of the week. I did all right at it for a bit, I coped, but nothing more than that. Anne wasn't interested in the music business, so I felt completely alone. I only had self-belief about making music into a career, I didn't have anyone else supporting me. As a result I began to feel very dissatisfied, very trapped. I was living a dream that stopped at seven every morning when I left for the factory, and started again at half past seven in the evening when I left the house. And I knew it couldn't go on.

I'd started getting offered quite good gigs from promoters, now that DJs had become more acceptable. I'd be given gigs playing in front of 800, 900, 1,000 people, at dance halls and swimming baths. I'd begun to build up a dedicated following, and the kids used to come and see me on a Saturday rather than go down to the Locarno on a Monday. It really hurt the Locarno's figures. This was a world where there wasn't a whole host of clubs, so if one was more successful than the rest, it took away from the others.

I made my nights different from the competition, more musical. We didn't have a live group playing at the Floorboards Club, just records. And whereas most people with small clubs would make them very intimate, I did the opposite. I made it very in-your-face, very up-and-at-you. Boom!

Because I've always been a friendly sort of bloke, I soon got to know all the kids. One Saturday night a kid turned up who was assistant manager of the Locarno, and he asked me if I wanted to do a spot down there on a Monday night, which I did. It was so successful, because many kids would specifically come and see me play, so he offered me the residency. I was probably making more money from doing the single gigs, but to be the resident DJ at the biggest club in Coventry was a massive leap forward.

It also meant that I was working until two in the morning, with obvious ramifications at home and arguments about me never being around. I knew that I had to decide what I was going to do, but I kept putting it off.

This was the time of the skinheads. I was playing Motown and a bit of reggae. I got a gig at Smethwick Baths promoted by an old friend of mine. They'd been having a lot of trouble with the skinheads, who'd threatened to smash up the town hall unless the council put something on for them on a Saturday night, so the council organised a dance. There was a huge stage with a disco rig and it was quite unlike anything I'd seen before. It was the first time I'd ever played anywhere so big with such a big booming sound. And it was heavy. I had the wrestler Giant Haystacks as my bouncer and I was thinking, 'Why does a DJ need a bouncer?', especially one the size of a shed. The organisers told me to get on and play records, and to carry on playing records whatever happened. If there was any trouble I was to tap Haystacks on the shoulder. Now that sounded a bit ominous for starters.

Anyway, off we went. They'd put a big fake floor over the swimming pool and all around were these people standing in little groups. Perched so high up looking down on them I could see distinct paths between the groups of people. It was all going well until at about half past nine, ten o'clock, an almighty fight started. There were bouncers to the left of me, bouncers to the right, chairs flying all over the place. I was thinking, 'What the hell am I doing here?' while in front of me a policeman was getting kicked and beaten, but I carried on playing. The fighting stopped as quickly as it had started and everyone carried on dancing. However, when the kids left at the end of the night, there was blood everywhere. It was horrendous.

I played this place every week for about three weeks and the violence was beginning to get gratuitous. I realised that the different groups of people I could see were all football supporters from teams round the West Midlands – Coventry, Birmingham, Wolves, West Brom, all the gangs in their crombies with their football badges on their lapels. And what was happening was that by ten o'clock they'd all had a bit too much to drink and one person would deliberately walk into the wrong circle so, wallop, it would all go off. Eventually they worked out that it was one particular West Brom fan who was starting it every time. By this time the council decided they'd had enough and they were ready to close it down, but the promoter was getting a lot of people in every week, and obviously making a few bob, so he wanted it to keep going. It was a lucrative gig.

One Saturday night I came in and the promoter said to me, 'I've got these two faces in tonight to help you out. If you see a problem, just point it out to them and they'll sort it out.' He introduced me to two short guys who must have weighed eighteen stone each, and spoke with real Cockney accents. They had a crate of Guinness each and they were playing cards at a little card table behind a curtain.

Half past nine and the usual fight started so I went and told these guys. Now, they were hard, but they were only little, and the skinhead causing the trouble was well over six foot tall and a good twenty-two stone. It didn't stop the Cockney faces going to try and sort it all out, though. They went up to this giant skinhead, but he looked down at the two dwarves and just laughed at them. That did it. One of the guys jumped up into the air and while he was still in mid-air he whacked this skinhead and broke his jaw. I was playing records and I could hear his jaw crack above the music, it was that loud. I can even remember the record that was playing at the time, it was 'Cherry Oh Baby'. And as the skinhead's jaw broke, it seemed as if everything went into slow motion. All the other skinheads just melted back in terror and the fighting stopped. The chap got hauled off to hospital and everyone went back to dancing, while the bouncers went back behind the curtain to play cards.

But it wasn't over yet. Near eleven o'clock there was a sudden uproar and all these police came through the door yelling 'Get the hell out of here, now!' The place emptied in five minutes. We went to the front steps and the street outside was solid with skinheads, all chanting 'We want the Cockney bastards! We want the Cockney bastards!' It looked like there were thousands of them and it was mayhem. The police were too frightened to tackle the situation because anything could have happened. Anyway, these two Cockney guys came out and said, 'Don't worry boss, we'll sort it out.' They went out to face the skinheads, who'd got the guy with his jaw wired up leading them. There was a stand-off. They kept taking a step closer to each other until suddenly the two Cockneys each pulled a couple of guns out of their coats, pointed them at the skinheads and said, 'If we're going, we're taking the rest of you with us!'

You've never seen skinheads run away so fast in your life. They dived into doorways, pillar boxes, letterboxes. It was like a cartoon and the street was empty in thirty seconds. The policemen went white and passed out. And these two Cockneys never batted an eyelid. That was my introduction to ballrooms.

The next day, a Sunday, I went to see Bob, the manager at the Locarno, to see about starting my job on the following Monday. Now, Coventry's Locarno was the most peculiar ballroom on the whole circuit because it was originally built as a department store until the council realised their city centre, designed as a prototype for the city of the future, didn't have any entertainment venue in it. As a result, they'd converted a huge store into a ballroom. They had to build a glass tower outside so that people could go up the stairs to get in. Bob had told me that every Sunday they had an Irish night, and to pop in to have a drink with him in his office beforehand to discuss terms. So down I went.

As I went up those stairs to see about my new job, there was a guy walking past holding his left ear in the palm of his hand, blood everywhere. He was being shouted at by a woman, who'd obviously bitten it off. Saturday night I've got people shooting skinheads, Sunday I've got someone with their ear bitten off! I knew I was going to be working in a whole new world. I took the job.

I used to have to do two sessions during the day on a Saturday: the under-12s in the morning and the under-17s in the afternoon. Then I'd have to sweep up the ballroom and change the lightbulbs. Saturday nights I'd work somewhere else. One night I was doing a club in Birmingham that rival gangs were trying to take over and I sat in the corner while people lobbed petrol bombs at each other. It was unreal. But back then four or five different gangs ran the nightclub scene and those people weren't saints.

Now, the Mecca scene was completely different. That was whiter than white and if you had a criminal record there was no way you would get a job. So I was moving between both these worlds and trying to fit into both of them. It was a very weird situation. The one thing that the two had in common was the violence of the crowds. In the sixties when you went out, there would always be a violent undercurrent. And the one thing you learned quickly was how to stop a fight. You were taught to spot trouble. Even today I can walk into any room and know if there's going to be a problem. At Mecca you were taught how to stop it before it started and doormen, inside the club at least, rarely threw a punch, whereas at private clubs violence was part of the entertainment. At the birth of club culture there was an uneasy peace between Old Britain and New Britain, with all these different gangs trying to muscle in on each other's territory, but doing it in a gentlemanly way. I remember seeing the Krays at a club in Birmingham; the owners were looking to expand their empire and had been approached by a gang from the North East, but preferred to get a London firm in. That sort of thing was just accepted. It wasn't unusual to see someone shot in a club, or they'd be taken out and you'd hear they'd been beaten to death with a baseball bat.

Of course the clubs didn't get closed down because the police didn't know it was going on. They never came into the clubs if they could help it. And police in 1968/1969 couldn't have controlled that violence. I saw violence every night. But I tell you, it wasn't half exciting.

There would be right royal battles all the time. Every town in Britain had the biggest, roughest families involved in some sort of feud. Friday night the families would end up down at the Locarno and the fights would start. The Locarno manager had almost judicial power, because it was he who decided whether they got in again the next week. As a result fights would end as soon as he came along. They couldn't afford to be banned because they knew that if they were they couldn't go along there the next Friday to have another fight. So you'd have this bizarre situation where guys would be put away for manslaughter, yet would be scared to death of the ballroom manager. The most violent of villains would be like teddy bears with the manager and the staff. One night you'd be chatting away with someone all friendly about records, then you'd read in the paper that they went out the next day and chopped someone else in half.

The DJ was seen as someone these people could trust. The men would usually ask me to look after their girlfriends for the night. They knew that all I cared about was the music, so they'd get all these girls dancing round in front of the stage by me and they knew I'd look after them. And because I looked after their girlfriends, the guys looked after me, so I was never in trouble. If anyone threatened me, these guys would have beaten them up outside. Mind you, some of the women were just as violent. I've seen women put stiletto heels through someone's skull, women who were the nicest girls you could meet in your life. I also met many of the music business legends at that time like Don Arden, the

Futrells, George Henry, people who were at the heart of a whole scene that you wouldn't know about unless you were part of it. There were people on that scene who were infamous; if you wanted to succeed at anything, you couldn't do it without going through them. And you had to learn where not to tread or your club would be closed down the next day.

By 1969 I was getting offered loads of work, I'd stabilised Mecca's audience and I was pulling in big crowds wherever I played, but I was still working in the day at G.E.C. Then, in 1971, I had my first son, Paul. And whilst it was wonderful to be a dad, I just couldn't cope with the responsibility. It was like being in a cage. The life I had outside the home was fantastic, musically and socially fantastic, but my life at home just wasn't working. I decided that the worst thing I could imagine would be that my son would get to fifteen and I'd still be working at the G.E.C., and I would blame him for me not having been able to make the most of my life. It sounds selfish, but that was how I felt. I left my wife and kid, and we got divorced several years later.

Around that time, one of the guys who used to book me all the time said to me one night, 'I've decided not to use you any more.'

'Why not?' I asked.

'Because,' he said, 'you've let yourself go. You're a scruffy bastard.'

And I was. I was fat, I'd got a big beard and long hair, but that was the look then. Unfortunately it wasn't the look he wanted. He wanted somebody smart, more old-fashioned.

That, on top of everything, was just too much, because this guy had given me a lot of work and had good contacts and I liked his clubs a lot.

I decided to go on a diet and change my lifestyle, while still working flat out. It wasn't a bright idea. I walked five miles back home one night in the pouring rain, having hardly eaten for weeks, and ended up catching pneumonia. I went home and slept for two days without waking up and when I did wake up my face was all swollen. I had to go to hospital, where they found I had 109 ulcers in my mouth. I couldn't eat, so I had to go on a drip and I lost three or four stone while I was in there. I shaved my hair and beard off, went and borrowed some clothes from a mate and went to see my mum. Now, I didn't even recognise myself in the mirror, so I shouldn't have been surprised that she didn't know who I was. The change in the way I looked was dramatic.

I knocked on the door.

'Yes?' asked my mum when she answered it.

'It's me, Pete,' I said.

'Pete who?'

'Pete, your son.'

And she fainted. She just couldn't believe it.

On the Monday I went to see the manager of the Locarno, having been off about six weeks.

'Hello,' I said. 'My brother's Pete Waterman. He's been off ill, so he sent me. I'm called Bill,' I said.

I played the show and it was brilliant. The place was jumping. The manager came up to me afterwards and said, 'That was fantastic. How do I keep you and not have to take your brother back?'

'Bob, it's me you prat,' I said. And he couldn't believe it either. He thought I looked so ill that he went and took me off for a steak, but I got the job back.

So I'd got back into the DJing, but was still working at G.E.C. At that time, the G.E.C. was in serious trouble with the Post Office and they weren't delivering orders of telephone exchanges in time, so the Post Office brought in a penalty system to try and make things a bit more efficient. I was senior shop steward, a right militant bastard, and I could see the company was in real trouble. Whereas a lot of the union guys didn't seem to really care, I did, because as much as I wanted good working conditions for the workers, I wanted a *job* for the workers more than anything else. The G.E.C. bought a guy called Peter Sawyer from South Africa in, and I met him at one of these meetings where we were having the riot act read to us about our inefficiency. Now he immediately struck me as a completely different sort of manager from the sort I'd encountered before. He was very fresh, on the ball about everything and very open.

He said, 'My door is always open for anyone who wants to talk to me about anything. If you've got a problem or you've thought of any ideas, just come in and we can sit down and talk about it, man to man. We might not agree, but I'm prepared to meet with anyone so that can we can achieve what we've got to achieve.'

That was the last thing he should have said, because if you say that to me you know that I'm going to be in sitting next to you next morning. And I was. I went in and told him that the problem wasn't the workers on the shop floor, it was the management. It was rubbish. They couldn't organise a strip show in a nudist colony.

'What's the problem?' he asked.

'Well,' I said, 'as far as I can see, no one wants to upset anybody. You can't prioritise things while they're running it all like a nice cosy little family.'

'What would you do then?' he asked.

'I'd get someone with the authority to cut through all the bullshit and get the jobs done,' I said. 'Give me that job and I'll show you how to get all the telephone exchanges finished on time. But, one thing. When I've done the job, don't ask me how I did it. That's the only condition. You may not like some of the methods, but I guarantee they'll be finished on time.'

'Right,' he said, 'you're on.'

Now, the main problem at that time was shortages in supply. You'd find a screw missing and it would hold everything up. You'd have a five million pound telephone exchange just waiting because no one could get a light bulb. It was ridiculous. There were so many departments and systems in place that no one had been able to cut through it before. But we did it, me and my boss Ian. If there was a job where every exchange was missing a tiny screw or whatever, I'd physically go over to the department where all these screws were just sitting in boxes gathering dust and tell the guy to issue them immediately. Then I'd go down to the shop floor and tell the foreman to stop whatever job he was doing and finish off getting the screws put in. And when we needed a light bulb, we didn't wait around for weeks until one turned up from the G.P.O. with the official stamp on it any more, we went down to the electrical shop in town and bought an ordinary light bulb, made a fake stamp and stamped the G.P.O. approval on the bulb. They were only ordinary bloody light bulbs that the G.P.O. were sending, but because they had the official stamp on they cost the company three times as much. It was stupid. And it didn't take me long to find that out. It was simple, but it just needed someone to pull it together.

Of course, I had an ulterior motive for doing this job. I wanted to spend more time in the record shops. I couldn't do that if I was working on the shop floor, but if I actually had permission to go flying about all over the place then I could nip down to Coventry city centre and go and look in the record shops. I worked out how to do this job and still manage to spend a couple of hours a day down at the shops. Unfortunately I worked myself out of the job because I was so good that we started to catch up with ourselves really quickly and got back on schedule. I knew that I'd done better than I ever would have in the company otherwise, but I also knew that I wasn't ever going to get any further. I wasn't going to get off the shop floor. I simply wasn't sixties style management material, because they were bringing in all these bright young people with university degrees. They were doing away with people who had worked their way through the system in favour of kids who'd studied the theories about management. That was all very well, but they still wouldn't have been able to find that bobbin that had been stuck on the back of the shelf in the stores for 36 months. I knew where it was, but that wasn't going to be enough for them to make me management. Much as I liked working for Pete Sawyer, there was no future at the company for me.

At the same time as all this was going on, I'd met a guy called John down the Locarno who was a coal miner. They'd come down from Wigan to the local colliery in Coventry. He introduced me to Northern Soul. It wasn't called Northern Soul in those days, it was just another sort of r'n'b music. He played me some of the records, and I checked more out for myself and started to play them. Before I knew it I was getting three or four hundred people at the disco in the ballroom on a Friday night turning up before the pubs had closed. Now this was unheard of. We'd got this little scene going between nine and eleven o'clock. I started advertising the nights in *Blues'n'Soul*. At the same time, Ian Levine was doing the same thing at the Mecca in Blackpool. There was another club called The Torch, and Alan Winstanley in Wigan where the Wigan Casino was just starting up. Before we knew it, it had become quite a scene. This is way before it turned into the big, organised thing that everyone goes on about so fondly today. Nevertheless something was definitely happening.

By the following year, the whole Northern Soul thing was massive and I was making far more money from that than from any of my other DJing. I did a Sunday night at a club called Mr George's in Coventry. It had been dead before, but they gave me a free rein to play whatever I wanted so I decided to play Northern Soul. At first that seemed a stupid idea because the Northern Soul kids had been out dancing until seven o'clock Sunday morning. Why were they going to bother going out again on Sunday night? I'll tell you why: because I'd arranged to do a club on a Sunday afternoon in Birmingham. Northern Soul fans travelled all over the place. They'd go out Saturday, then along to Birmingham on Sunday afternoon and to Mr George's on Sunday night. It was a phenomenal success, so much so that we had to close the doors at half seven. We had to stop advertising it, too, because it was getting embarrassing. It was crammed. You couldn't move. People would be coming from North Wales, Liverpool, Wigan, and Manchester, and there'd be 1400, 1500 people there. It was amazing.

I've got two best mates. One is Keith Jackson whom I have known since I was one year old. The other is Tilly Rutherford. He was a great musical influence in Coventry during the sixties and we worked on mobile discos together. Tilly and I decided we were going to open a record shop, because there was nowhere you could get all these Northern Soul records. So we opened a stall on a Friday night and all day Saturday selling records, and I juggled it with my slots at the Locarno. We called it the Soul Hole because it was in the basement of a clothes shop. It was all bootlegs and obscure records that we'd picked up from all over the place. It started to do really well, but eventually we decided we'd just got too big.

Around this time I was approached by the manager of Virgin Records in Coventry, who asked me if I wanted to go and see Richard Branson and Nik Powell. The idea was to do a deal whereby I could rent the upstairs of the Virgin shop to sell singles and black records, because Virgin didn't sell either (although they did sell Bob Marley – we weren't allowed to sell Bob Marley). So we did a deal with Virgin and suddenly found ourselves selling records in a very big store. We were then given other opportunities to expand in the Virgin Group. We'd very quickly gone from a hole in the ground to a quite big shop, courtesy of Virgin. This was getting serious and I just couldn't fit in everything that was going on in my life. It was all a bit too much. It was mind-blowing really. I was DJing six nights a week, running the shop *and* working at G.E.C. I knew it was time for me to pack in G.E.C.; I'd gone as far there as I could. I had to take the next step into the music industry full-time. My divorce had come through and it was time to move on. I resigned from the G.E.C.

Also, around that period, local radio was really making its mark in Britain. The first commercial stations like Capital, BRMB, Trent and Radio City had started. Because there was a kind of independent presence in the provinces, CBS Records had set up promotion offices in Manchester, Glasgow, Southampton and Birmingham. It meant that, for the first time ever, the record industry wasn't based entirely in London; suddenly it was on your doorstep. It was only promotion, but it was there.

I got to know a lot of the promotion guys at the company, but looking back it's easy to see the naivety of the operation. These guys weren't really promotion people, they were salesmen who'd kind of fallen into jobs that were created for them. There wasn't such a thing as a promotion man before and now it was a career.

A bunch of DJs like myself were getting courted by the promotions departments. I'd already had ten years' experience, so I was there at exactly the right time, as the whole industry was booming and completely changing. Other record companies were sending people out of London; labels like ABC, Probe (which went on to be MCA and Universal), Bell Records, a whole load. In the matter of a couple of years the DJs had become very important. And Birmingham and the West Midlands were more important than just about anywhere else because they had loads of chart return shops, so if I played a record at one of my gigs it would create a trickle of people who would go out and buy the record, enough to make a blip that would give it a chart position. For the first time ever I could actually influence something on a wider scale. I'd get people coming up to me offering me free records, offering to take me out, whatever, just so that I'd play what they were promoting.

Now you don't have to buy me. If I like your record, I'll play it. You don't need to bribe me to play your records. The whole concept had never even been mentioned before. This was a whole new ball game.

One of the nicest of the promoters was a guy called Lee who worked at Probe. He was a gentleman, but his product was terrible. Still, you always wanted to do him a favour because he was such a decent guy. His best mate was Peter Powell, who was a DJ in Birmingham at the time. Lee was trying to get Peter a job on Radio Luxembourg, which he eventually did. I wasn't particularly interested in radio, because I liked the buzz of playing in front of a live audience in a ballroom.

One day Lee came up to me and told me he'd got a record, but he wasn't sure if he liked it or not. He was a bit confused by it. He played me 'Do It Again' by Steely Dan. It just blew my mind. It was awesome, so I started playing it. And while it didn't go on to become a hit, I'd started raving about Steely Dan to everybody. Consequently, when their next single, 'Reelin' In The Years', came in, he brought me an acetate and asked what he should do with it, who would like it, what I would suggest. All of a sudden people started coming up to me with other records, asking me my advice on how to work them. I wasn't just DJing any more, I was offering advice on promotion.

I had a meeting with Nik from Virgin one day and he asked me if I'd help with the promotion of a record a mate of his was doing, someone called Charlie Gillett. I met Charlie and I was immediately impressed. I'd never met anyone before who was as knowledgeable about music. I mean, he was like an encyclopaedia. And he loved all the same stuff as me, especially an old r'n'b DJ called Mike Raven. I got all this promotion sorted out for Charlie's record. I got TV people involved, I got the record on Radio One's playlist, everything. It gave me the confidence to go from being a big fish in a small Coventry pond to deciding to really have a go at doing something outside the small pond. I never got as far down the line at that time as actually putting a record out, but I'd certainly got the bug. The whole idea didn't seem entirely inconceivable.

I'd seen the way that the music business was changing beyond all recognition, and I knew I wanted to be part of it. But there was a vital part of my musical education that was missing. There was only one thing I could do. I had no choice: I had to go and live in America.

4 T.S.O.P. – The Sound Of Philadelphia

I T WAS 1973 and it was time for me to put the final bits of the jigsaw together. Time to stop just sitting on the sidelines and start participating. I'd been so inspired by American music. I'd talked to people from American companies on the phone, and met them when they came over to England. Through those initial contacts I had a standing invitation to go over to Motown and to Philadelphia International to meet Kenny Gamble, Leon Huff and Tom Bell.

So I thought – and this was the kind of arrogance that was motivating me at that time – that what I would do was make a radio show about r'n'b. Not the r'n'b that Mike Raven played, which was serious soul, but a different side of it, *pop* r'n'b. Motown, Three Degrees, Billy Paul, that sort of thing. I bought myself a little tape recorder, booked myself a ticket and jumped on a plane. I'd decided to go to Philly rather than Motown because Philly seemed like the coming thing. Motown, I'm sorry to say, seemed to be over. I don't think anybody else thought that, but I did. It seemed to have lost its edge now it had moved to Los Angeles, while Philly still had that edge.

The decision to go to America really was a spur of the moment thing. I'd be surprised if there was more than three weeks before me deciding to go and actually getting on the plane. I remember that by the time I left the idea of the pop r'n'b radio show had turned into writing a book about the mechanics of the r'n'b industry. The trip to Philadelphia International was going to be research. Now this was ambitious to say the least, writing a book about the ins and outs

4 3

of an industry I'd never witnessed before. Not least because I couldn't actually read or write. However, I knew that there was more to r'n'b than met the eye and that I couldn't quite understand what it was.

The only way that I was going to be able to find out was by actually going out there and immersing myself in the culture. Live, if you will, like an American black person for a while. As a white kid from Coventry I couldn't get it. All I knew was that black American records gave me goosebumps, but I never got that same reaction from English records. I just couldn't work up that enthusiasm. Why did records from a culture I knew nothing about excite me, whereas records from my own society left me cold? Records being made in Britain didn't seem to have the integrity or honesty that American records had and I just couldn't work out why.

So, armed with forty quid and a plane ticket, I went out there. Of course everyone thought I was a nutcase when I told them I was going, or that I was bullshitting, but I eventually persuaded them that it was a real plan. A friend's sister lived in New York so when I got off the plane I turned up on the doorstep of her and her flatmates' apartment on New York's Upper West Side. What they must have thought of me I don't know, but they were good enough to put me up overnight. I made the call to Philadelphia International, and they told me I could go there in a couple of days' time. So, over to Philadelphia I went and turned up in the morning at the Gamble and Huff building on South Street. And I was met with total surprise. They were all asking, 'Who the hell are you?' I showed them the letters I had from major people in the CBS hierarchy and told them that all I wanted to do was see what was going on.

One of the girls there, Mary, took a bit of a shine to me. She was the only other white person at Gamble, Huff and Bell Productions and about the same age as me. She could see that I was enthusiastic, while everyone else just seemed a bit bewildered by the fact that all I wanted to do was hang around and ask questions. I sat around and, at first, everyone gave me a pretty wide berth. Slowly it dawned on me that I actually knew more about the music than they did. After a couple of days I started wondering what had gone wrong. I mean these people were black, but that was the only difference between them and me. We were all human beings. And they were just ordinary guys, not supermen. Watching the company work it didn't seem like there were any magic tricks going on. There were no magic buttons. The way things got done was just through hard work. That was it. Nothing more.

I started watching them at work. They had the Spinners in at the time. The Detroit Spinners as we know them, but they were called the Spinners in America. The Stylistics were in as well, and I noticed on the board that Tom Jones was due any day. To me, it was fantastic; to them, it was just a job. I'd come to study magicians, but found I was studying a workplace. I was in exactly the same environment as G.E.C.: a place of work.

I was still a DJ. At that point I wasn't a studio person, so the process of making records had previously seemed something very glamorous. It was like a lightbulb coming on above my head, the realisation that this was just a job. I mean, they might have come into work in jeans, but they were still clocking on and clocking off. Then it dawned on me why black records and white records were different. For the white bands, making music was a luxury, something glamorous. For the black guys, they were coming in and doing the job of making records so they could pay their rent. It was their living. People in the British record industry treated it as art. Here it was necessity.

They used to have a board with dates written on it that were deadlines for people to submit their songs for various artists. If those songs didn't get picked then the songwriter might not be able to afford their rent the next week. I talked with Gamble and Huff, and Kenny in particular was very forthcoming. He made me see that these guys were basically cotton mill owners – but instead of selling shirts they were selling songs.

They'd created a community in which people were taken care of by their boss, the guy who made sure that everyone got their social security or their dentists' appointments on time, that they got their letters or their mortgage was paid. Kenny Gamble had created a social welfare state; a microcosm within Philadelphia. Just the same as Berry Gordy had done with Motown in Detroit and then in Los Angeles. They'd created places where everyone was taken care of from cradle to grave within that community. They didn't have to worry about anything apart from writing songs.

It was British Railways personified.

For the black record producers and writers in the stables I adored lived in a great work community, a family. It was a lifestyle, not an indulgence. And that made me not just a fan of the music, but also a massive fan of the ideology. This was completely different from the way that the record industry worked in England. In England in the early seventies there was still the Old Boys' network. It was beginning to break down, but it was still full of Oxford and Cambridge University graduates. There were people working there who came from pre-pop music days, people who were just paid to do a job and didn't really understand what they were doing. There were people like Mickie Most and Tony Hatch making records that I liked, but they weren't serious records and it was obvious that there was no social awareness to what they were doing. Songs like 'Devil Gate Drive' by Suzi Quatro and 'Blockbuster' by the Sweet were almost made in a vacuum. Great music, but the acts were more important than the songs.

Britain was still showbiz, but the records I liked listening to from America were about life itself. They were about sex, love, and death, so Les Gray from Mud singing about Tiger Feet wasn't quite the same. He was a lovely guy and a great showman, but the song wasn't exactly 'Standing In The Shadows Of Love' or 'How Sweet It Is' or 'The Year Of Decision' or 'When Will I See You Again'. One's a catchy song knocked out by people who don't really feel anything. The other's a song written about the realities of life.

I was never particularly hungry to experience American culture itself, but I couldn't help but be impressed the first time I saw the sheer size of the buildings, the trains with graffiti on them, all that urban life. And I'd never seen a real black community before, which made for some strange experiences. For instance, when I was in New York I'd gone up to Harlem to see James Brown and War. I nearly got killed. I'd just gone and stood in the queue and this guy came up to me and said I couldn't go in because I wasn't black. When they realised I genuinely loved the music and that I must have been possessed by incredible bravery or, more likely, complete naivety, they befriended me, and got me a really good place at the front. They couldn't believe that this white kid with flares and a floppy hat on who looked like Dick Turpin actually liked James Brown. So I'd gone from one end of the spectrum, where I thought that black people had a hard time, to the other where *you're* having a hard time, and black people hate you. It was very confusing, but I wasn't about to take the blame for the sins of white Americans.

A very famous record came out around that time by Richard Pryor, called 'That Nigger's Crazy', in which he takes the piss out of a white man. I *was* that white man. It was recorded at Cherry Hill Latin Casino where the O'Jays were performing. I was at the front on the Philadelphia table, the only white guy in the place. Everyone had been warning me not to sit anywhere near the front of the stage, but I didn't understand why. Richard Barrett, the Three Degrees' manager, who I got on really well with, decided to have a bit of fun and made me sit right by the stage. So Richard Pryor walked on and the whole place was full of big black guys. The whole Philadelphia International hierarchy was there because not only were they recording the album, they were also giving out million-sale awards to the O'Jays for 'Ship Ahoy', which was their big record at the time. Not only was I the only white guy, but because of the heatwave that had been going on in the city, I was lobster-pink. I might as well have had an arrow painted on my forehead.

Pryor just started ripping the piss out of me. I was brought up in quite a conservative home, so when someone started talking about my sex life on a big stage in front of three thousand people, with a spotlight on me, I was just dying. And the more he went on, the more the audience was whooping! I was getting my arse kicked big time. Then he turned onto the black guys and it got even funnier. I'd never seen a comedian like that before. But that night, going into a black supper club and seeing Richard Pryor playing in his own back yard, for the first time I was seeing building an act around social observation. Of course I *was* that social observation, and I can tell you, it wasn't comfortable. I saw what it was like to be in the minority. Even at Philadelphia International I'd never really experienced that, because I'd been sheltered in the Philadelphia family. It was an eye-opening experience and my first appearance on a Number One record, but I can't say I really enjoyed it. I couldn't stay in Philadelphia because I got homesick. I had to come back to the misery and the wet, but I stayed there a month.

I'd learned that the great records were made by people who took it seriously, people who weren't just playing at it. That these people were passionate about every aspect of their music. And the songs were about their community. Even the dance songs were, at their heart, about community, a community which was everything.

I finally felt like I understood what it was that had appealed to me about those records. I don't know if I was looking at England through different eyes when I got back, but I certainly felt different. I felt that I'd seen the future. And not just the records, but the whole American culture in general had shown what the future was going to be like, from Saturday morning kids' television to great big shopping malls to great big, thick Sunday newspapers. Britain suddenly seemed small and old-fashioned. Subconsciously I could see that Britain was about to change, that the American dollar was going to come in and change the country forever. Working-class kids like me were no longer going to be bullied. No one was going to tell us any longer that we couldn't get on because we hadn't been to Cambridge or Oxford. Britain was going to go through a revolution.

Everything in Britain seemed more amateur than ever. I mean, before I'd gone away I won the DJ Of The Year award from CBS Records, and they gave me a cup. A bloody cup! Can you imagine nowadays if you gave Fatboy Slim a cup? But that's what it was like then; it was playtime. They didn't think of giving you any cash for doing their promotion, they just patted you on the head and gave you a poxy cup.

In America I'd also seen the beginnings of what we now call club culture. The black clubs were still chicken-in-a-basket supper clubs, but the gay club scene was just starting, and all the records that were played were black. But in Coventry I couldn't just play James Brown and War all night. It just wouldn't have worked. We were still a white culture, so something like 'Me And Baby Brother' by War would have completely bewildered a white audience. 'Sex Machine' by James Brown worked because it was uptempo. 'Get Up Offa That Thing' or The Isley Brothers' funk stuff just didn't connect with anyone outside a small enclave in London or the deepest parts of Birmingham.

When I got back, the Philly thing really started to take off and songs like 'Backstabbers' and 'Love Train' and The Intruders' 'I'll Always Love My Mamma' were hits. By the time they'd been hits here, the people back in Philadelphia had moved on to stuff like 'Ship Ahoy', the slowed-down 'If You Don't Know Me By Now' by Harold Melvin and the Bluenotes, 'Me And Mrs Jones' by Billy Paul, all that stuff. Culturally, they'd become a very black company. They'd done the same thing as Motown, moved left of centre and towards a more stylised black sound.

A lot of this was because of the way that black and white radio stations in America never crossed over since they both had very definite identities. While I was over there Joe Jackson was one of the very few white people who could get on black radio. In addition, the radio stations were driven by payola. Personally, I don't think that payola detracts from the records themselves, but I saw people getting given drugs, yachts, cars, just to play records. You listen to something like 'Shaft' and you're hearing the beginning of the mythologising of a black Mafia, a culture of black payola. It was accepted as part of the promotion. And there was nothing subtle about it; everybody knew what was going on. If you didn't bribe the DJs you didn't get your record played. And, on top of that, black stations didn't play white records. So when the O'Jays made 'Ship Ahoy', they made it sound exactly like they knew black radio stations wanted it to sound. And, ironically, one of the country's biggest black DJs got in trouble when I was out there for taking a boat as a bribe.

So the black dance records in America were becoming completely polarised, increasingly mystifying to white kids in Northampton. Even in America, white people didn't listen to black music. They can pretend now that they did, but let me tell you, they're lying. It was an insular, self-driven scene. In England black and white DJs worked together and colour wasn't an issue, but that's because the records weren't as entrenched in their own culture. And people who loved the records loved them because of what they sounded like rather than as symbols of anything. You'd get white guys like Don Christie in Birmingham who loved reggae more than any West Indians. There weren't any rules about what you were supposed to listen to. That was the difference between the two societies, and maybe it still is. People mix here in working class societies far more readily than they do in America. Growing up in Coventry, you'd be in the middle of a completely multi-cultural society and people accepted each other. I didn't like the separatism of America.

One of the other things I'd loved about Philaldelphia was that the producers had their own studios. Over here that simply didn't happen. People would hire places when they wanted to make records. And they were pretty bloody sterile places. They were like government buildings, based around a rigid BBC mentality. There was something far more dynamic in Philadelphia. I'd seen the future in America and I wanted a part of it.

So when I got back in the summer of '73, I was pretty full of myself and hugely enthusiastic. I was busy DJing, building up big crowds, packing people in to places like Tiffany's in Coventry, and wondering what was going to happen next. Around this time I also introduced a concept I called my Loon Hour. It was something I did at the ballrooms to combat the fact that black r'n'b had started to get all weird. I used to play the soul tunes, but in between I'd play Gary Glitter or Suzi Quatro, songs like 'Devil Gate Drive'. Then throw in a few slowies, a bit more r'n'b and a bit more glam rock. It was an hour where there were no boundaries. Very pop. And when glam started to get boring I stopped playing it. I timed it right. If there's one thing I'm good at, it's knowing when to jump off the barrow. That's because the public are fantastic, but they're hard taskmasters. They do get fed up very quickly. And you have to give them exactly what they want, because they drop you if you don't. And with any trend there comes a point when you start to dictate. That's when it becomes very dangerous. The quality goes out because the business comes in.

Now one of my best contacts at the time was a guy called Steve Collier who was head of promotions at CBS Records. He was the one who'd got me all the introductions at Philadelphia International. Anyway, I called up Steve one day and he said, 'I'm leaving CBS and I'm going to Magnet Records as head of promotion, and I want you to come and meet the head, Michael Levy.' I think it's safe to say that I'd never, ever played a record on Magnet. Their main act was Alvin Stardust who was a lovely guy, but I never played his records. 'Steve,' I said, 'I hate their records, mate. What's the point of me going to meet the head of a label whose records I hate?' But Steve kept going on to me about how Michael was this diamond, this fantastic geezer and how I had to meet him. I asked him why. He said he was going to get me a job with Magnet. I couldn't imagine anything worse than working on Alvin Stardust records, but finally, after a whole summer of pestering me, he managed to persuade me to come down to London to meet Michael Levy.

Levy had had this idea of starting a part-time promotions department. I'd be paid just expenses and a small fee, but I'd be going round radio stations all the time and I'd be able to drop my DJ tapes off as well, so I'd have the opportunity to do a bit of free advertising of my own services. I'd get in the frame and I'd be getting paid for it. Suddenly it didn't seem such a bad idea. I didn't have a driving licence at the time, so quite how I thought I was going to get around all the radio stations I still don't know, but I got on a train and went down to London. I went into the offices and the first person I met was some guy in a suit, the smartest man I'd ever seen in my life. He looked to me like he'd just walked out of a shop window. It was Michael Levy.

He had a glass table and a big cigar and he sat there and gave Steve and me a lecture about his record company and what he wanted to do, and then he offered me the job, but the more I thought about it, the less sure I was that I was the right person. Steve and I went off to lunch and I said to him, 'Look, I can't do this job. He's an impressive bloke and everything, but I just can't sell something I don't believe in.'

'Go and tell him then,' said Steve. 'If you feel so strongly about it, go and tell him you think his records are crap. Don't tell me, tell him.'

So we go into Levy's office and Steve says to Michael, 'Michael, Pete is one of the top DJs around and he thinks your records are rubbish.'

I thought Michael was going to jump over the desk and strangle me.

'You've made a lot of records, have you then?' he asked.

'No,' I said, 'but I've played a few hits. I know what a good record sounds like and let me tell you, it doesn't sound like anything you're putting out.'

So Michael got out this big reel-to-reel tape player and played me some songs, asking me what I thought of them.

And at each one he played, I was going, 'Crap. Crap. Crap.' I hated them. By now he was fuming, because he'd never had a kid coming along slagging off all his records before.

Then this song started playing. And I knew within ten seconds that it was a hit.

'What's this?' I asked.

'What do you think it is?' he replied.

'It's a smash,' I said.

He went, 'You dozy bastard. This is just a demo. It's not even a proper record.'

I said, 'I don't care what it is, it's a hit.'

He told me it was a guy called Pete Shelley, Alvin Stardust's producer. It was a song called 'Gee Baby'.

I went back off to Coventry and a week later Steve rang me to say that Magnet were going to put 'Gee Baby' out as a single. It was a real soppy-poppy song so even my mates were taking the piss out of me. They were telling me I was supposed to be a soul DJ, but I just loved that record. Everyone thought I was crazy, but I rang up Steve and said, 'You've got to get this record on the radio. It's going to be huge.'

He knew Tony Blackburn who was doing the *Breakfast Show* on Radio One. I said, 'Steve, get him to play it and it's a Top Five record.'

'Are you sure?' he asked.

'I'm sure, Steve, just trust me.'

He couldn't see it himself, but he managed to get it as Tony Blackburn's Record Of The Week. And it went straight to Number One.

I got a call from Michael Levy's secretary. She handed me over to Michael. 'I want you to come to London and listen to some songs,' he said.

So I went back down to London, met Michael again and he sat me in his office with the smoked salmon sandwiches – first time I'd ever had one of those in my life – and played me some more songs. They were going with some other record for the Pete Shelley follow-up that was due out the next week, but I thought it was rubbish and I told them. By now Michael Levy was twitching on his seat. But they played me another demo and, again, I thought it sounded like a hit. It was a song called 'Love Me, Love My Dog'.

And I went back up to Coventry.

I got another phone call from Steve. He told me Levy wanted to offer me a job. I didn't want a job. I didn't want to work for a record company. But Steve persuaded me to go down to meet Levy *again*.

I went down to see him at a Magnet Christmas party at a club called the Barracuda. I took down one of the records I'd been playing a lot. It was a reggae record that I'd picked up while I was out at Philadelphia. We'd gone to Jamaica on a weekend break and I'd found this record called 'Hurt So Good' by Susan Cadogan, produced by Lee Perry. It had been put out by a guy called Dennis Harris, who had a little company in Stoke Newington called DIP Records, and I played it at the Magnet party. Ringo Starr was there with Lynsey De Paul and he loved it. He said if I went round his office he'd do me a deal for it.

Anyway I had this meeting with Michael, and he told me they'd decided to go with 'Love Me, Love My Dog' for the next single. He asked me to become Pete Shelley's assistant for £100 a week. That was a lot of money then; I'd probably only have been making £45 a week DJing. £100 a week seemed so much it terrified me. I took the job.

*　　*　　*

When I first went in to work, Michael asked me about the Susan Cadogan record. It was, along with a song by Junior Byles called 'Golden Locks', one of the two real underground reggae records I was playing. They weren't pop reggae records at all like the Greyhounds or Bruce Ruffin that were doing the rounds at the time. The two records I had were very raw, very Jamaican. And of course Michael thought they were terrible.

I started working with Steve in that first week of January 1975 on 'Love Me, Love My Dog'. Once again we talked the record up, played it to the right people and got Tony Blackburn's Record Of The Week. Michael Levy thought I had golden bollocks by this point, so he reconsidered the Susan Cadogan thing and decided to do a deal. I phoned up Dennis and we got him in from Stoke Newington. It was quite a sight when he met Michael Levy for the first time: a huge West Indian street guy and Michael, the ultimate Jewish business-man. Talk about ethnic minorities clashing.

Michael could be ruthless. But he agreed to pick the record up.

Now, I started officially in the music business on 1 January, and within the week I was down at the cutting room at the Beatles' Apple Studios. They were just about the only group who had their own studios, and the atmosphere was much warmer, much more exciting than those sterile old places that bands usually used. It was obvious that the Beatles had picked up their way of working from what was going on in America.

Apple used a guy called Malcolm Davies and I took the record down to him. While I was there, Lennon was doing something in one of the studios with Phil McDonald, it was a real hive of activity. Malcolm was cutting a Crusaders record which was one of the greatest twelve-inch records you ever heard. I found the technical aspect of cutting records intrigu-ing so I was asking, 'Why do you do this? Why do you do that? How do you get this or that effect?' It was the first time I'd ever worked with a cutting engineer and the first time anyone had bothered to actually explain to me the technique behind the process of physically making a record. You'd never have got that at one of the stuffy studios that other people used. At Apple, Malcolm was just one of the lads. He was very approachable, and wasn't precious about what he was doing.

I told him I loved the Crusaders' record, and that I'd been playing it on import for months. Then I played him the Cadogan record and he told me it wasn't even in stereo. It was two-track mono like the old Beatles records, with the voice on the right and the track on the left. But he loved it; he got John Lennon and Phil McDonald in too and they were all raving about it.

I couldn't believe it. I'd been in the music business a week and I was in Apple Studios with one of the Beatles and they were raving about one of my records. It was like a dream.

Being a Jamaican reggae record, of course the track you were hearing was a copy of a copy of a copy. And at the very beginning there was even the sound of Susan tuning up. Malcolm was a genius though; using the Apple equipment he cleaned up all the noise that had worked its way on from previous crappy pressing companies, spliced it down to a really good edit and made it sound fantastic. And it was still just a two-track mono record. I took it straight back to Tiffany's in Coventry and it sounded like a different record, even better than before. The kids went wild when they heard it. It had presence, it was more direct, it had better bass on it and it had been sped up slightly.

Malcolm had all this incredible experience. He'd been working at EMI since 1957 and had cut every Beatles record, so he knew every trick in the book. The first record he cut was 'How Much Is That Doggy In The Window?' for goodness' sake. And Phil McDonald was engineer for Lennon and the Rolling Stones, so between them they'd turned what was a good reggae record into a fantastic one. Now, I hadn't a clue what they had done to it, but when I played it out I could see how they'd just taken it to another level. So there was this reggae record on DIP Records, and another completely different version of the same track on Magnet Records. And 'Love Me, Love My Dog' about to be a hit. All in the first week of my job.

5 D.I.S.C.O.

I 'D ACTUALLY TURNED down Michael's original offer of £100 a week because it frightened me too much. I took £60 a week because I thought that was probably what I was worth. I had no idea what the job really entailed, and I didn't know how long it would last, so I didn't want to become too dependent on the money. I said to Michael, 'I'll take £60 a week and we can review it four months down the line.' I didn't know if I'd still be there four months down the line, but Michael agreed with the proposition.

I was the only non-Jewish person working in the office. There was a kosher fridge and a non-kosher fridge. Every time I put a bacon sandwich in the fridge, when I came back it would have gone and there would be a pound note there. I was making 30p a sandwich! I always made sure there were four sandwiches in the fridge because it meant I had a free one.

The phone rang one day and it was Pete Shelley.

'Nip down to the recording studio, R.G. Jones,' he said, 'and do me a backing track for "Love Me, Love My Dog". Speak to a guy called Jerry Kitchener and tell him I sent you and do me a backing track.'

I didn't have a clue what he was on about, but I put the phone down and got the tube out to Wimbledon to R.G. Jones. When I got there, I gave them the tape and watched them make another backing track out of it. And I remember when they turned the faders up I heard a piano bit that wasn't on the record. I realised that by taking the piano off they'd made one song into a completely different one. This was all part of my education about how to play around with all the elements that make up a record.

The backing track was for Pete's appearance on *Top Of The Pops*. In those days you'd go down to the BBC at Lime Grove Recording Studios and they'd record it all in the morning. Then you'd go off to where they actually filmed it all and there'd be a rehearsal in the afternoon and, after that, they'd film the whole thing live. It was the last outpost of a ridiculously strict organisation. It was all still run by military types and the unions completely controlled things. You couldn't even move your own drum kit. A stage hand had to move it for you. Those were the rules.

Because there were fewer than five people in the band, we were allowed to use the backing track, so we didn't have to go to Lime Grove. We just went straight down to the filming, and that's when it started to get messy.

Steve had decided that, frankly, Pete wasn't Mr Personality. Lovely man, but not exactly overflowing with charisma. Pete didn't want to be; he was an A&R guy and record producer who'd just kind of fallen into the role of being a pop star. Steve wanted to up the game plan for TV, so he decided to get a dog. You've got to have a prop, right? The dog of choice at the time (the dog *par excellence*, if you like) was King, the English Sheepdog that was on all the Dulux paint ads. So Steve, being a promotions guy, decided that Pete was going to go on *Top Of The Pops* with King. He rings around all the dog breeders, gets the number for King's owner and, sure enough, books the dog for the programme.

I walked into the studio and there was this huge dog standing there. I mean, enormous. It was like a polar bear or something. And it wasn't just sleeping, it was running about all over the place. I asked the owner how on earth it was going to stand still during the show and she said, 'Oh, it's OK, we just spike a bone with peppermint and nail it to the stage. I promise the dog won't move.' No one seemed to have any better ideas, so that's what we did.

Pete's only a little guy, and he was a bit nervous about this huge dog, but Steve was trying to reassure him. 'Just sing your song and look at the camera,' he said. 'Give the dog a stroke every now and then and you'll be fine. And, if you're really worried then, for safety's sake, wrap the lead around your hand.'

So they start the filming and Pete's singing away, 'Love me, love my dog . . .' when all of a sudden the dinner bell goes and a stage hand walks on, pulls out the bone and takes it off the stage. Whoosh! The dog goes bombing off down a corridor, dragging Pete Shelley after him. And Pete was really hurt. He'd fallen off a four-foot stage.

The whole place just fell about. There were people standing there with tears running down their faces. By now the dog had got the bone and the owner was going bananas. It was like a circus.

We eventually got the dog back and patched Pete up, nailed the bone back on the stage and got ready for the performance. Twenty minutes went by and then suddenly this dog started doing its doings on the stage, right in the middle of the live recording of the song. So the camera discreetly moved up and Pete tried to carry on singing with a great big, steaming poo right under his nose. *Top Of The Pops* isn't all glamour.

The record went to Number Two in the charts and I managed to talk Pete into coming up to play at Tiffany's. The poor guy walked out on stage and everyone started shouting, 'Where's the dog?' And that taught me that the dog had become the gimmick for the whole song. People weren't buying the Pete Shelley record, they were buying the dog.

At the same time the Susan Cadogan record came out, but although we'd sold 20,000 copies on DIP Records, DIP wasn't registered with the chart-return shops, so it wasn't showing up on the charts. So we rung up this woman called Win Barton at the British Market Research Bureau who put the chart together, and told her that the record on DIP was the same song as we had out on Magnet. We asked her if she could add the DIP sales onto the Magnet ones and she was happy to do so.

The week before I'd been down to Radio One to promote the record. Paul Burnett who did the lunchtime show quite liked it. I started talking it up as potentially the biggest single of the year and eventually got it made Record Of The Week, which meant Radio One played it every day. Now it was time to promote it to the shops.

So come Easter Weekend, I drove around like you wouldn't believe. I didn't actually have a driving licence, but I got a car and drove anyway. I went to Newcastle On Tyne, from there to Sunderland, Doncaster, York, Leeds, Liverpool, Formby, Manchester, Warrington, Sheffield, Nottingham, Derby and Rugby. You can imagine how many miles that is.

I went into the office a week later and they told me that the sales figure for the record was 16 copies. 16 copies! At that point I wasn't sure whether that was good or bad. I didn't know whether it was supposed to sell 16 or 16 million. I didn't have a bloody clue, but everyone kept on coming up and saying, 'Never mind, you did your best,' so I guessed it was supposed to have sold more. Then, a day later, the chart came out and it was the highest new entry, in at Number 26 or something! Everyone wondered how you could get the highest new entry when you only sold 16 copies. Of course, everyone had forgotten the 20,000 that Dennis had put out on DIP which had been added on, plus the fact Dennis had so much of his stock out there. Add to that the Record Of The Week on Radio One and all the promotion I'd done and it suddenly kicked in. We had a hit and we got *Top Of The Pops*.

I'd forgotten what Susan Cadogan actually looked like, because it had been so long since I'd seen her. The pictures Dennis had were awful. There were no videos in those days, so having to worry about what a singer looked like didn't really matter unless you were doing TV.

Steve found out that her father was the main Baptist minister of Jamaica, and that she was the librarian at Kingston Library. We put a call in and asked her if she wanted to come over and do *Top Of The Pops*. She said she couldn't get time off work, but we finally persuaded her that she had a hit and that she was going to make lots of money and she had to come over.

So she got on a plane and we arranged to meet her at the airport. Tuesday morning we were at Heathrow waiting for the Air Jamaica flight with the chauffeured limo, but because we didn't really know what she looked like I was holding up a big sign saying 'Susan Cadogan'.

This woman walked out of immigration. Six foot two, bald as a coot and with only one eye. She came up to us and said, 'Hello, I'm Susan.'

Steve and I just looked at each other. ' We're dead!' we both thought. We couldn't take this woman to Michael and tell him she was going to be famous. She was scary.

This being in the days before mobile phones, Steve went off to find a phone box and made some calls. We had to get this sorted out somehow. Back he came and told me he had a plan. We drove to Ozzie Clarke's, the dressmaker's. He was a friend of Steve's and he made Susan a beautiful red dress. Then to Vidal Sassoon's to get a wig made. All this in a mad rush because she had to be on *Top Of The Pops* the next day. Finally we drove off to the London Eye Hospital so that they could make her a glass eye in 24 hours, because the one she had made her look like Columbo.

And I swear to you, when she walked out on that stage on *Top Of The Pops*, she was the most stunning, elegant performer you could imagine. She looked fantastic, like a young Shirley Bassey.

The record went to Number Two. It was only kept off the top by Tammy Wynette's 'Stand By Your Man'.

In those days you weren't supposed to be on *Top Of The Pops* for two weeks running unless you'd gone up the charts. Susan Cadogan was the only person I knew of who was on there three weeks on the trot, because the producer Robin Nash loved her so much. And within weeks we'd sold three, four hundred thousand copies of the record. I was the king of the castle. It wasn't a bad job at all – not for sixty quid a week!

I was also working on the Junior Byles reggae record and a song by Guys And Dolls called 'Whole Lot Of Loving' which had been written by Barry Manilow's writers. I'd managed to get the Guys And Dolls song made Record Of The Week on Tony Blackburn as well. The job was taking me down all sorts of new avenues. However, it was quite a combination, DJing in clubs at night and sitting in a London office all week meeting people who were famous in the British record industry. I'd be having a cup of tea with John Lennon one day and the next hanging out with the Wombles. I was still living in Coventry and I commuted to London to get in by nine o'clock every morning. I'd initially tried staying with a mate of mine in Wimbledon, but I could never find his house so I kept having to get the train back up north anyway.

I was still getting a buzz from DJing and I enjoyed being around my old mates, but it was increasingly becoming a 'Jekyll and Hyde' situation. You can't tell your mates you were hanging out with John Lennon without them either not believing you or thinking you're showing off. It was a surreal sort of existence. Magnet was a genuine phenomenon. It was a little independent company, set up by an accountant, that had taken on the majors and started to beat them at their own game. It was turning out a lot of hits. At the time I wasn't aware of the enormity of it all. I don't know how many of us were, but in hindsight you can see that the whole dynamics of the industry were starting to change.

In January every year there's a music industry festival in Cannes called MIDEM. Michael decided I ought to go. Now, other than America and a school trip to Belgium I'd never been out of Britain. Suddenly I'm being sent to the South of France. Other people might have thought that was fantastic, but I was more worried that I was going to lose four nights' DJing. But I had to go.

I had no idea where I was supposed to be going and what I was supposed to be doing. All I knew was that I had to get the plane and work on some stand that Michael had. They'd got an apartment for me for nine days. This for a kid from Coventry who couldn't speak French – who couldn't even really speak English properly! And another thing, I was down there on my own. They just put me on a bleeding plane and waved me goodbye. I had no one to help. And I couldn't even pronounce Cannes, let alone pick it out on a map. A Black Country boy in the South of France really is like a pork chop at a synagogue.

I got out of the airport and was a bit shocked to see all the police had guns, so I thought it might be a good idea to get a taxi to where I was supposed to stay. Londoners are sophisticated and know how to hail cabs, but I wasn't used to all that. There weren't more than a dozen cabs in Coventry and you only ever got to see them at two in the morning. I wasn't confident about even getting out of the airport.

Luckily, as I was walking out I met a guy called Grant Goodchild who worked in the accounts department at Magnet. He was actually there to pick me up, although no one had thought of telling me. I hadn't expected any kind of organisation, especially since they'd packed me off with only twenty quid in francs.

The apartment was really posh and I began to get quite excited about it all. We went down to the Palais de Festival and there was this amazing scene going on. There were loads of little stalls, but it wasn't like the National Exhibition Centre. Nowadays there is far more of a trade-show feel to it all, but at the time it was nothing like that. It had only been going for a few years and really hadn't found its feet.

Like at the Film Festivals today, people used to do stunts on the street to publicise records. One campaign really caught my eye: a photo of a pair of breasts and a set of handcuffs. And underneath, the words 'Silver Bird Convention – Save Me – Jupiter Records – Stand 231'. The posters were everywhere. In the streets, in the cafés, everywhere. Just the tits and the handcuffs. It was a fantastic campaign because everyone was talking about it, wondering what the record was all about.

I was sitting in the booth the first day and these people kept on coming up with tracks to sell. And, to be fair, most of the stuff I heard was absolutely diabolical. Every twenty minutes or so, though, I'd hear a noise through the wall; the sound of some record being played. The bass drum was so loud it was coming right through the walls from a few booths away. These weren't soundproofed booths, they were basically wooden photo booths that you decorated yourself and then fitted out with a tape player or you hired a record player. Really basic. By lunchtime I was dying to find out what this incessant noise was, so I went along to the booth and there were the two most gorgeous German girls I'd ever seen, with thigh-length boots on. I was gobsmacked.

A guy came up and I told him I was from Magnet and asked him what the record he'd been playing was. He wouldn't tell me, but said that he already had a deal for the record in England.

'Yeah, OK,' I said, 'but can I hear the record? I've been sitting in a booth just down from here all morning and it's been driving me nuts. Can I just hear it?' So he played me the record, and by God it blew me away. I was riveted to the spot, and instantly got goosebumps. The guy looked at me as if I needed oxygen.

'What's the matter?' he asked.

'This record,' I said, 'it's absolutely unbelievable. I've got to have it. I don't care if you've already got a deal. You've got to break the deal and do one with me instead. I am the only man in the world who can break this record.'

They had a deal with Robin Blanchflower at PRT, but I knew that no one understood how good it was better than me. I *had* to have it.

Another immaculately dressed guy walked in, and they started talking to each other in German; I could tell it was about me. I don't speak German, but 'dumkopf' is 'dumkopf' in any language. Eventually the new guy turned to me and said, 'I'll tell you what we'll do. We'll wait until Wednesday and if Robin Blanchflower hasn't come to the stand to sign the deal, you've got the record.'

We shook hands on it. The guy was Ralph Siegel and it was his record label. So I went back to my booth and said, 'Hey, I've just done a deal with Herman the German next door.'

And the guy working with me said, 'Are you mad? Michael's Jewish. He'll *never* do a deal with a German.'

'I don't care,' I said. 'I was told to come here and pick up records and that's what I'm doing. The war's over. It's not my problem.'

'He won't sign,' they said. 'Let's see you try and sell it to him.'

I knew from the 'Hurt So Good' record by Susan Cadogan that Michael would license stuff in if he thought there was a bob or two in it. And I knew that this record could be huge. So I came up with a sneaky plan. I figured that if I met him off the plane I'd be in before anyone else could talk to him. He'd be in a good mood because he was in the South of France and I might be able to convince him to do a deal.

So I collected him from the airport and all the way from Nice to Cannes I wouldn't stop going on about this record and how he had to pick it up.

'OK,' he said. 'Take me to the stand.'

He heard the track, and although Michael didn't know himself whether the record was any good, he trusted my enthusiasm and agreed to pick up the song if the PRT deal didn't happen.

Afterwards he said to me, 'What are you doing to me? You've got me doing deals with Germans. And not only that, but you've gone for the biggest record of the festival. These guys are going to hammer me.'

'What do you mean, biggest record of the festival?' I asked.

He pointed out that the record was the one with the tits and the handcuffs poster. I hadn't realised. And because it was such a high profile advertising campaign, he was going to have to shell out loads to buy the record. I was in deep trouble.

I went down to the coffee bar and did my best French accent as I bought an orange juice and a ham sandwich – those were the only two phrases I'd picked up. There were two guys at the bar next to me and on their jackets it said 'Midland International'. I'd done promotion years earlier on a record called 'Doctor's Orders' by Sunny, and a fantastic American cover version by a girl called Carol Douglas had come out on Midland International Records. So I got talking to these guys and told them how much I liked the Carol Douglas version. It turned out one of them was Eddie O'Loughlin, who'd produced it. And the other was Bob Reno, who owned the label.

So I said, 'Listen, if you want a hit, do yourselves a favour and get up to Ralph Siegel's stand and check out a record by Silver Bird Convention called "Save Me". It's a huge hit.' I knew that Eddie would understand why I liked it because he'd made Carol Douglas' 'Doctor's Orders' and I could see we were both coming from the same place. I knew Eddie must be into clubs.

Off they went and a few minutes later they were back. They loved the record and they'd bought the rights for America. They insisted on taking me out for lunch and told me that if we were putting out 'Save Me' in England, they'd wait and put it out in America on the back of our success. I'd only been in the business eighteen days and here I was doing deals with all these people who'd been in the business for years! Bob Reno was behind big labels in America like Buddha (although I didn't know that at the time), and here he was under the impression that I actually knew what I was doing. I didn't at all, I just loved the record.

Wednesday came and there had been no sign of PRT so the record was ours. Michael was shitting himself; he was white when he signed the deal. To this day I don't know how much it was for, but it must have been a considerable amount. The world was changing, and whereas MIDEM in the past had been basically a market for little publishing deals, we'd turned it into a shop window. We'd done a deal there that changed the record industry. This was serious money now, and MIDEM would never be the same again.

That's been acknowledged since, and at the festival's 25th anniversary I was given the keys to the city of Cannes and made an honorary French citizen. All to do with the part I played in turning MIDEM into what it is today.

While I was in MIDEM that first time I also managed to set up something of a restaurant institution. We used to get forty quid a week for expenses and it was always thirteen or fourteen quid a meal just to eat. There were a load of us young lads there, and I was hanging out with two guys, Chris Hill and Nigel Grange. We were finding it very difficult to feed ourselves, so we decided to look for some restaurants in a back street called Rue D'Antibes. I came across a place called the Blue Tulip and went in to ask if they did any special deals. Not speaking French it was pretty hard to make myself understood, so the owner went into the back and came out with the chef, a guy the size of a house. He went, 'Hey up lad, what da thee want?' He was from Leeds!

I explained we were all down for the festival, but we couldn't afford to eat on the Croisette. I asked him if he'd do a special set meal for the lads, and I guaranteed I'd fill his restaurant every day if he did. All I wanted in return was a free meal each day. He agreed to the deal and did a forty-franc meal each day, for which you got three courses and a glass of wine. And in the evening he did a hundred-franc meal. I tell you, by the end of the next day you couldn't get near the place. It was packed.

Come Saturday night he was so pleased with the custom I'd brought in he threw a massive party with free food and drink. It was one of the greatest parties I've ever been to. And ever since then, all the cheap menus during MIDEM are on the Rue D'Antibes. Nowadays it's even spread to the Croisette. And that was all because of a deal at the Blue Tulip with the chef from Leeds in 1975.

I came back from MIDEM having had a great time. Things were going well with Magnet. By Easter we'd broken Guys and Dolls, and Susan Cadogan was beginning to happen. And I had this record called 'Save Me'.

By this time the band were just called Silver Convention. They'd dropped the 'Bird' from their name because of the sexual connotations. Malcolm Davies and I felt that although the record was really good, it wasn't quite right, so we went into the studio and edited it. We spliced it around and looped the chorus. It sounded brilliant.

Back then there were no 12-inch singles. Chris Hill and I were into American records and out there they'd just started pressing 10-inch records. I decided to cut 'Save Me' on a 10-inch 78rpm disc. If you cut it and play it on 10-inch at 78, you get incredible volume because you get so much more movement with the stylus. It makes the record so much bigger.

We made a 10-inch record which, of course, most of the public couldn't play – but the ballrooms could because they still had the old Goldring decks that played 78s. And the records sounded so much better. Within a week Chris and I had both come up with a variation. We'd put out records on 12-inch that played at 45rpm. It was the same concept as with the 10-inch, but it meant people could play them at home. That was the first time anyone put out commercially available 12-inch records.

The record created a real buzz, but only just got into the Top Forty. No one else ended up putting the record out. When we got back the producers had sent over a new Silver Convention song called 'Fly Robin Fly' which was actually far better than 'Save Me'. We were already underway with the 'Save Me' promotion though, so we had to go through with it. By early summer we'd put 'Fly Robin Fly' out and it was literally flying all over the world. Eddie and Bob at Midland International had managed to get ABC television in America to use it in the background, when they showed their yearly footage of people diving off the rocks at Acapulco. That got it a huge audience and from there it just took off. Within a few weeks the phones at Magnet were ringing constantly with people asking where they could buy this record.

By now I was intrigued about just where Silver Convention were coming from so I flew out to Munich. When I got there I found a very strange scene going on. There was a big studio in Munich called Musicland where Michael, one of the Silver Convention producers, was based with Giorgio Moroder. They'd brought in a whole load of British session musicians and two or three black girl singers whose husbands were in the US forces based in West Germany. One of them was called Donna Summer. What I'd thought was a whole nation-wide movement was in fact based around a very small circle of people.

What it immediately reminded me of was Philadelphia International. Or Motown. This was the whole family thing again. It might have been unusual in the European record industry, but to me it seemed a perfectly natural way of doing things. I loved the idea of everybody being on the payroll, and turning up for different sessions with different producers as entirely different groups. It seemed a great way to make records.

I became very friendly with these guys. They'd seen what Malcolm and I had done with re-editing Silver Convention; in fact they originally thought we'd re-recorded it, and so they started copying our ideas with all their new tracks. Pretty soon they were asking me for advice on how to construct the records and how to market them.

Everything I was touching was turning to gold. In the first quarter of that year, Magnet had 12.2 per cent of the British sales market. That was unheard of. One day they played me a record by Donna Summer and it was quite obvious that it was just her with the guys from Silver Convention. It actually wasn't a very good song. But then they played me 'Love To Love You Baby' and I knew that was a smash. They'd originally done a deal with Creole and with Neil Bogarde at Casablanca Records in America. And the plan was to break the record out of America. I came along and told them I wanted to break it out of England. I didn't have a clue what was going on on a global scale. There was no masterplan to make loads of money. I was just thinking about Tiffany's in Coventry, and what would go down well there. My mission was just to keep people dancing. And I reckoned if I could actually make the records then I could keep myself at Number One as a DJ because I'd have the records before anyone else. I was like a donkey with strawberries. It was the ultimate DJ trip.

What I liked about the songs was that they were basically white versions of Philadelphia records. They sounded like Barry White or the Three Degrees but with a bass drum that white people could dance to. And that four-on-the-floor, tight polka bass drum was what made them stand out. The quality of the string arrangements put them on a par with the Philadelphia records, but the bass drum made them sound completely different. No one else could see the correlation, but I knew that I could drop the songs into my soul sets and no one would imagine they were German. Ultimately it's the solidity of the rhythm that makes a record. On Motown and Philly Records it was the backbeat. On the German records it was an even more direct drumbeat.

Because I loved the sound of these records so much I was hanging out in Munich just giving these people advice on how to play around with the tracks, add bits here and there or take things away; doing it purely so that I could have some good records to play when I DJed. I'd also get calls from the Midlands International people asking me to sort tracks out for them. I was happy to; I loved it, I was like a kid in a candy shop. I had absolutely no idea that what I was doing was having an impact on any wider scale.

One day *Billboard* started calling it disco and they rang me up to talk to me. Next thing I know they're calling me 'The King Of Disco'.

This is something that I want to get on record, because whenever I read so-called histories of disco all I read is people getting it wrong. *I* was at the heart of it. Without me going to the South of France and picking up the Silver Convention record, it wouldn't have happened like it did. That opened the door for Donna Summer and Boney M and everything that went after. All the other guys like Larry Levan who claim responsibility may well have played it, but they were trying to keep it underground. We took it overground. Naively for sure, but we took it overground all the same. We loved the records and we didn't see it as separate from mainstream pop music. There was no cynicism, no desire to become billionaires. And there was no need to think about how to sell it because it was made for a specific purpose: so that the people dancing to it could enjoy it. In a way that was the best kind of marketing of all. And all the DJs across Europe understood it without having to explicitly think of it as a white version of Philly soul.

There was no ego there. I wasn't looking at myself and thinking, 'Aren't I bloody brilliant'. I was just doing what seemed to me to be a great opportunity to be at the very heart of making records I loved. And suddenly I found myself in the middle of an amazing boom.

6 Fool If You Think It's Over

I GET NERVOUS WHEN PEOPLE tell me I'm a genius. Usually it means you're about to be ripped off. So I kept my head down and kept doing what I was doing. I carried on with Magnet and kept up the DJing in Coventry. Meanwhile, I'd somehow managed to stumble into consistent success.

At the end of the first month at Magnet I was in Mayfair Studios with Pete Shelley when Michael Levy came down. He took me out for a sandwich.

'I can't sleep at night,' he said. I asked him why not.

'It's the money you're getting. I don't feel happy with you getting £60 a week. You're getting a hundred a week and that's it. I don't want to hear any of your bloody backchat. And we're backdating the money from when you first started.'

On top of that I was also getting bonuses depending on the success of the records I'd picked up for the label. Just for Susan Cadogan I got a bonus of £15,000, so by the middle of June I was seriously wealthy. And it all happened so quickly. I bought a cottage for £12,500 in the countryside just outside Coventry. It was an amazing change in lifestyle, but I still kept on with the DJing and everything because it was something I loved doing; I was building a reputation for playing records that no one else had because I was cutting them all from acetates. That actually meant more to me than the money.

Early in the summer I signed another first. In the sixties I'd been a huge fan of the Four Seasons. One day a guy walked into my office and played me a reggae version by

Adrian Baker of the Four Seasons' 'Sherry Baby'. This was the first time anyone had put out a cover version of a pop song, but we went on to have a massive hit with it. Then people realised that radio liked to play records by other people of songs they knew. Major record companies hadn't thought of it before, but of course we'd been playing cover versions of reggae records on the club scene for ages. This was just the first time anyone had thought of taking it into the pop world. I remember even Michael Levy said to me, 'You can't put this song out; it was a hit for the Four Seasons.'

'Michael,' I said. 'That was twenty years ago.'

'I know,' he said, 'but people aren't going to want another version.'

But they did. It was a big hit.

Within six months I'd stacked up all these firsts. And they came about simply because all I'd done was make records that entertained people and made money. And the reason I'd done that was because that was my job. Every night I worked at the disco I kept people dancing. If you played something people liked, they danced. If you played something they didn't like, they walked off. It wasn't rocket science.

That dancefloor was the best acid test there was. I'd brought that mentality into the record industry; for fifteen years I'd been used to the snap judgement of someone saying 'That's a piece of shit' and walking off the dancefloor. So that became the way I'd respond to things I heard. No messing about with endless meetings, just this is great, or it ain't. End of story. And hard though it may be to believe, that was something people weren't used to. Although I was new to the record industry, I had a wealth of experience in club or popular culture. So I applied that knowledge to the record business.

I had the advantage, as has happened throughout my life, of being there at the very beginning as the world changed. Record companies had never been so hands-on before. It was only a couple of years since they'd launched their first promotional offices. The companies were beginning to change the way that they perceived their customers bought records. Now there was a far more bluntly direct route between the A&R and the record company and the consumer. And with Silver Convention I was even asked to put together the public image of the band. The American sleeves had a fifteen piece orchestra on the cover! I thought they looked awful, so I got three girls on the cover to give them that look of the Three Degrees. Because it looked better, the public perception of Silver Convention became my perception of Silver Convention. The girls, not the orchestra. I wasn't thinking of myself as an image Svengali, I just wanted something that would look good. There was no premeditation behind any of the things I was doing then. What seemed right: that was all.

Magnet had built up 12 per cent of the British singles market without me having a clue as to its importance. Similarly, I didn't know how much money I'd made for Silver Convention or for Michael Levy or for Midland International. They were all just brothers in the dance trade to me. Looking back it was all so naive, so tiny. There were so few players.

American rewrites of dance music history try to build it into some artistic spectacle, but the bottom line behind any successful trend is that someone, somewhere, has got some money. It takes someone with money to take the trend from the boondocks and put it into the mainstream arena.

Where was the volcano that knocked the dinosaurs out? We were the volcano. My attitude to the job did begin to change as I got more successful and got paid more. When I was on sixty quid a week it was just a kind of extra bit of fun to go with the DJing. When it was a hundred quid and all the bonuses were coming in and I'd got this Golden Boy tag, suddenly it became very different. I couldn't eat at the Parsons Nose chippy in Coventry and do an advert over the mic at two in the morning in return for a free bag of chips. I had enough money to get whatever I liked, and I wasn't used to that feeling. Very quickly my life started to change.

My parents just couldn't deal with it at all. I took my first silver disc home, for 'Hurt So Good', and got a nail out to hammer it up. My mum wouldn't let me. 'I don't want the neighbours to think you've gone big-headed,' she said. And if Peter Shelley came round to the house in his Rolls Royce he wasn't allowed to park outside the house, because my mum reckoned the neighbours would think it was the tally man come to repossess the furniture. He had to park around the corner. When I got the big bonus cheque I took it round to show my mum and she fainted. She thought I'd stolen it from the accounts department and tried to get me to go and give it back to Michael. They just couldn't comprehend that anyone could make that amount of money from records. I'd been there six months and already I'd earned more than my dad had earned in his whole life. You can see how alien it must have seemed to my mum. She never understood the record industry and how it was everything to me, never understood why I left my wife for it, never understood the kind of money it generated. But she loved me, so she just let me get on with it. She thought one day I'd grow out of it and get a real job. My dad was the same; he never understood it either. I think it was because there was no one else in the family with that kind of determination or drive or enthusiasm. No one else who was determined to succeed at all costs. As very religious people, I think my parents may have thought there was something slightly immoral about it all.

For me it was a fantastic time. I went out to the Disco Conventions in New York and started to meet the Americans making disco, people like Bernard Edwards and Chic. Along with Chris Hill, who had been one of the most influential soul DJs in the South of England, we were talked up as England's version and got a lot of respect from the people we met there.

One day in New York I got taken to a studio to give some advice on a record that some people were putting out. I gave them a few suggestions because I could see that what they were trying to do was make a Donna Summer record. That record turned out to be Sylvester's 'You Make Me Feel Mighty Real' and, yet again, I'd been there advising at its inception.

I did enjoy the New York disco crowd. It wasn't unknown for me and Chris Hill to go down Studio 54 naked except for socks on our privates. The American crowd were chic dudes and we weren't, we were just scruffy bastards. But people knew they could do business with us and that we knew what we were on about.

I'd be jetting about all over the place by this time. One week it would be New York, the next it was Germany or

FOOL IF YOU THINK IT'S OVER

France. They were very exciting times. Magnet was a label based on homegrown talent, but it hadn't been operating on a large enough scale to be considered a proper record company. It had been more of a production company. Without realising I'd turned it into a record company and we were so successful that we'd blown the majors out of the water. We'd taken away their domination, and the majors obviously weren't going to sit back and let Magnet and the other independents that came in our wake take such a huge share of the market. I put together a meeting with some of the others, trying to establish an alliance of independents to try and counter the majors who were obviously starting to gang up. It never came to anything, but it was clear that we were in a vulnerable position. The majors had seen how lucrative disco was and they just muscled in and took it all away. You'd have American record companies spending half a million on a record, while I was expected to compete with a budget of ten thousand pounds. It just wasn't possible. And the more it became about big business the less interested I felt. The thing that had attracted me in the first place had been the records. Now, the records themselves had become the least important part of the equation and the passion had gone. I became very disenchanted.

At the same time we got hit with a lawsuit from Lee Perry, who claimed that Dennis hadn't had the rights to put out the Susan Cadogan record. We looked into it, and found the rights had been sold three times over to a load of different people. I was caught up in the middle of all that and it was a nightmare. Worst of all, I hated having to do what I was told.

It was a lot easier when no one took me seriously, when it was fun. By now it had gone from being a job to being a lifestyle. And I wasn't prepared to live my life having to justify restaurant receipts while being expected to work 23 hours a day. I felt like I was selling my soul.

I'd met a chap called John who'd brought in a tape with three songs on. At that time, Island Records used to open their studios for a couple of hours a day when anyone could go in and do demos as long as they got first refusal. And this was one of the tapes that had come out of it and been passed on by Island. The tracks on the tape were rock songs. Now I don't profess to be a rock expert, but I do like good rock. And this was good rock. The singer had a fantastic voice.

'Actually,' said the guy, 'this bloke used to be signed to Magnet, but Michael dropped him.'

The singer was called Chris Rea.

I went up to Michael and said, 'Do you know who this Chris Rea is?'

'Yeah,' said Michael. 'We dropped him. We can't re-sign him.'

'We've got to,' I said, 'he's really good.'

There was massive resistance to me re-signing him to the label, but what I will say for Michael is that although he can be a ruthless businessman, if he can see someone genuinely believes in something he'll support them all the way. So we got Chris Rea back. I went up to Tyneside to meet him and got on really well with him. And I loved the songs, in fact I was so caught up listening to his tape in the car on the way up that I drove straight into the back of a transporter carrying six brand new Jaguars from the factory.

The first track I'd heard on the tape was 'Fool If You Think It's Over', which went on to be a huge hit and a song that's still played today.

Magnet had got A&R people in who seemed to me more like businessmen. I felt as if they were trying to control me, because I was seen as this wild bohemian. The whole Chris Rea project was suddenly taken over, and other people were deciding who he was going to work with, who was going to produce him, whatever. I felt that I'd been pushed out of involvement in it all. Anyway they stuck to their plans and they got Chris into the studio where he made the most godawful album you've ever heard in your life. It sounded like a wimpy Cat Stevens. There were all these keyboards on it for some reason, which was obviously stupid because Chris Rea's strength comes from the combination of his voice and a guitar.

I was supposed to sell this record to EMI in Germany, but it was the biggest pile of nonsense I've heard in my life. It was really poor; even Chris' manager had rung me up to tell me it was a crap record. Like I hadn't noticed. It just wasn't going to happen.

Michael eventually realised the same thing. So he got Chris back in the studio to make a record with Gus Dudgeon, who'd done Elton John's stuff. It was a very brave move on Michael's part to just bury the debut album and finance a completely new one. It was a giant leap of faith, but it established that Michael was thinking like a proper record executive. The album went on to be very successful, which was a vindication for Michael. And it proved that he was able to support real talent.

We did have problems with Chris' name. Michael didn't want him to be called Chris Rea because he said everyone would nickname him Dia-Rea. So out of the blue one day Michael announced to me that he'd come up with the name Benny Santini.

'Benny Santini!' I squeaked. It was quite possibly the worst alias anyone had ever even considered. Chris was horrified when I told him, so we pestered Michael into changing his mind and Chris got to stay as Chris Rea. But he did call the album *Whatever Happened To Benny Santini?*

Michael's best friend and lawyer, Tony Russell, went on to become the industry's biggest lawyer. He was feared and respected in equal measure in the business. He was married to a girl from Coventry, and we got on really well. We shared a villa at the following year's MIDEM; it was the Guinness family's villa in Antibes. Michael was there to do a Chris Rea deal with United Artists in America, the biggest, most happening label at the time.

The label boss was Artie Mogul and we threw a party for him out there. He turned up with Don Arden, another of the legendary music business managers who'd got quite a reputation for being something of a hard man. There were more guns at this party than Elliot Ness ever saw in his whole life. The whole place was surrounded with armed bodyguards. None of it bothered me, because I'd been around gangsters all my life through working in the ballrooms. Don was actually a really nice guy; a bit abrupt, but basically a bloke from Manchester who'd had to do what he felt necessary to succeed.

Artie had an appointment with Michael to sign the deal, but he kept on putting it off. He used to stay up all night gambling, playing cards, a real typical old-school American boss. Eventually Tony and I went up to his suite with Michael to see what was going on. Artie was sitting there completely naked except for a towel. And he just looked up, grabbed the contract and signed it like it was nothing; for although this was a deal for an enormous amount of money, to him it *was* nothing.

At that point I realised just how fed up I was with the whole business I was involved in. It had moved so far away from what I loved about it in the first place. It was all deals and ego and nothing to do with music. I've always admired Michael Levy and I always will. He took me out of Coventry and gave me a chance when no one else would, but what was happening with Magnet just didn't appeal to me any more. I'd been there two and a half years and I couldn't really see it interesting me any longer. I had a passion for what I did that wasn't being satisfied.

I'd formed my own band on the side called JALN. It stood for Just Another Lonely Night. I'd got a band from Birmingham called Superbad who played with me. It was no great shakes, but it was fun and I was doing my own thing, which was most important. I got far more satisfaction from that than I did at Magnet. Music had got so boring. The American labels in particular were churning out stuff in such volume and with so little imagination that it just sent you to sleep. Everyone had their own label, and 99 per cent of the records were awful.

I decided that the music business wasn't for me any more. I couldn't be honest about it; the excitement had gone for me. The money was too big and, though it might sound stupid, I was groaning under the wealth. I just couldn't handle it. I think it was the greed that put me off the most. Every time you did anything new, someone wanted a part of it. It was relentless. Furthermore, I felt I'd lost touch with real life; I spent all my time on trains or planes and in studios. Tilly had brought in bands like Darts and Matchbox to the label and they didn't interest me in the slightest. I did have some fun when I discovered a boy band of the time called Stephenson's Rocket and wrote their first two hits, but it was only a brief diversion from a way of life that was driving me mad.

So I decided to jack it all in and go off to be a coal miner.

7 You're The One That I Want

I T WAS 1977, I WAS BORED, AND I NEEDED a focus. I actually applied for a couple of jobs in the record business, but didn't even get a reply. That was quite strange since I was obviously way more qualified than most of the other people working in the industry, and had a great track record. Maybe it's just as well I didn't get the jobs, as I might not have ended up where I am today, but at the time I did find the rejection quite insulting. I'd had enough of it all and I wanted to do something completely different.

If you're going to get back to real life then you've got to do it like you really mean it. And you can't get a much harder job than being a miner, so that appealed to me. I felt I had to purge my soul, get it all out of my system. I'd got lazy and overweight and didn't like what was going on in my life. I had no friends. And so I was like one of those guys who's been sitting in a steam room for ages, and then goes and jumps in the snow. I wanted to give my system a serious shock. There was never any question of me dropping out. Quite the opposite, I was dropping back in, if you like. I had to know what the pain of work felt like again and it was only by getting my body back into shape that I'd be able to get my mind back in shape. I'd been dealing with so much crap in the record industry that I'd forgotten what real life was like. I wanted to do something basic and honest.

So I went to the Coventry Homefire plant and got myself a job as a miner. The job interview went well, basically because they didn't ask any questions. They just wanted someone big who wouldn't mind swinging a shovel two miles underground. That was exactly what I wanted to do. The coal industry was still fairly healthy and it seemed like a good idea at the time.

First day at work I got in the cage and it took me down to the bottom of the shaft where a guy came up to me and said because I was such a big lad he needed someone like me to work for him on the surface. So I got back in the cage and went straight back up again. I found myself doing concreting for them all day, just laying concrete outside.

I was DJing that evening and I met a bloke in the pub beforehand who told me he wanted someone to do some concreting for him. So, with about five hours' experience, I got a job with him for forty quid a day. That was the end of my very short career with the Coal Board. But the hard work at the concrete company seemed even better.

A day later and by Christ was I regretting it. It was the hardest job I have ever had in my life. The company had come up with a completely new concrete treatment whereby the concrete had no sand in it. And they were getting loads of work repairing the city centre car parks around the country that had started to crumble to pieces.

I went down to the site, which was a three-storey car park. They had the biggest cement mixer you've ever seen, and they delivered the aggregate for the mix thirty lorries at a time. I was mixing it all with a power-assisted scoop and heaving in these huge bags of concrete. I must have lifted a hundred and forty bags by three o'clock that day. It wasn't like being in the record industry any more.

A lorry pulled up and there was another huge lorry delivering bags of cement from the Blue Circle factory in Rugby. Now, Rugby is only ten minutes away from Coventry so the concrete was still red hot. And I had to stack it while it was still so hot that it burned your hands. I tell you, if you want a way to bring you back to reality quickly, making concrete is hard to beat. I was dead by the end of the first day and the whole of my back was covered in blisters from where the concrete had burned me when I slung the sacks on my back. The labourers were moving this stuff around like it was popcorn, but I was completely knackered.

I went home and had a bath, leaving a permanent rim round the side, because concrete really stinks. By the next day I couldn't move, but I was determined not to be beaten so I stuck the job out for the whole summer. And of course I woke up every day wondering what on earth I was doing, but as the job went on I found I was thinking so much more clearly. I was probably the richest labourer in Britain, but I was focussed on what I was doing. I really wasn't thinking about getting back into the record business.

Punk was starting to happen and I'd seen the Sex Pistols when I was working at Magnet. I really enjoyed them and loved bands like the Stranglers as well. I'd started to play punk as a DJ and went down to all the punk clubs even though I was ten years older than anyone else there. I loved the energy, and although Magnet had never signed punk acts I knew a lot of the people from other companies who were involved in the scene. In punk I'd seen a way of working that inspired me. I was very drawn to that whole do-it-yourself ethos and the anti-establishment thing. While it wasn't as outrageous as I would have liked, and was still controlled by a lot of public schoolboys, it was still pretty good fun. If the Pistols thought they were about anarchy they should have lived with me for a few years, then they'd have seen what chaos was really like.

I'd pretty much cut off all my links with people from the music industry by then. One of my few real friends from that world was Peter Collins. He was a small record producer whom I'd bought some stuff from towards the end of my time at Magnet and we'd got on like a house on fire. He was a lovely little Jewish kid who'd been brought up in a posh house with servants and wasn't the slightest bit streetwise, but a great lad. He lived in Soho and every hooker around knew what he looked like because he wore a great big cowboy hat. They used to say hello to him when they saw him in the street. And he was so innocent he didn't even realise they were on the game. He was, however, very, very talented and came from a folk rather than rock'n'roll angle, which set him apart from everyone else. We used to ring each other every week; he was the only person I'd really stayed in contact with in the record industry.

My friend Chris Mason who'd worked with me at the Soul Hole record shop was now running the Virgin Records shop in the arcade in Coventry. He'd heard on the grapevine that there was a new band in town who were looking for management. So, one night I went up to a local pub called the General Wolfe to see this group called the Automatics, who were great. Jerry Dammers, who was the leader, had fused punk and ska and come up with this totally original sound. But the amazing thing was, they were toasting in the band. I was very impressed with them because they were quite simply unlike anyone else around. Two of them, Lynval and Neville, were dancers I knew from DJing. I knew another couple of the band from local groups. They had a singer called Tim at the time who looked like James Dean, and they played 'Too Much Too Young', 'Jaywalking' and 'Concrete Jungle' and that was it. I was smitten. I asked if I could manage them. They were only too happy to agree. Without planning it, I was back in the industry.

I rang around everyone I knew and told them they had to come and see this fantastic group. By then they'd changed their name to the Coventry Automatics and changed their singer for Terry Hall. Now, Terry was not then a singer, but he was a tremendous entertainer. I didn't get it myself at first, but Jerry Dammers did and he brought Terry in. Jerry is a genius. I've always thought that and the music he was making then was far ahead of its time. All the people who'd come into the industry at the same time as me had now started to get high-level jobs in the companies. We'd all cut our teeth at the same time so I rang them all up and tried to persuade them to see the Automatics. A few of them went along to gigs, but surprisingly they didn't like them much. I was astounded that they didn't love them. The whole urban sound of the Automatics seemed completely natural. There was nothing faked about it. It seemed like that was exactly what the record companies should have been signing, but they didn't seem interested.

I got £600 together and we went down to Berwick Street Studios in London to record demos of three or four songs. They were utterly brilliant. Really raw, really exciting. I took the tape around to a few people and yet again absolutely nobody was interested. I had the publishing and I was the manager and as far as I was concerned they were the greatest band I had ever seen. I couldn't understand it.

A few months later they changed their name to the Specials, started the Two-Tone label and became a phenomenon. But back then no one would touch them. And I was running out of time, both financially and emotionally. I just couldn't get them a deal.

The 1978 MIDEM was coming up, so Peter Collins, bless his heart, offered to pay for me to go out as long as I tried to sell some of his records for him. He kept on hassling me about getting back into the record industry and the excitement of being around Jerry Dammers and his band had rekindled my enthusiasm. Plus, it was winter and who wants to work on a building site in the winter? You don't need much encouragement to go to the South of France.

So I went down to MIDEM and tried to sell the Coventry Automatics, as they were still called. Yet again, no interest. I was so depressed about it all because it was obvious to me that they were an extraordinary group who were going to have a lot of hits. If anything, they were too far ahead of their time, and that's why no one else could appreciate how good they were.

One of the most important things about me is that I'm the luckiest guy in the world. Things happen to me without me trying, and they've kept on happening throughout my life. As soon as one door closed another opened. It was the same at that MIDEM.

I was sitting having a cup of tea when I felt a pat on my back. It was Eddie O'Loughlin from Midland International, and he told me he was currently Number One around the world with the *Saturday Night Fever* soundtrack. Then and there Eddie offered me a job doing John Travolta's A&R. I had no idea that Travolta could even sing because of course the *Saturday Night Fever* songs had been by the Bee Gees, but Eddie assured me he had a good voice and that the job would be right up my street.

I took the job, thinking of it more as a way of opening a few doors for me to publicise the Automatics. I didn't realise that Travolta would go on to be just about the biggest star in the world at the time. I helped chop and change some things around with a number of the songs on *Grease*. The album was being put out by RSO in America and their boss, Robert

Stigwood, has my greatest admiration for what he did with the Bee Gees. But over here the record was coming out on another label, and that was a different story entirely. The people involved in putting it out didn't have a clue. They had no idea about which singles to put out and spent all their time in meetings without actually doing anything.

It seemed perfectly simple to me. All they had to do was put out 'You're The One That I Want' by John Travolta and Olivia Newton John and they'd have a Number One. Then on the back of that they could have a whole load more hits off the album. It didn't seem to be something they needed to have meetings about. It was like shelling peas. When I suggested it they all looked at me like I was mad. And they had all these convoluted plans for the record that would have taken away from the simple fact that it was a great collection of pop singles. I spent all my time on the phone to the Americans trying to get them to persuade the British end to see some sense. I got my way in the end and, sure enough, it panned out exactly like I'd predicted. The *Grease* album was just about finished and, along with the phenomenal success of the *Saturday Night Fever* soundtrack, John Travolta was established as a major star.

It was very useful for me to actually witness celebrity on the scale that Travolta had attained, because it taught me just how important the concept of the pop celebrity was becoming. I remember sitting with Travolta in a New York steakhouse when the President of the United States came up and asked him for an autograph. When the President is asking for your autograph you know you're famous! Travolta was a nice bloke, but I think it was the concept of his celebrity that intrigued me the most.

I'd also started doing a column for a trade magazine called *Record Business*. Peter Harvey would ring me up and I'd tell him about the hottest new records. They gave me the pen name the Disco Duck. I must have been the only journalist who couldn't read or write, but I was good at picking up the big new records. So I was responsible for tipping 'Instant Replay' by Dan Hartman, 'Y.M.C.A.' by Village People, a whole load of stuff. It kind of gave disco a second wind. I started getting people ringing me up asking me to do consultancy work on disco records. That was what I'd tried to get away from and now I was right back in it again. It was clear by now that I wasn't just dipping my foot in the water, I was back in the record industry full-time. I had all these different things on the go at once and that kept my interest alive. I was doing what I wanted to do and working for myself.

I was still very friendly with Peter Collins. His ex-partner got married to Tom Jones' piano player's daughter and they had moved abroad to set up the biggest nightclub in Bermuda. It was an enormous place, something like Studio 54. And because I gave it a plug in my column he flew me out there, and I had a great time. One night I was in the club having a beer with John Lennon, who was separated from Yoko at the time, and we were talking about disco, as you do. The idea came up for a Disco Convention in London and the guy who owned the club said he reckoned he could get the Bermudan government to sponsor it. Now, when I'm excited about an idea, I do my best to make it happen. It seemed to me that the Disco Convention thing was a very exciting idea. So we hired a place called the Venue in Victoria and got a whole load of acts on. And we had a competition there, where the first prize was a week's all-expenses-paid holiday in Bermuda. It was a huge success.

I'd only been back five minutes and I'd got Travolta, the Disco Duck and now Britain's first Disco Convention. I was certainly establishing myself, although I wasn't making much money out of it all. I mean I only had enough left over at the end of each week to buy a couple of model railway engines. But at least I was enjoying what I was doing, and by the end of 1978 I had a fabulous reputation. I spent the next year trying to calm it all down a bit; just letting things tick over and trying to think about where I was going with my life. I still did a bit of promotion and carried on with the column, but it was all a bit less frenetic than the year before. What I did do was go back into the studio again and get my nerve back producing and writing. Nothing big, just keeping my hand in.

Meanwhile the Automatics had become the Specials, and though I'd had to end my involvement with them a while earlier because I simply didn't have the time, people still remembered that I had been raving about them before anyone else. It consolidated my reputation even more. By the end of 1979 I was sure that I wanted to stay in the record industry. This time, though, I wanted to do it on my own terms. It was the first time I even considered the idea of having my own label. I'd been right about the Specials and that vindication gave me a lot of confidence.

At the 1980 MIDEM I met a man who was to change my life forever: Salvador Chianti, president of MCA Music. A true Sicilian gentleman, very dapper and more charismatic than anyone I've ever known, I met him through Leeds Levy, who was being groomed by Sal to be the next president of the company. Sal wanted to retire and Leeds was a real go-getter. It was obvious that he was going to hand over the reins soon.

They invited me to have tea with them at the Inn On The Park in London the week after I got back from MIDEM. I went along and, out of the blue, Sal said to me, 'How do you fancy a job?' Now, the last thing I needed was a job. I had enough of them already! My life wasn't particularly going anywhere, but I was quite happy with what I was doing. Peter Collins was starting to get successful as a producer and I was helping him out. I wasn't looking for any more work. But Sal wouldn't take no for an answer. He told me he wanted to give me a job working at Leeds Music, which was a music publishing wing of MCA. My job would be to go in and modernise it with my own independent production company based in the building. I was expected to bring in songs by new artists and just shake things up a bit. At the same time I could carry on with the other work I was already doing, using their place as a base. They'd give me a good salary and an office on Piccadilly. I liked the sound of an office on Piccadilly; it felt like I'd really hit the jackpot.

But then they took me down to see the building. It was magnificent from the outside, but you walked in and it was 1953 all over again. Honestly, it looked like some office from just after the war. It was as if the whole place had been caught in a time warp. And it might as well have been a bank as anything to do with the record business. I could see immediately that modernisation was going to take a lot of work.

They introduced me to Cyril Simons, who was to become my mentor in many ways. The two of us together were like Morecambe and Wise, opposites in the extreme. Cyril wasn't a risk-taker; he was a veteran of the old-style music business and a publisher through and through. If you had cut him he would have bled musical notes. I was for taking chances, he wasn't; he was 1953 whereas I was 2003. On the face of it, it was a complete mismatch, but here I was, expected to work for a company where they had a sherry break at eleven every morning!

Still, the prospect of working there kind of intrigued me and I accepted the job. They gave me a cupboard for my office and a girl called Suzie as my assistant. With Sal's approval, I set up a production company with Peter Collins that would be based there, called Loose Ends. The idea was that if you were at a loose end, we were the people to call. So I was working within this giant of a music publishing company, but had the freedom of my own production company as well. It was a pretty odd state of affairs, but I've never done things the conventional way and it worked well for me.

I don't think Cyril Simons was very happy to be working with me at first. This was a man who must have thought his life was going to run along the same sensible, conventional straight path forever. He didn't want anything to ripple his pond. And then I came along and I must have seemed like I was from hell, his worst nightmare. There weren't going to be ripples from then on, there were going to be tidal waves.

I think he saw my arrival as the end of his reign. The threat wasn't specifically from me, the problem was that the Americans had installed me there. So from then on it was going to be them dictating the running of Leeds Music. No matter how successful it was, it was old-fashioned and institutional, and the one thing the Americans wanted to get rid of was the concept of the record industry being run as an old-fashioned British institution. So the Americans just threw me in like a big bomb and waited for me to go off.

This was exactly what I'd predicted years earlier: that the American Way would eventually control the British record business. The Americans liked me because I was basically an American in a British body. I thought like them, had the same enthusiasm as them and believed in being direct. I wasn't going to take any prisoners. And I think they thought it would be worth it even if I only lasted a year and killed everybody – at least I would have initiated change.

The Americans had started to think globally, too, bringing in lawyers and accountants and starting to roll their products around the world without having the British there as a pain in their arse. It was the beginning of the industry becoming truly modern; as the eighties began, the new broom came along with the new decade.

Cyril had been there since the fifties and had run a very successful publishing company. He wasn't dynamic and he didn't court publicity, but he was a great old-fashioned publisher. He knew the business inside out. When you sat and talked to him about deals, you realised that his knowledge was staggering. He'd really earned the right to his comfortable lifestyle, but that knowledge wasn't enough any more. The MCA group was looking to expand at a quite phenomenal rate and the whole idea of that was completely alien to Cyril. He constantly advocated caution. What he didn't understand was that MCA were trying to establish brand identity for the label before the phrase 'brand identity' had even been coined. I understood exactly what they were doing and how MCA wanted a greater presence. They wanted to rationalise and bring the record company and publishing together. Now they thought that would never happen if they had someone just come in and work for Cyril, because Cyril wouldn't have let it happen. He would have just put obstacles in the way. The only way forward was to give someone like me the power to change things. I actually think it was unfair of them to put Cyril in that position because he'd done good work and continued to do good work for MCA. He was the master at what he did; he knew the back catalogues inside out, knew how to play one deal off against another, he knew it all. He was entitled to be a respected senior citizen of the record industry, but the Americans seemed adamant that things had to change.

It took a while for Cyril to realise that I was being honest, but I eventually convinced him that I had nothing but respect for him. He used to sit and tell me about the old music publishing days when it really was a cut-throat business. While I'd been on the common playing records in the fifties, he'd been on the phone to America doing deals for publishing, establishing the base for what the industry had become. It was fantastic just talking to him, and before long we had a relationship that was the complete opposite of what I think the Americans had intended. He could be a difficult man to get along with, but he was honest and I admired his experience and his integrity. I had the enthusiasm and the dreams and the knowledge. I wanted to dominate the world and he just wanted to dominate his bridge club. And in a strange way that meant we actually worked really well together, so while the Americans had intended for me to upset the whole apple cart, that didn't actually happen. I may have come in firing on all cylinders, but I wasn't going to let it fall apart. I'm like that. If you throw me in the shit, I've got news for you: I'll find a fucking paddle, and you'll find me sitting at the front of the canoe. I'd had affection for Cyril from the first ten minutes of meeting him and I wasn't going to be a part of destroying him. So in the end we actually managed to establish a working relationship. He taught me a lot of what he'd learned over the years and having him around was invaluable.

Way back at the second MIDEM I ever went to, I'd met David Croker. He'd discovered Elton John, and put Elton together with his manager John Reid. David had left EMI to go and run Rocket Records, which was Elton John's label. David was a lovely guy; the most laid-back person you could imagine. He had a razor-sharp knowledge of popular music, and we struck up a friendship based mainly around our mutual knowledge of pop trivia. In fact, because Elton John was on MCA in America, it was David who'd recommended me to Sal Chianti and Leeds Levy for the Leeds Music job.

I'd done some work for him over the years with acts like Judy Tzuke, who was very popular in the seventies, because David was trying to build Rocket into a proper company, not just a vehicle for Elton. He was one of the few people who really appreciated the Specials, and in fact Rocket tried desperately to sign Madness at one point. In 1980 he asked me to go and help out with their A&R department occasionally, working with Sally Atkins. Rocket wanted me to go on Elton John's tour of Russia to do A&R back-up, but I simply didn't have the time. They still wanted me to do some stuff for their label though, in terms of giving the company a younger image. I'm not being rude, and David's no longer with us unfortunately, but he would have agreed that at the time trying to get any band managers to take Rocket records seriously was just about impossible. Artist's own record labels are seen by most people as an indulgent whim.

I went in there and decided to place an ad in *NME* saying that if anyone wanted free studio time and the chance of a break into the music business then they should ring Rocket and we'd sort it out. Suddenly we had about three hundred bands on the phone. So Sally and I dashed around seeing them all and, once we'd ditched all the cabaret singers, we tried to sort out the good ones. We had an idea for putting out a compilation album of the best ones, so suddenly I found myself producing something like fourteen bands. We hadn't made any judgements on particular musical styles, so it was a really diverse bunch. The theory was that the cream would rise to the top. We were going to put the record out for sale and see if anyone picked up on the acts. And it gave me a chance to hang out at Rocket. I never met Elton there, but the luxury of his lifestyle had rubbed off on the place. Every day for lunch we had a bottle of Chablis and a baguette. Before that I'd only ever had a bottle of Vimto!

It was a trip through fantasyland being able to choose all these acts, but very hard work and on a budget of something like three and a half grand. We were working 24 hours a day. The album eventually came out and it got pretty good reviews. It was the first time anyone had done anything like it and it was good for Elton's image because he got a reputation for being a good guy, helping out bands that were just starting. A few acts did come out of it, though, that were a cut above the rest.

One of them was the Lambrettas, who were part of a movement of mod bands that were around at the time. Obviously they were just ripping off the sixties, but they weren't bad at all. Rocket decided to put out a single by them, a cover of the mod standard, 'Poison Ivy', and David asked me to produce it. So I did and it sounded really good. Rocket created a label especially for the band and we called it Two Stroke as a tribute to the Specials' 'Two Tone'. I'd asked Jerry's permission and he thought it was really funny. The record came out and it was a massive hit, the first one in years by anyone other than Elton John that had been a hit for Rocket.

I loved the work I was doing for Rocket, but I hated being part of the office. I'm not a political animal. They had Eric 'Monster Monster ' Hall there and he was a great promotions guy, but then they started getting him involved in publishing and as far as I was concerned, he just wasn't the right person for the job. It wasn't playing to his strengths. It seemed like the people at Rocket really didn't focus enough on making themselves into a proper record company. There was too much flair and not enough of a work ethic. That said, the flair was pretty impressive. John Reid and Elton John were actually the most tasteful people I ever met, even if you might not think so because of Elton's flamboyant image. In private they did everything with incredible taste, and in public they had glorious style and panache. I remember going to a Christmas party where the cabaret was a bunch of Liverpool dockers in drag, and there were people sneaking off and snorting coke off Rolls Royce radiator grilles.

In 1980 I also got married again, to Julie. A year later, we had a son called Peter, my second child. I was hoping that perhaps this time I could balance work and my private life, though sadly once again things would not work out, and we would split up four years later.

Work-wise, the eighties had begun pretty spectacularly for me, but I had no idea just how much more exciting they were going to get.

8 Pass The Dutchie

THE EXPERIENCE I'D GOT FROM MCA and Rocket was a wonderful education, but there were other people who, in the early eighties, set me on the road to where I am today.

A vital figure was Dave Robinson, who ran Stiff records with Jake Riviera. Stiff was just about the best independent label in Britain and I loved the acts they'd signed, like Elvis Costello, Wreckless Eric and Madness. I'd first met the Stiff people when Elvis Costello was recording the *My Aim Is True* album ('Red Shoes' by Costello is one of my favourite songs of all time) and because I was stuck in London for the night I'd sat in the studio and pretended to be a tape operator.

Dave is one of the business's most colourful characters: a wild Irishman just bursting with ideas and a completely unconventional way of working. I rang him up at his office once and his secretary said, 'He can't talk right now because he's out on the pavement having a fight with the Damned. If he wins, he'll call you back in a bit.' That was typical Dave.

Dave had heard some of the production stuff that Peter Collins had done with Matchbox and he'd liked it, so he said he'd think of us if he had any stuff we might be interested in.

One day he rang up and said, 'Watermax' – that was his nickname for me – 'Watermax, I've got something you might be interested in.'

So we went down to the Stiff HQ, which was based in a taxi office near Paddington, and he showed me these fourteen or fifteen girls who he said were in a band called the Belle Stars. He played me a demo tape of four of the worst songs I'd heard in my life. Or, technically, three and a half of the worst songs; there was something half-good about a number called 'Sign Of The Times'. Incomplete, but quite appealing in a Motownish way.

'It's right up your street, Watermax,' said Dave.

Around then we'd been working with a guy called Pete Hammond who had a studio called Tooting Sound in South London, and we'd become friends. So I told Dave I'd do it if we could work with Pete Hammond. A week later we went back to Stiff and by now the Belle Stars had gone from a fourteen piece to a five piece. They were nice enough girls, and a complete mixture of personalities in the group, but as I recollect they weren't exactly in love with each other.

Peter Collins, Pete Hammond and I went down to Trident Studios to record 'Sign Of The Times'. Pete Collins had a Linn drum machine, which was pretty new back then, and we asked the band if we could use it. The drummer wasn't having any of it, and said we had to use her real drumming. We had to sit with the drum machine under the mixing desk playing it over her drumming and every time she stopped we'd turn it off. If we were a bit late hitting the button, we told her that it was really her drumming, but that there was a delay in the studio.

We finished the record and it came out surprisingly well. It sounded like a hit.

When we took it back to Dave Robinson, he listened to it, then said, 'OK Watermax, speed it up a bit.'

'What do you mean, "Speed it up",' I said.

He told me that he had this theory that when they played a record on Radio One it automatically slowed the record down by three beats per minute. Quite where he'd got this bit of advanced physics from I don't know, but he was convinced of it.

Now some people have perfect pitch. I've got perfect rhythm. I know exactly the right speed for any record and speeding this up made it sound awful. We managed to dissuade him.

The video had lasers in, which was pretty spectacular for the time, and the girls had a pretty good image. The song was a big hit, and because Dave saw that we'd been able to handle working with the Belle Stars, who were a volatile bunch, he got us to produce their next two singles, 'The Clapping Song' and 'Iko Iko'. Two more singles, two more hits. 'Iko Iko' was so successful that there was even a cover version of it in the charts at the same time. The experience of working with the Belle Stars was going to stand me in good stead for handling Bananarama years later.

Dave, who'd by now moved offices to Bayham Street in Camden, started to employ us more and more. I think he saw Peter Collins and me as a cheap-rate version of Langer and Winstanley, the production team he had for Madness. One of the people he threw our way was Tracey Ullman. He told me he had a singer whom he wanted to cover a song called 'Breakaway', which I knew as an old Irma Franklyn B-side, a real old r'n'b favourite. Now I hadn't watched Tracey on her *Three Of A Kind* TV series where she'd got a reputation as an impressionist comedienne. I never watched TV. She could have been anybody. We went down to the studio and she asked me who I wanted her to do the song as, which I thought was a bit odd. Then she did it as Lulu, Diana Ross, all these different people. I was falling about with laughter and said to the other people in the studio that she ought to be a comedienne They thought I was taking the piss, but I genuinely didn't know who she was.

That song was a massive success and brought out one of Stiff's real strengths, the fabulous stable of girl singers that the label had.

One of the best singers and songwriters, not just on the label, but that Britain has ever produced, was Kirsty MacColl. She wrote a song called 'They Don't Know About Us' for Tracey, and Dave had me polishing it off at the studio in the middle of the night, with me getting Kirsty and Dave's wife Rosemary to add Shangri La-type backing vocals. It was the best song Tracey ever recorded and Dave gave me something like £30 for doing it.

The day after I'd first played it to him, I went into Dave's office and he said he'd decided not to release it because it didn't 'swing along'. I explained that everything didn't have to 'swing along' and that housewives everywhere would be singing along to it when they were doing the ironing. It went on to be Tracey's biggest hit and the record that broke her in America, a place that has completely taken her to their heart. Now she's a big star over there, and I sent Dave an ironing board painted gold when it got to Number Two.

Dave loved gadgets. He bought a brand new Merc and had one of the first mobile phones, back when mobiles were the size of fridges. He smashed it to pieces one day when he rang me up on it and I got him angrier and angrier by pretending I couldn't hear him. His office was full of whatever happened to be the newest gadget he could find.

He brought some of that obsession with gimmicks to the label. The promotional items would be ridiculous. For instance, because Madness had a song about it raining, he decided to shrink wrap Pac-A-Macs to all the singles. He hadn't even considered just how bulky that would be, so the office ended up full of Pac-A-Macs. He didn't think about how to market things in advance, he just went ahead and did it to see how it would turn out. And he brought that spirit to the videos that went with the songs. For Madness's 'My Girl' he dropped a piano off a crane onto a pianist sitting on the ground in the middle of a muddy park. It missed taking the guy's legs off by a fraction of an inch, though Dave was completely oblivious to it all. He just thought it was a great idea. Stiff was beginning to get in real financial trouble, but it was the only record company in the world that had its own Film Department.

The fact that Dave was making easily the most inventive videos around actually worked against him, I think. Like with Madness's 'I Like Driving In My Car', the 'beep-beep' car noise came from the video first, so the producers would often have to tailor the song to fit the video. This meant that the videos ended up becoming more artistic than the bands or the songs.

Dave was ostensibly a rock'n'roller, whereas I was a Motown man. I was convinced that Motown would last longer because it had a more specific brand loyalty. Rock'n'roll is all just about the flavour of the week. The way that music was going in the early eighties, rock wasn't particularly rebellious any more. Dance music, or more particularly the hi-energy of the gay disco scene, was the new underground. And Dave hated that music.

Still, I did bring him one more success. At MCA we'd picked up the rights to the song called 'Pretend'. It was originally a hit as a ballad for Nat King Cole, and that was the version that Cyril was thinking of when he bought it. I'd heard a country version by Gerry and the Pacemakers and I thought that way of recording it had potential too. That was a good example of the way that Cyril and I found common ground.

MCA had had a big hit when Shakin' Stevens did a cover of the rock'n'roll song, 'This Old House'. We offered 'Pretend' to him, but he turned it down. So, thinking back to my Magnet days, I realised it might be good for Alvin Stardust to do. I rang him up and he agreed to do it, so I put the money up and we recorded it. I decided to play it to Dave, without telling him who it was, and he loved it. When I revealed it was Alvin Stardust he was horrified, but then he realised that it might be so odd for Stiff to put it out that it was worth doing. He did the tightest deal in the world with me, but agreed to release it. Then, just before it was about to be released, he had another of his changes of heart. He'd come to the conclusion that it wasn't going to be a hit.

'Dave,' I said. 'I promise you this will be a hit. I'll make you a bet: if it's not Top Five, you keep all my royalties. If it's Top Three, you double them.'

'OK, Watermax,' he said. 'I like a bit of a flutter.'

It was a big hit all over the world and I got the double royalties. I knew that boogie rock'n'roll could fly across the globe. I wasn't thinking like a marketing man, I was being instinctive, and once again I was right.

Stiff was to end up being bought out by Trevor Horn in 1984, and Dave moved to Island Records. In a way it was the perfect plot, because he ended up doing the marketing for U2 and brought to U2 the kind of approach he'd had with Madness. If anything, he made them the rock version of Madness. Of course they went on to become the biggest band in the world. At the same time, Island, which had built a reputation as a credible sixties label, had turned into something that appeared to me to be run by smooth LA executives. Dave isn't a smooth LA executive, he's a rock'n'roller from Camden. So Island kind of consumed him and, to those who had known his earlier, maverick self, he lost that greatness that he'd had at Stiff. However, I can't overstate the importance Dave Robinson has had on my life. On the one side I had Cyril at MCA exercising caution and giving me this incredible business education. On the other I had Dave championing blind faith and pure enthusiasm. Having those two very different people around me at that time was so important.

Dave Croker had left Rocket by now and gone to work for Hansa Records where he was working with the Thompson Twins. He'd also picked up a deal for licensing stuff to Sire Records. He asked me if I had anyone he should check out and I told him that, as it happened, I did.

I'd been with Jerry Dammers to see a band called the Piranhas, and I thought they were fantastic. They were one of those new-wavey pop bands that came out of the whole post-punk thing and what I liked most about them was that their line-up included two guys called Johnny Elmer and Bob Grover who wrote really good lyrics. I'd got all their records and particularly liked one called 'Coloured Vinyl' which was about how all the record companies were putting records out on coloured vinyl. It was written wittily enough to actually make it one of the smartest attacks on the record business I'd heard at the time. In their set they used to do a cover version of a song called 'Tom Hark', which I knew from my old ballroom days. I got in touch with the band, told them I was a fan of the original 'Tom Hark' and asked them if they fancied putting out a new version with new lyrics to come out on Sire.

They were well up for it, so we went down to Pete Hammond's Tooting Sound to record it. It was Cup Final Day on the hottest day of the year and we still didn't have any lyrics as we travelled down on the tube. Then these two old women started gabbing away in the seats opposite us and Bob and I just looked at each other. They'd been wittering on about war and holidays and what they were saying was so scatty that we knew it just had to be a song. We got to the studio and Bob wrote the lyrics down in the loo, in all of five minutes. Then we went into the studio and the drummer, who was called Dick Slecsic, put down the beat. It must have been 110°F in the studio. Dick did the drums in three minutes and passed out. The B-side was called 'Getting Beaten up' and the chorus went, 'Getting beaten up/Is part of growing up.' I loved the Piranhas.

We got Sire to put it out with a lovely glossy sleeve covered with instructions on how to do the dance and, yet again, I found myself with a big hit on my hands. Even today you hear the tune being sung at football matches. Classics last forever.

I had my fingers in all these different pies, and it seemed that everything I was doing was successful. As you can imagine, by the middle of '82 Loose Ends was flying and Peter and I were the golden boys.

That summer MCA Records and MCA Music started to move closer and closer together. They brought in a new A&R chief called Charlie Ayres and he immediately signed three groups. The first was Tygers Of Pan Tang, a thrashy heavy metal band. The second was Nik Kershaw. The third was a group of young kids from Birmingham called Musical Youth. Charlie asked me if I'd like to produce the new signings.

Tygers Of Pan Tang were a proficient metal band, and if that style of music is played well, I'm all for it. I didn't think that we'd be the best people to produce them, but I was prepared to give it a go.

Nik Kershaw I loved right from the start. He reminded me of Elton John. From the demo I heard, I could tell he had at least eight good songs so I told MCA that they should forget about signing him for a singles deal and make it an album deal, because he obviously had real talent.

Musical Youth I'd already heard from listening to John Peel. They were really young kids, but they were making these amazing reggae records. I didn't need persuading to produce them.

The track that Charlie played me was called 'Pass The Coochie' and it was nine and a half minutes long. Now there was no way that Radio One were going to play a record nine and a half minutes long, so we chopped it down to four minutes, tightened it up a bit and used that as the arrangement for the version that Musical Youth would record.

We went to Birmingham for the recording session and it was chaos. They all had their families there and there were people all over the place treating it like it was a big party or something. Someone had decided that we had to change the title from 'Pass The Coochie' to 'Pass The Dutchie', because a 'coochie' was a spliff, but a 'dutchie' was a cooking pot. To be honest, I never completely bought the cooking pot explanation. I'm sure it was just some West Indian Brummie bullshit, but I couldn't be bothered arguing, so we recorded it as 'Pass The Dutchie'. But when I heard the tape of the version they'd done I hated it. It had no spark. Completely lifeless.

Peter agreed, but MCA wanted to release it. They thought it was great just because they were caught up in the idea of the band rather than the song itself. There was no way I was going to let them put it out, so we took the band to Peter Hammond's studio in Tooting and did it again. We added a bit of percussion and extra keyboards and this time it *was* brilliant. I took the tape to MCA and played it to them and it was great. You got goosebumps listening to it. It bit your arse bigtime. They knew that was the version they had to put out.

Musical Youth went straight to Number One. The record was selling something like 89,000 copies a day. I was sitting at home watching *News At Ten* when suddenly they announced the headline, 'Reggae Boys From Birmingham Have Number One Hit.' It was extraordinary! I'd produced this record and it was on the news! Their promotions guy, Peter Price, had pulled an amazing stroke where he'd turned a music story into a national news story. It was the first time that had ever happened.

At MCA Music we thought we'd done the deal for Musical Youth's publishing on the record. After all I'd been given the project and brought it all together. We'd been talking to the original writers, but somehow we never managed to close the deal. It was one of those typical reggae record 'later' deals. The one where people would be saying, 'Yeah man, later' to you all the time.

Anyway, I went to the party MCA had thrown to celebrate the record getting to Number One and in walked Peter Price with Richard Branson. He announced that Richard had the rights to the publishing. Branson clearly knew nothing about the background, but it appeared to me as if Peter had talked to the management and played both ends off against the middle. I felt disappointed that we'd built the whole thing from nothing and had it taken away from us. A couple of weeks later Peter Price went to work for Richard Branson. It may well have been coincidence, but it felt wrong to me.

We decided to record the first Musical Youth album in Los Angeles. Getting away from Birmingham was the only way to escape the quite extraordinary tabloid interest that was resulting from the band's success. Musical Youth came from the heart of the city's West Indian community, and there was a great deal of inter-island jealousy going on, as people connected with the band with roots in different parts of the West Indies started slagging each other off. The boys were at the centre, everyone trying to sell their stories to the press, and journalists were coming up with tenuous links to some so-called criminal element in their not-so-immediate families. It was madness. They'd got a new manager and whereas the old manager had been the father of one of the band, using their fame as a way of acting out his own fantasy of success, the new guys had lost that personal link with the band. The Birmingham Education Authority had insisted that all royalties go to a fund that they would manage, and that was just about the only sensible decision that came out of the whole thing.

Musical Youth were actually the first black band ever to get their video on MTV, so right from the moment we arrived at LA Airport, they were recognised wherever they went. Usually when you're famous in Britain, you go to America and, because of its vastness, you're anonymous. However, because of the MTV thing they were even more famous in America than they were in Britain. We were staying at a lovely villa in the hills and there'd be people like Diana Ross, Bill Cosby and even Mr T ringing up asking to meet them. It was bizarre.

While we were there, there was work to be done on the Nik Kershaw project as well. I'd come up with the idea of using Jerry Hay, who'd worked on Michael Jackson's *Off The Wall* album to do a brass arrangement on Nik's single, 'Won't Let The Sun Go Down On Me'. I met Quincy Jones at the studio and he put me in touch with Jerry and we did the track. MCA hated it and said you couldn't put out a contemporary pop record with brass on it, but of course they were wrong. We did it and it was critically acclaimed as a great arrangement. And, obviously, it sold a whole load of copies.

I should have been sitting on top of the world, having been responsible for the best-selling single of the year in Musical Youth and giving Nik Kershaw a big hit, but it all seemed to have gone sour. Stiff was in big financial trouble and the Piranhas had fallen out of favour with Sire. It was the same old story: record company politics. I didn't want to be involved. My job, as I saw it, was making hits; that's been the cornerstone of everything I've done. If someone has a better song than I do, I'll use theirs ahead of mine. I'd rather have a small percentage of a hit than a big chunk of nothing.

A record producer's royalty is the lowest on any record, and with Peter Collins and I working together it meant the royalty was split in two. We weren't on buttons, we were on half-buttons, and yet we were supposed to take all the flak. My salary at MCA was only £10,000 a year, plus expenses, which wasn't much even then. The A&R chiefs were getting ten times that, despite the fact that it was us doing all the work. The company weren't paying enough for Loose Ends to work for them exclusively, which is why we were involved in projects for so many different people. The bottom line was that we were still the most successful independent producers in the country. Our most recent job had been a load of production work on Matt Bianco for Warner Records, which showed we were being trusted with shaping bands that were being heavily pushed in the pop market.

Unfortunately Peter Collins was getting more and more into rock production and his wife seemed to think I might be a bit of a bad influence. The whole company was constantly dealing with other people's problems rather than our own strengths. We decided to split up. It was amicable, but it was a split.

My second marriage was in trouble by this time, and I'd separated from my wife, so I decided to visit Canada with my new girlfriend, Carol Wright, who was a manager working for Virgin. While I was there I went into a radio station called

CFNY to talk to them. As I sat there, every record they played was one of mine. They didn't believe me, because it didn't say 'Pete Waterman' on the sleeves, it said Loose Ends Productions. Yet again I felt like I'd been left out in the cold. Here I was, responsible for the bulk of the songs they were playing and yet no one knew who I was.

My Canadian contacts were pretty strong back then, in fact I'd brought a couple of Canadian producers whom I'd known from the disco days over to England: Ian Gunther and Willie Morrison, both of whom had good reputations in disco circles. Willie was amazing. He was a Jewish-Scottish-Canadian who later became a Buddhist. They were great producers, and what with their circle and going out with Carol, I spent a lot of time in Toronto. I even got myself lawyers and accountants over there.

After Loose Ends folded, I went to my lawyers in Toronto and formed two new companies. One was called PWL – Pete Waterman Limited. The other was a publishing company called All Boys Music. I chose the name initially because my kids were all boys, but I also thought about the marketing aspect. I'd always liked the old ads for a chocolate bar that Fry's did called Five Boys Chocolate. I had absolutely no idea about the whole Boystown gay disco buzzword, although later I was to have gay friends who thought it was the best company name in the world. So, I had my new company. Now I had to do something with it.

Early in 1983 I had another pivotal experience when I went to see David Bowie play at Milton Keynes Bowl, as part of his Serious Moonlight tour. I'd met Bowie several times many years earlier and been impressed, most of all by his knowledge of r'n'b.

It was a big stadium gig and I had no intention of going to stand down the front so, because I knew some of the people who'd put the gig on, I went and stood at the back by the mixing desk.

It was one of those moments where a light comes on above your head and you wonder why you've never realised what it's all about before. I'd always liked the way Bowie reinvented himself and when 'Let's Dance' came out I thought it was one of the best things he'd ever done. Seeing him play that day, though, I suddenly realised what was so good about what he did. It was pantomime. *Smoke and mirrors*. I couldn't believe it had taken me so long to see it. The best thing about Bowie was that he wrote great pop songs, but disguised them as something else. His pop songs were skewed and perverse, but they were still pop songs, and they got the audience excited. Every time he did a hit they went bananas, every time he did an arty number they went quiet. It was just old r'n'b with costumes.

I went to see him again on that same tour in Germany, France, LA, London and Toronto, but after Milton Keynes I didn't watch him on stage, I just watched the audience. The reaction was the same wherever he played. I understood the global simplicity of pop. I'd got it.

One good thing that came out of the Musical Youth session in LA was that I'd got a phone call from Lamont Dozier, my all time hero. Part of the Holland/Dozier/Holland team that had written so many Motown hits, classics such as 'Stop! In The Name Of Love' by the Supremes, and 'Jimmy Mack' by Martha and the Vandellas. He said he wanted to meet Musical Youth because his kids were really into them. I said I'd be only too happy, but it would cost him two hours of his time while I quizzed him about Motown.

We met up and got on really well. We arranged to meet the next day, then the next and before long we were friends. It was like my fantasy come true to be hanging around with him. And he filled in all the gaps for me about Motown. It was the last bit of the puzzle in my r'n'b education.

Lamont was a lovely guy. Far happier cooking than writing songs, as I found when I went round his house. He had a kitchen range that was like something you'd find in a hotel, but no gold discs on the wall.

'Why's that?' I asked him.

He took me up to the attic and it was packed, floor to ceiling, with gold discs piled high. 'Where do you think I'm going to find walls for those?' he said.

After a few more meetings, I suggested that he come back to England with me. I loved the idea of him writing songs for contemporary pop artists.

We rented a house for him in Marble Arch and I introduced him to people I knew in the business. One of them was Phil Collins, whom he went on to work with later. Initially, the important thing was to get his profile raised again. One of the problems we had spotted was that, whereas nowadays MTV and the American influence has established American as a global language, back then the things he was writing were full of phrases that were alien to the audience over here. He had one song called 'Greedy To The Bone' which didn't mean anything to a British audience. And I remember he had another, which went on about 'blinders'. I didn't have a clue what that meant until he explained that they were what Americans called 'blinkers'.

The thing about Lamont was that his brain was split definitively into left and right, with both sides working at the same time. Because of that he played piano in a really unusual way, and created all these odd elements in his songs. And he'd done it time and time again.

We went out in London to a restaurant to celebrate his birthday and he ended up at the piano playing his songs for three hours. And every single one was a hit. He said, 'I only ever wrote one song. I just did it 66 times.' What a wonderful man.

I introduced him to Alison Moyet, who was looking for some new songs, but he couldn't come up with anything for her. Then one day I was driving home to Crouch End, where I was living, listening to a programme called *Round Table* on Radio One. I heard a song that had a line in it that went, 'Invisible, feel like I'm invisible'. The phrase stuck in my head and next time I saw Lamont I told him about it. He sat down there and then and wrote a song. 'Invisible' became a big hit for Alison Moyet. It was copyrighted by All Boys Music, my company, and it was written by Lamont Dozier. That was something I never could have imagined all those years earlier, playing Motown records on the common.

Lamont stayed in London for a few months, but there really wasn't enough work for him, so he went back to America.

As for me, I was about to begin my greatest adventure yet.

9 The Upstroke

I SPENT A LOT OF TIME IN LA in 1983 and while I was over there I'd met a girl who was, let's be honest, a hippie. We used to go to bed at night with joss sticks and candles and all sorts of weird stuff around us. I really liked her and I lived with her for a few months in an amazing, enormous apartment block where everyone else was gay except for me and this girl. And this was no ordinary gay community because everyone was creative, working in film or photography or TV. They were the elite, so it was like living with the Mafia because they all had so many important connections. I'd hung around with a lot of gay people before, but this was a wild, dynamic community. There were parties every night and a lot of people exploring both the gay scene and the ecstasy culture, which pretty much went hand in hand on their scene.

I'm not a drug person; I never have been. That's not some moral standpoint, because I l know some great records have been made by people off their heads on drugs, but doing drugs over any period of time for a social purpose was something I never needed. Imagine me on speed! It just doesn't bear thinking about.

AIDS was just beginning to hit the community then, though no one around then knew what it was. The big theory at the time was that it was Legionnaire's Disease. Now, for the first time I saw HIV deaths, and it was heartbreaking. Though I didn't share the sexual inclination of all these gay people around me, we had initially bonded through a love of the gay disco scene and I'd been inspired by all the creativity going on. When people started dying I realised that these were people I'd loved, even though I hadn't known them long. And I witnessed the way that an HIV death in a gay relationship was almost inconceivably tragic. There was so much vulnerability and pain. It was awful.

While I was living with my hippie girlfriend, I had another slump into introspection. I had so many ideas and plans that it felt as if my head might explode. At the same time I'd been through a whirlwind couple of years where I'd been behind a lot of successes and I felt they'd all been taken away from me. The experience at the Canadian radio station kind of summed up the way that it seemed that everything I'd done creatively had been rubbed out. I was spiralling into the worst despair I'd ever experienced.

A friend of a friend in LA was a woman who'd tragically lost her son in a car crash. The only thing that had kept her from falling apart after his death was a consultation she'd had with an astrologer whom my girlfriend knew. I'd witnessed the way this mother had been saved from total breakdown by the astrologer, so when my girlfriend suggested I should have a consultation too, I agreed. The astrologer was called Shelley Von Strunkel. These days she's famous, with columns in newspapers all over the world, but back then she was simply someone who had helped out someone I knew.

I went to her house for the session and it was full of charts and stuff. I was the biggest sceptic in the world and it seemed like the only things missing from her place were witches' hats and broomsticks. It felt like I'd finally gone all LA and I wondered what my old friends back in Coventry would think of what I was doing. Spiritually I felt so low, I had nothing to lose.

Shelley just asked me for the details of my birth – 15 January 1947, 11 p.m. on a Wednesday in Coventry, England – and nothing more. I was determined not to give anything away by blurting out stuff about my life, but she didn't ask any questions anyway. She just put a blank tape in a tape recorder, turned it on and started to tell me things.

Shelley made it clear that she didn't tell futures and wasn't about to announce that I'd get hit by a bus on a Thursday in twenty years' time. She would just tell me about myself. And she just came out with all this stuff that blew me away. She told me stuff about my mother, who'd died in 1970, and about my sister; things I'd never told anyone before. I couldn't believe that she knew the things she was telling me. She said she thought I was in communications, but she didn't quite know what. And then she told me about all my weaknesses. She came up with this analogy about a parking meter, told me that I spent my life waiting until the needle was almost into the red zone then rescued it. And how I really liked working in the red, but pretended to myself that I didn't. She told me that I was the most traditionally romantic, sentimental person that she'd ever met, and that I should place people around me to make the building blocks for what I wanted, so that it wouldn't fall apart when I started flying about creatively all over the place.

'You're really interesting,' she'd said.

My ego had liked that. But then, despite the positive observations about me, she'd cut right to the core of who I was with her criticisms. I'd created a shield around myself and she'd smashed right through it and seen the real me. I don't think I'd even realised myself what my limitations were until she pointed them out. And I certainly hadn't realised how I could capitalise on my strengths.

Before going to see Shelley I'd had a meeting with Steven Spielberg. He was a friend of friends on the LA scene and he had connections with MCA through their filmmaking arm. His company had offered me $250,000 to work for him running a company based out of London that would bring in new acts and music for soundtracks to his films. It had been a tempting offer.

After the meeting with Shelley I turned him down.

Lamont Dozier had stripped away the veneer of the myths about Motown and the history that had meant so much to me. Bowie had done the same with the fundamentals of fame. And Shelley had made me focus on *myself*.

On 10 January 1984 I flew back to London. I still didn't have a masterplan of how to make it all work, but I knew I had the key to the door. All I needed now was to know where to find the door itself.

* * *

Stiff had given David Croker and me a room in their offices to use, even though we didn't realise at the time that they were about to be evicted. I'd left MCA and decided to strike out on my own, so money was tight. Royalties are paid twice a year and I knew I had a big cheque coming in April for stuff I'd done with Musical Youth, Nik Kershaw and Matt Bianco. Until then, though, I had to think about short-term cash-flow.

I'd expected to be inundated with work, but because the records had had 'Loose Ends Productions' on them, rather than 'Pete Waterman', no one contacted me. I was working at the office with Dave Croker and a girl called Nancy who was Nik Kershaw's manager's daughter. We used to ring each other up in the office just to check the phones hadn't been cut off, because no one else was ringing us, that was for sure.

Two years earlier, Pete Collins and I had worked on the worst record we ever produced for Loose Ends. We were so embarrassed by it that we'd given the record company their money back. It was by someone called Chris Britten and it was called 'One Nine For A Lady Breaker', cashing in on the Citizens' Band radio craze. It was actually a great little pop song and Chris was a good singer, but the production just didn't work. We'd done the B-side down at MCA's studios in Piccadilly and that didn't work either. The whole thing was something that Pete Collins and I would have rather forgotten.

Since no one was ringing us at the new company, even a wrong number would have got an appointment to meet up with us. A couple of weeks into an operation that seemed to be dead in the water, the phone rang.

'Hi,' said the voice. 'This is Chris Britten. I don't know if you remember me, but you produced one of my records. Can I come in and see you?' he said.

I checked my diary, which had tumbleweed blowing across it.

'How about tomorrow?'

The next day I'd been to a meeting with my solicitor and I was half an hour late back to the office. When I got back there were two blokes in reception.

'Hello,' said one of them. 'I'm Chris Britten. Actually my real name's Mike Stock. And this is my partner Matt Aitken.'

I didn't know it at the time, but Stock, Aitken and Waterman started that second. Mike played me a demo that he and Matt had done. It was called 'The Upstroke' and they'd done it under the name Agents Aren't Aeroplanes. It was a good little song. Not quite focussed and it didn't quite work, but it was promising.

We got talking and I played them a record that I'd got in LA by the SOS Band called 'Just Be Good To Me'. It was produced by Jimmy Jam and Terry Lewis, who were just about the finest producers in the world.

We had some keyboards in the office and Mike and Matt sat down at them and started playing along to 'Just Be Good To Me'. They weren't playing what they thought they heard, they were playing the actual chords. It was then I realised they were unlike anyone I'd ever worked with. They didn't just approximate what they thought the record sounded like, they saw exactly how it was made. I didn't know it at the time, but they'd both been in cover bands and when they were playing they wouldn't just be impersonating, say, Chic, they'd be replicating exactly what Chic would play. Knowing the difference between what a record sounded like and what it really was; that was a subtle but important distinction. Some people would hear a record and try to copy a B Flat that they thought ought to be there. But r'n'b records were never that simple; there'd be a B Flat with an inversion or something. And Mike and Matt were the first people I'd ever met who could listen and work that out.

It was a gift from heaven to meet people who could comprehend that structural element. I knew that the way forward for what I wanted to do would be to make simple songs that had those musical variations in the chords. If we disguised the simplicity of great tunes with complex chords we could make hits. That was the secret.

Mike and Matt understood what I wanted. I don't think they particularly understood *why* I wanted it yet, but they knew what I was on about. The year before, I'd got a job for the Canadian producers, Willie and Ian, whom I'd brought over, doing a record by Brad from the Specials. We'd sold it to RCA Records after dealing with an A&R man, Peter Robinson. I decided to take him Matt and Mike's track, 'The Upstroke'. He liked it.

At that time I was sharing a flat with a bloke called Barry Evangeli who'd started a gay disco label called Proto. We'd just got kicked out of the Stiff buildings and needed a base. He said he had a suite of offices nearby and that I could move the company in. In fact it turned out to be a room with a settee above his dad's Greek restaurant next to Camden Town tube. I still took him up on his offer. Barry had just signed up a girl called Hazell Dean who was about to release a big gay disco record called 'Searchin''. It wasn't quite right, so he'd got me in to help. To tell the truth Proto was a bit all over the place at the time; as a company it struck me as a bit chaotic. But Barry did have a fantastic promotions guy called Nick East and I was glad to help Barry out at Proto.

I proposed to Peter Robinson that I would arrange for 'The Upstroke' to come out on Proto and I'd sort out all the promotion for it – then RCA could buy it with the buzz already having been created. He was well up for it, even though it was the sort deal that people just didn't do then. To me it just seemed like a good way of working it.

I got Mike and Matt into Marquee Studios to record the single. Before they started, I told them, 'I don't want any traditional instruments on it.' I didn't want guitars or violins or even pianos that sounded like pianos, I wanted it to be really innovative. You've got to realise that, because of all the work I'd done with Loose Ends, I'd built up a studio's worth of fabulous equipment. We had really good synthesisers that were almost as good as top producers like Trevor Horn would use. This equipment was integral to the records I wanted to make. I had a vision of Motown-type songs with more modern chords and techno, gay disco rhythms. I wanted to make technologically brilliant records. The best gay disco producers in New York, people like Bobby O, were still forced to make records for something like a thousand dollars on relatively basic equipment. No one was taking it seriously outside their small circle. I wanted to move it on.

The first version that Matt and Mike did was OK, but it wasn't innovative enough. I asked them to do it again and to really push themselves, to make the most modern record in the world.

The final version was excellent and we put it out.

John Peel picked up on it. He raved about it and played it on his show on Radio One, so history can confirm that the first person ever to play a Stock, Aitken and Waterman track on the radio was John Peel. I'd been an admirer of his for ages, so it was a dream come true for him to play the record.

However, it had to have a public image and Matt and Mike weren't a real group, so we got in a couple of girls to front it. We couldn't afford any styling, but we just about managed to carry it off. Most importantly, the record started to create a buzz. John Peel came down to see us and played it every night. The music papers liked it and the DJs and audiences on the gay scene welcomed it as a record unlike anything else around at the time. Peter Robinson liked it too. I felt like I finally had a purpose, and I realised that within that independent gay disco genre a record like 'The Upstroke' would sell enough to pay for the next record you wanted to release. I knew I wanted to invest more, but in the meantime I'd found a marketplace where there were no rules apart from that as long as you made a good record, you'd be able to make the next one. You weren't going to become a millionaire doing that, but you could keep your company ticking over.

I looked at Proto and I saw a pointer towards the future.

Maybe it was because I'd become so strong-willed, maybe because Barry just wasn't as driven as me, that I was able to make the records I wanted to make. I wouldn't say I bullied the people around me – although they would probably say I did – it was just that I had a vision, and I didn't want anyone to compromise that vision.

In 1984, when the Stock, Aitken and Waterman partnership was coming together, the record industry was in the biggest turmoil it had experienced for many years. Record sales were plummeting and the marketing men had taken over and gone wild. There was no focus to it all. I looked at it and thought, 'This is interesting', and all the important stuff I'd learned from the previous couple of years suddenly came together. I thought that I might just have a chance of sorting the whole thing out myself. If a little company like Proto could make money, then anyone could make money. Barry hadn't been in the business long enough to have any kind of real experience and Nick was just a great promotions guy. I saw that there were innovative people around me who didn't have any great knowledge of the business. I could supply that knowledge. They were pulling me in and I was bringing their ideas to life.

Mike, who was four years younger than me, and Matt, who was four years younger than Mike, were, as far as I was concerned, the most talented people I'd ever met. But they were completely different characters.

Matt was originally from Coventry, which was something we had in common, but he had gone to live near Manchester when he was young. Mike was from Margate, the son of a successful salesman. He was a very scholarly person and had gone to Hull University as well as winning a RADA scholarship. Matt was smart too and, as far as I understood, had been an accountant of some sort at one point at Salford Town Hall. Mike was studious, he was the clever driving force. Matt was one of the best guitarists I've ever heard. The most important thing was that as a combination they worked well.

They both had solid musical backgrounds, particularly Mike, whose brother had been lead violinist in a major German orchestra. They'd both been in bands that played Barmitzvahs, but not amateurishly. Mike had taken it so seriously that when he'd turned up to play it had virtually been the Mike Stock Show, with proper keyboards and an incredibly accomplished level of musicianship. He'd advertised for someone to join his band and that was how he met Matt. Anyone who has ever met Matt and Mike will tell you that they were the sort of people who, if they did anything, would do it properly, so I can imagine that their band must have been quite something. Mike's knowledge of music and his grasp of the theory behind it all was awe-inspiring, perhaps because of his academic training. He was wonderfully thorough at understanding musical structure. He was obviously the leader of the two and you sensed it had been that way since they first met.

I actually liked Matt a lot, too, but his personality was such that he never liked to admit that he was letting you like him. It always seemed that any comment you made, no matter how innocent, was taken as some sort of snide remark. He came across as not having much confidence. Matt lived in a squat and had the worst car I'd ever seen in my life. Superficially Mike's life seemed more stable, because he was living with his wife Bobbie who was a schoolteacher, and he had a studio in the basement of his house. But they were in dire financial trouble, the pair of them.

But apart from all this, Matt and Mike were the most talented people I had ever met – they just didn't know what to do with that talent. So, though 'The Upstroke' was their idea, it was me that pushed them into shaping it into something I could sell. I'd taken something unformed and basic and ended up with something truly original. The record created a huge buzz on the gay circuit because it sounded different from all the records around at the time.

The way that we put the record together pretty much became a blueprint for the way that we would work together for the rest of our partnership. The creative contribution from each of us would vary from song to song over the years, but if we were to have badges pinned to our lapels, then Mike's would read 'The Songwriter', Matt's would read 'The Musician' and mine would read 'The Producer'. Ostensibly there were three different roles for the three of us, but that was only a theoretical arrangement. Some days one person would contribute more than another, and some days the roles would be changed around. Nothing was written in stone.

The best thing about Mike was that he knew what I wanted almost before I could put it into words. I'd come into the studio with simple melodies and simple lyrics and Mike would turn them around and make them work. The beauty of the way that our relationship developed was that all three of us were integral to an extraordinarily smoothly running machine. Right from the beginning we began to understand that when we were on form all three of us could work together almost telepathically.

Barry had just signed an American star called Divine. He was a cult figure, a huge transvestite who'd appeared in movies by John Waters. A real larger than life figure, but one of the loveliest people I've been blessed to meet in my life. He and his manager Bernard were wonderful, elegant people.

Divine was releasing a song called 'So You Think You're A Man' and his management were looking round for producers.

They'd considered Ian Levine, who was one of the top gay disco producers in the country, but in the end they approached us. Though we were the new kids on the block, as far as I was concerned, no one else was in our class. I had experience and over the years I'd amassed a studio's worth of high-tech equipment that no one else could have even afforded to hire on a daily basis. Matt and Mike had toys to play with that others could only dream about.

You've got to remember that technology was a lot different then to what it is today. You couldn't drive more than one synthesiser at the same time and everything wasn't neatly set up on a computer screen like it is today. It was a technically demanding business and we were right at the cutting edge of technology. Matt used to read the manual and then spend three weeks working out how the equipment worked. Since all the programming was done in real time, they'd have to spend days putting a track together, not hours like now. I knew that the Divine record would be our big break. I don't know how, I just knew. He'd been big on the gay disco scene for a couple of years, but if we could take him into the pop charts, it would be a real coup. So we went down the studio to record the single and Mike and Matt actually taught him how to sing properly. He did the track with proper singing on it then got a cab to the airport to fly back to America.

Barry came down to the studio to hear the track, but when we played it to him he was horrified.

'Why's he singing?' he asked. 'I don't want singing, I want shouting.'

So we rang the airport and got them to send Divine straight back. He came in, did the whole thing shouting rather than singing, in one take, and headed off back to the airport.

'That's better,' said Barry.

We played around with the track and tightened it up a bit. I knew it was going to be a hit because it was so camp. If it had started off 90 per cent camp, it was 120 per cent camp by the time we'd finished with it!

Barry brought in a company called Impulse to promote it. One of the guys they had working for them was an old friend of mine from the Midlands whom I'd known as a DJ and

promotions man, Steve Jenkins. He'd also done the promotion on Hazell Dean's 'Searchin'', so he and Barry got on well.
I knew that gay clubs would love the Divine record, but I
could also see that it would spill over into the Mecca-type pop
clubs because it was basically a very funny song. So I told
Steve to get it into pop outlets. A lot of other people around
me didn't seem to think that was a great idea, they were just
thinking of it as a gay disco record, nothing more. Nevertheless Steve agreed to give it some pop promotion.

The song was almost immediately Number One in all the
gay charts and everyone was really pleased and surprised. I
wasn't. I mean, it was obvious it was going to be a big gay hit.
A huge transvestite singing 'So You Think You're A Man'? I
wasn't expecting a medal.

Then the real charts came out and it was Number
Eighteen. I'd been right. Everyone was calling me an arrogant
bastard, but I wasn't arrogant, I was right.

The big test was going to be *Top Of The Pops* because I
knew when Divine turned up the BBC were going to have a
heart attack. And sure enough, they freaked when they saw
him. So did the viewers, and by nine o'clock in the evening
after his *Top Of The Pops* performance the switchboards were
clogged with complaints. The next day a cab driver told me
he'd seen the show and that Divine was the ugliest bird he'd
ever seen, even uglier than his missus. When I told him
Divine was a man he almost drove into a tree.

Around then, Matt, Mike and I started thinking about what
we were going to call our team. So we got three pieces of
paper and each wrote our surname on them. Then we
shuffled them around to see which order looked best.
Eventually we came up with Stock, Aitken and Waterman,
which even though it sounded a bit like a firm of solicitors,
had the same rhythm to it as Holland-Dozier-Holland. So
Stock, Aitken and Waterman it was.

Even though we'd had a hit with Divine, money was still
tight and I was ploughing everything we were making back
into the business. And because I was the only one with any
money at all, I had to pay all the bills. None of us were eating
regularly, and by the time Friday came around and the
woman in the flat above me cooked liver and bacon for her

husband I had to be held back from going and ripping it off his plate. And I don't even like liver and bacon.

The important thing was that we were building a public image – and that meant no one was going to see just how poor we really were. Whenever I had a meeting I'd go to the person's office. They'd never be allowed to come and see me.

One day Barry came up to me and announced that, as a Greek Cypriot, he'd somehow managed to wangle the job making Cyprus' entry for the Eurovision Song Contest. By 1984, Eurovision had become a joke and a not very funny one at that, so quite how we'd managed to get involved in it all I didn't know.

He wanted us to come up with a song and produce it. I thought it was terrible idea, but Matt and Mike were really into it and they had a little rock and roll song that they wanted to use. It was going to be recorded by Andy Paul. So I came up with the money and we did it. It was a pseudo-Elvis Presley song sung by a man with the hairiest chest in the world, and a picture of Cyprus on the record sleeve. I jetted off to Luxembourg with Barry for the contest, but we couldn't even get a hotel in Luxembourg so we had to stay in France and travel over the border each day. When we got to the event itself it was like a different world. This wasn't the music business, it was just a freak show. And I knew we had as much chance of winning as I had of becoming Prime Minister. I was sitting in the audience thinking, 'What am I doing here? Have I worked all these years just to achieve this?'

There were so many political undertones to the voting. If a country gave Greece top points they'd give Cyprus none, and vice-versa. It was ridiculous. I think we came about fifteenth. Afterwards, though, we had a great party in the bar with the dancers and the people from British Forces Network who were covering it for the radio. All these Spaniards crashed it at one point, and because the Spanish have completely different musical tastes from anyone else on the planet, when they started singing I had to throw them out. It was a great party though. I've never seen so many gorgeous girls surrounded by so many wallies.

Sometime next morning I went straight out of the hotel bar and got a plane home. I didn't even go back to France to pick

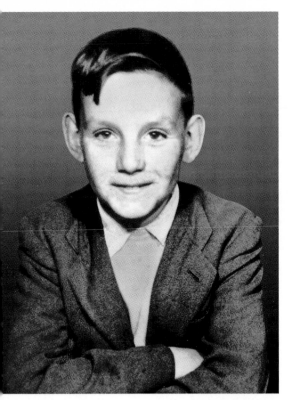

TOP LEFT: *A post-war child in a world about to change. Me aged 7.*
TOP RIGHT: *On the day of my first wedding, with best mate Keith Jackson.*
ABOVE: *My dad John with my children Charlie, Paul, Little Pete and Toni.*

TOP: *Peter Collins and I celebrate the success of The Lambrettas'*
'Poison Ivy' with the band and Radio One DJ Mike Read.
ABOVE LEFT: *A hero for all time. Peter Collins and I with Motown*
songwriting genius Lamont Dozier.
ABOVE RIGHT: *Dressed for success. Me in 1984.*

TOP LEFT: *With one of pop's great characters, Pete Burns (second left) and the rest of Dead Or Alive.*
TOP RIGHT: *Us against the world. Mike Stock, Matt Aitken and I.*
ABOVE: *At Boston's fish market with Bananarama's Keren, Sarah and Siobhan as 'Venus' goes to Number One in America. The wildest girls in the world.*

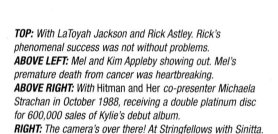

TOP: With LaToyah Jackson and Rick Astley. Rick's phenomenal success was not without problems.
ABOVE LEFT: Mel and Kim Appleby showing out. Mel's premature death from cancer was heartbreaking.
ABOVE RIGHT: With Hitman and Her co-presenter Michaela Strachan in October 1988, receiving a double platinum disc for 600,000 sales of Kylie's debut album.
RIGHT: The camera's over there! At Stringfellows with Sinitta.

OPPOSITE: Especially For You. Pop's King and Queen, Jason Donovan and Kylie Minogue.

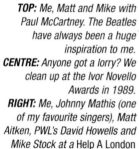

TOP: *Me, Matt and Mike with Paul McCartney. The Beatles have always been a huge inspiration to me.*
CENTRE: *Anyone got a lorry? We clean up at the Ivor Novello Awards in 1989.*
RIGHT: *Me, Johnny Mathis (one of my favourite singers), Matt Aitken, PWL's David Howells and Mike Stock at a Help A London Child function in 1989.*

TOP LEFT: With pal Steve Jenkins from Zomba records and ex-Manchester United footballer Mark Robbins, now of Walsall FC. Dreaming of Walsall winning the cup…
TOP RIGHT: Just call me Casey Jones. Trains and railways remain a love of my life, and here I am on my Flying Scotsman.
ABOVE: You can never have enough cars when they're as beautiful as this.

TOP: *More stuff for the wall. Steps' first single, '5,6,7,8' received a silver BPI award – the first of their many gongs.*
ABOVE LEFT: *The techno Abba. Steps' 'Deeper Shade Of Blue' look.*
ABOVE RIGHT: *At the Music Week awards in 1999, where I won a Strat Lifetime Achievement Award for outstanding contribution to the music industry. l-r: MW's Steve Redmond, me, DJ Paul Gambaccini and longtime friend Michael (later Lord) Levy, who gave me my first break at Magnet Records.*

up my things, Barry had to get them for me. I vowed never to do the Eurovision Song Contest again.

We were getting regular work for Barry now, and he asked us to come up with the new Hazell Dean single. Everything was done on such a tight budget then that there wasn't much money for demos. You had to do all the research and development of your song in your head. You worked on the hoof.

Matt and Mike had written a song called 'Dance Your Love Away' which seemed a rubbish title. One day I was up in Coventry and Mike rang me up to play me the song down the phone. I changed a bit in the chorus to the words, 'Whatever I do, wherever I go' and that became the title of the song. We were literally writing and arranging it over the phone.

We went to record it at a studio called the Workhouse in the Old Kent Road in South East London and as we started working on the track it took on a life of its own. We played around with it and did some edits, entrusting one bit to an engineer called George Chambers. He accidentally edited all the drumbeats backwards at one point so the beat kind of turned on itself. I hadn't noticed until I took it down to a place called PRT where Malcolm Davies was working, to get it pressed.

'That's a great idea doing the beat backwards,' he said. Since everyone else who heard it agreed, we had to pretend it was deliberate, not just a silly accident. But because that mistake had given the song such a distinctive sound, it became a big hit.

While I was working at Mecca we'd hosted events twice a year for disabled kids through the Spastic Association. I'd seen that handicapped kids had a great capacity for enjoying themselves at the events, really letting go – but only if it was pop. More recently I'd become a patron of a camp in Surrey for children with spina bifida, called Woodlarks, and I used to take pop stars down to meet the kids. Soon after the Hazell Dean record came out, I took her there. We were driving across this bridge in a little village in Surrey when I saw the kids from the camp canoeing, and they were all singing, 'Whatever I do, wherever I go', at the tops of their voices. It was the first time I had ever witnessed the public picking up on one of my records, and suddenly I was aware of how pop music can transcend your own small circle of people and become public property. To see people enjoying themselves at something I'd made was a kind of freaky experience.

That record launched Stock, Aitken and Waterman into the pop market. We still only saw it as a brief foray into pop from the dance scene; there was no way that we had suddenly decided we wanted to make pop records. This success was just a bonus. Quite a bonus considering it sold 300,000 records.

We paid for the pressing of the single with an American Express card. We paid the American Express card with a Visa card. We paid that with MasterCard. And MasterCard we paid for with American Express. We were experts at juggling credit. In a moment of indulgence we took out a full-page ad in *Music Week* with a picture of two hands, one handing over an American Express card to the other. It was headed, 'Hazell Dean – Whatever I Do' and said 'That'll Do Nicely' underneath.

Making a hit is difficult enough, but when you actually have one it creates a whole load of cash-flow problems, because you have to pay for pressings and promotion before you get the money in from your distributor. You press an initial amount of records and then when it starts to take off you have to press a load more, but you don't get the money from the distributors for the first sales until eight or ten weeks later. So you feel like you've hit the jackpot, but before you can collect, the bailiffs have got you by the collar and they're beating you up on the pavement.

So we had a hit, but we were never afforded the luxury of sitting on our laurels. And that could well have been the making of us.

10 You Spin Me Round

B ARRY ASKED US TO DO THE DIVINE follow-up, a song called 'I'm So Beautiful'. We did, and it was a superbly technical record. A pile of shit, but superbly technical. Barry insisted on doing a 12-inch remixed by Ian Levine and they sped the record up and it sounded ridiculous. As far as I was concerned, they'd actually killed the record before it had even had a chance. That was it. I'd had enough. I did my records the way I wanted to do them and I didn't want anyone messing around with them, I didn't want anyone else involved in what we were doing.

To compound the situation, we were doing a Hazell Dean album and, again, other people were brought in. We'd made the album on a shoestring and put everything into it. I'd even put some of my own money into it because I wanted to make the album so much. It seemed like a good experience, a way of really stretching ourselves. Then, when other people got pulled in to work on it, it seemed a familiar story: I do all the work and set it up and someone comes in and takes all the credit. No one had made a hi-energy album before, yet it was still being taken out of our hands. We weren't indulging in high art, we just wanted to show how to make lots of gay disco hits on one record. Rocket science never cropped up.

There seemed to be too many secret conversations at Proto that I wasn't privy to. I sort of got the feeling that all in the garden wasn't entirely rosy. I'm not saying we were never paid. We were. But I always wondered, rightly or wrongly, if we earned the full amount we should have. For instance, I also found out that, unbeknownst to me, a deal had been done on the B-side publishing of the singles we'd made. No one had told me about that, and yet we were supposed to start signing contracts on it all. I told Barry I wasn't going to agree to it. Publishing was supposed to be All Boys Music: no one had any right to make deals on our behalf. Overall, I got the impression that everything wasn't as straight down the line as I'd presumed.

But, hey, we'd learned a lot and had a Top Ten record. And more importantly, people were talking about us. As a team we'd begun to make an impact. People started to ring up with a passing interest in getting us to work for them. No one actually offered anything, apart from Mark Dean who had a project on Wham!'s label, called Girl Talk. I don't think we ever actually finished the record, but at least there was interest.

We were sitting around the office dreaming up our fantasies about conquering the world when there was a phone call.

'Hi,' the voice said. 'It's Pete Burns from Dead Or Alive here.'

There have been maybe a dozen extraordinarily important moments that have made me what I am today. That phone call was one of them.

Pete Burns was an outrageous-looking singer from Liverpool. He'd been in a band called Nightmares In Wax at around the same time that the Teardrop Explodes and Echo and The Bunnymen had formed. And he'd established a reputation for himself as something of a flamboyant outsider on the whole Liverpool scene. He also loved gay disco.

I didn't know any of that at the time, but I'd seen pictures of him and remembered him. Once you'd seen him you weren't likely to forget him. In many ways, he reminded me of Divine. What's more, Pete understood what we were doing. He's very, very smart when it comes to pop.

'I'm doing a record,' he said. 'And I want you to produce it. I've got a deal with CBS.'

I was interested, but when I met with their manager Martin Barter, it turned out that they wanted us to produce three tracks for them for a pittance. We argued over it for a bit and eventually he said he'd go and talk to Muff Winwood at CBS about it.

He came back a few days later and said, 'We've talked to them and Muff Winwood doesn't think you're a record producer.'

I'd known Muff for years. The whole Chris Rea thing had come out of studio time provided by Muff when he was at Island. I found it hard to believe that Muff wouldn't know who I was, but I bit my lip and set up a meeting with Pete. The first time I met Pete Burns he blew me away. He had this amazing charisma, and he effortlessly dominated the room with his presence. But I soon found that the best thing about him was his savage wit. He was so sharp, he could have put a racehorse down from three hundred yards, just by saying something. He was relentless. And you couldn't take offence because what he was saying was so funny. But it soon became clear that he actually thought I was an old queen and that Matt and Mike were two young boys that I had in tow. Because I was becoming respected on the gay disco scene, he just assumed I was gay. Admittedly I did have green and red hair and a red leather suit with a yellow stripe so it might have been an easy mistake to make. I was camp without realising it.

He played me demos of three or four songs that were OK, but nothing special. I loved his personality, though, and we got on like a house on fire. His boyfriend, the band's drummer Steve, was just as engaging. I liked them, and I knew I wanted to work with them.

Pete was brutally honest with me, which makes a change in this business.

'I've come to you because I want you to make me a Hazell Dean record,' he said. 'We loved that. It's the best hi-energy record we've ever heard and we've been into the scene for years. That's what we want.'

By this time we'd sort of fallen out with Proto, or at least assumed there was no money left in the pot, and we didn't really know where the Stock, Aitken and Waterman thing was going to go. So we did a contract with CBS for three tracks; the deal was that we got £500 each. The only part I wouldn't bend on was the question of royalties on 12-inch singles. People didn't get royalties on them back then because they were seen purely as promos. Only 10,000 would be pressed, because they were just viewed as a gimmick.

I went into CBS and said I wanted royalties on the 12-inch singles. They'd never had anyone ask for that before. I mean, major record companies would budget around the fact that they were going to sell 3,000 12-inches, maybe a few more if they could get a nice sleeve or coloured vinyl. They were an indulgence, so they thought I was an idiot. £500 in advance and a royalty on something they didn't even sell? They jumped over the desks to sign the deal. What they didn't know was that, working as independent dance music producers, we had made our living on the fact that we could sell 18,000 copies of any 12-inch we made. And that level of sales had given us cushion money for anything we went on to do. We weren't going to be able to buy Ferraris and Rolls Royces, but at least we weren't going to have to catch the tube home at night. We were actually a lot poorer than Dead Or Alive thought we were, because we'd built up this image of being famous, hugely successful record producers. In actual fact, at that point the cash-flow problems meant that all we really had going for us was our self-belief. Still, we agreed to produce Dead Or Alive at Marquee Studios in London.

Back in the Magnet days I'd met the engineer there, Phil Harding, and I'd liked him. I respected his ears because it seemed he understood what great records should sound like. By 1984 he was chief engineer at Marquee Studios and I'd done a deal where I'd bring bands in and use him in return for preferential rates. So, with money tight, it seemed like the best place to use.

There's a pub called the Ship on Wardour Street in Soho, just down the road from where the Marquee Studios used to be. We used to have to get a pint between the three of us and two empty glasses, then make it last three hours waiting for the band to come in and buy us a round on their daily expenses. We knew how to time it exactly right, so they'd come in just as we were down to the last mouthful. We weren't going to let on to them that we didn't have a pot to piss in. The only way we could keep the momentum going was by pretending we were rich.

On the first day of recording, Dead Or Alive came into the studio. They played us a couple of songs that were later to end up on their first album. Pretty good songs, but nothing exactly out of the ordinary. Then Pete said, 'Oh, we've got a song we wrote this weekend as well.' And he put on a tune called 'You Spin Me Round (Like A Record Baby)'.

It was fantastic. Easily their best song. I knew it was the one. But I was trying to act cool; I knew that the song was a smash, but I also knew I didn't have the budget to produce it. The contract we'd signed meant that we had to produce three tracks and all three tracks were named. This one had only been written the day before, so it was nowhere on the contract. The priority, contractually, was simply to produce the other three songs. 'You Spin Me Round' wasn't named in the contract.

How on earth was I going to get a budget for us to produce this song? I loved it, and Pete knew I loved it. He wanted me to just go ahead and do it, but I knew the contract wouldn't allow it. It was so frustrating.

I talked to Pete and we decided to sort of half-work on the songs we were contracted to do while, at the same time and on trust, concentrating on 'You Spin Me Round'. We'd use what we were supposed to be doing as a way of trying to pull in the budget for a song that I already knew would be massive.

Three days into the session it became clear that Pete and Steve from Dead Or Alive just didn't get on with Matt and Mike. The band were ready to throttle two of the producers and it was only Wednesday. Those were easily the most violent sessions I've ever seen. The thing was that Mike and Matt could be quite arrogant when they wanted to be. Matt had programmed the whole of the bass and everything on the record and he'd done a great job, but the band saw it as him and Mike trying to take over the whole thing. And Tim Lever and Mike Percy, who were the real musicians in Dead Or Alive, didn't take kindly to Mike Stock and Matt Aitken saying, 'You're taking too long so we're going to play it ourselves.' Not that Mike and Matt couldn't have necessarily played it better, but it's just not the sort of thing you're supposed to suggest to the band you're producing. And band loyalty being what it is, Steve and Pete were obviously going to stand up for the others in the band. The atmosphere seemed to be constantly on the edge of physical violence.

I don't sit in the studio during the whole recording process. I'm a dipper; I dip in, I dip out. And I make instant judgements on what I hear, changing things that don't immediately sound right. So I was back at the office when Pete rang up. He told me in no uncertain terms to get down to the studio before Steve chinned Matt and Mike. I went down and told the two of them to go off and have a break. Immediately. And they did. Whether they realised they were about to be beaten up I don't know, but if they hadn't left the studio there would have been bloodshed.

I sent Dead Or Alive home too. It was all too fraught. I told them that Phil Harding and I would finish off the record ourselves.

Listening to the tapes of what had been done so far, it was obvious that there was something magical about the record. And Matt and Mike's programming and arrangements were fabulous. You shivered just listening to it. Phil and I were determined to make it the most barbed, amazing record we'd heard in our lives. We wanted to make a record so sharp that it would cut through steel girders. It had to be supremely dynamic.

Phil and I spent all night working on it. At three in the morning the computer on the mixing desk crashed, and we had to wait for a guy to come up from Southend to fix it, so it was six before we could start working again. I'd been up for twenty-four hours by this point and I was exhausted. But we carried on and by half past nine in the morning we knew we were milliseconds away from making it work. Then Phil turned up one of the instruments and instantly it all came together. It was what we'd been working through the night to achieve, and we'd finished ten minutes before the band were due back in to hear it.

When the band turned up I told Phil to turn the speakers up so loud it would deafen them. He did. And we played it to them.

Within seconds Pete was literally leaping up in the air, whooping. And the longer it went on, the more excited he got. But after about ten seconds of the record I'd looked at Phil and realised that, through sheer exhaustion, we'd actually made an enormous gaffe on the record. Originally we'd had something like thirty seconds of one of the instruments at the beginning of the record and then it had dropped out. In our hurry to finish the track we'd forgotten to drop it out on the finished version, so it was in all the way through. We'd kept the repeats on by mistake and it had stayed in through the whole song.

'That synth going all the way through is fantastic,' said Pete. 'What a brilliant idea to keep that going through the whole thing.'

I'd been panicking, because if that record hadn't worked, we would have had no money and that would have been the end of the business. We'd used up the twelve grand that we'd got for the production and also the fifteen hundred quid that we'd split between us as our wages. I'd concentrated on 'You Spin Me Round' because I knew it was a risk we had to take, but it had to be right or we were dead.

I was living in Crouch End in North London and I drove home having been up for a day and a half. I must have played that song twenty times in the car on the way home and each time I heard it, it sounded better and better.

I played it to Matt and Mike and the first thing they said was that I had to take out the synth sound which went all the way through because it sounded ridiculous. I told them that I couldn't because the band loved it. And we didn't even have the money to take it out if we wanted to. The budget was gone.

Martin played the track to CBS and they loved it. They gave us £36,000 to do the rest of the band's album.

Working with Pete Burns was one of the most wonderful experiences of my life. We had arguments at times, but ultimately it was a pleasure. He's volatile and often misguided, something he would probably admit himself, but one of the most entertaining human beings I've had the good fortune to work with.

'You Spin Me Round' hit the clubs and it was like Cadbury's Smash, it was so instant. You put the water on and it went 'Boom!' What we'd done on the record was roll all the real bass off, so it didn't have a proper bass guitar any more. It had hard bottom end. It was a technical thing, but it made the record sound more modern than anything else around. We'd also exploited the fact that at that time every Mecca-type club had something called a sound-to-light system; the sound of the record would affect the way the lights functioned. I'd worked out years back that handclaps and cowbells sent the light system nuts. So I'd put cowbells and handclaps all over the place on the record. You put it on and you had a light show.

As a result the DJ in the club would put the record on and because of what we'd done with the bass, it wouldn't distort. It basically sounded louder than anything else and came leaping out into your face. Meanwhile the lights would go barmy. You'd get instant reaction!

To be honest I'd nicked most of the ideas from 'Ride Of The Valkyries' by Wagner. We'd sampled the Vienna Philharmonic all over it with all these string sounds. Dead Or Alive just seemed like they ought to involve over-the-top opera. I'd gone into high camp without thinking about it; I've always loved Wagner and Pete seemed perfect as a vehicle for that kind of flamboyance. Furthermore, no one else was sampling like we were sampling. Nowadays it seems like old hat, but back then it was unheard of.

I started to get people ringing me up asking about the record, and Simon Bates on Radio One began playing it every day, religiously.

On the first week of its release in the autumn of 1984 it went to Number 41. The next week it went to 47. Then back up to 41. And down to 48. It was bobbing up and down the lower reaches of the charts for ages.

Coming up to the Christmas period I'd been booked to do some DJing in various places. We'd got a Fairlight, which was the big new piece of technical kit at the time. We'd used it all over Divine's 'I'm So Beautiful' and the tracks we'd done for Dead Or Alive's album. I'd got hold of some BBC sound effects albums and on one of them there was the sound of two dogs having intercourse. Now, me being me, I thought I had to put it on a record. So Phil Harding and I pressed up this acetate of 'You Spin Me Round' with the sounds of the dogs yelping and stuff over the top of it, and I called it the 'TDF' mix. TDF: Two Dogs Fucking. At all the gigs I played it sent the audience mental. I had one bloke come up to me and offer to give me a hundred quid for it there and then – it was a winner every time I played it.

I came back after the Christmas holidays and there was a phone call from Muff Winwood's office at CBS. They wanted to know what on earth this TDF record that everyone had been raving about was. They'd had orders for it coming out of their ears, so I told them it was Dead Or Alive, and just something that I'd come up with to play when I was DJing.

Then Pete Burns rang me up. 'What's this TDF mix?' he asked. I didn't know quite how he'd react if I told him it was Two Dogs Fucking. I sort of thought he'd appreciate it, but he could be so unpredictable that it might have cost us the working relationship.

So, off the top of my head I said, 'Oh yeah, Pete. TDF . . . that's the Tour De Force mix.' I don't know where it came from, but it sounded viable.

'Tour De Force. Brilliant! I love it,' he said.

And the buzz on that mix was the final shove we needed. From just scuffing round the edges of the charts it went straight into the Top Twenty the next week. Then we got *Top Of The Pops* and, like with Divine, the visual force of Dead Or Alive's image, combined with the quality of the record, meant that everyone wanted it. It went Top Ten, Top Five and then Number One. It was the first Stock, Aitken and Waterman Number One.

And it wasn't just successful in Britain, it was massive everywhere. All over Europe, in Japan and America, suddenly everyone was talking about Dead Or Alive's TDF record. We'd taken the original concept, added a sexually humorous joke that seemed perfectly natural in a gay disco culture and taken it overground. The gay audience got it immediately, but the heterosexual audience didn't have sex in discotheques then. They held hands and danced with each other. They just liked the noises.

But the best thing was, the 12-inch sales were enormous, and we got paid on all those sales. We'd been doing the gay disco, high energy, Boystown, call-it-what-you-will thing for a good few years by then. And from that original Bobby O, New York inspiration, we'd taken it somewhere else. We were the masters of the art and the world was our oyster.

Then Pete came up with Dead Or Alive's follow-up single, 'In Too Deep'. It was a smashing song, but it wasn't 'Spin Me Round'. It was a different sound and although we agreed to produce it, I didn't see why there was any value in deliberately abandoning a formula that had been so successful.

Pete wanted thirty different sorts of song on one album, so one minute it would sound like Dead Or Alive, and the next like Michael Jackson, and the next like Wham! It just wasn't working out for us, so we stopped working with them. I've worked with a lot of artists in my life, but the one person that I think I could really have done amazing things with is Pete Burns. If he'd given me more control over the direction the band went in, I think we could have taken Dead Or Alive onto a whole new level. Some of the projects we'd started to work on were quite outrageously inventive, and I hope pop's history books give him the respect he deserves.

It was obvious that we had to move forward. We'd had a taste of what we were capable of and now we had to build on it. We had to write our own songs and get into a situation where we were no longer in the pay of anyone else, financially and creatively. We were going to rise or fall by our own talent. And of course there was the necessity to earn money to live. Doing our own thing became the next goal. If we were going to do ourselves justice, it was absolutely imperative.

At the end of 1984 we'd been approached by Tom Watkins, the manager of the Pet Shop Boys. He'd got an act signed to EMI called Spelt Like This and he wanted us to produce it. There was a massive record company campaign behind the project and we'd got sucked into it. Before long it was clear to us that the whole thing was basically a front for Tom Watkins' ego. It was just an exercise in marketing and self-promotion. It wasn't something we were either used to or happy with, but we'd started working on the Spelt Like This album, and it was becoming a nightmare.

During the recording with Dead Or Alive at the Marquee I'd realised that the quality of the sound wasn't good enough for what I wanted. We were making great records, but the technology of the place simply couldn't match the potential of the sound we wanted to make.

Way back from the end of the Magnet days, I'd built the production company around buying pieces of equipment and using that equipment when producing records, rather than shelling out to rent stuff off the studios. So I'd built my own collection of toys and I'd taken them to the studios where we were working. If we used them the record company paid; if we didn't they'd saved themselves the money they'd normally have to pay for hiring an all-inclusive studio package. And since we were using the Marquee a lot, all my equipment was just piled up down there.

In the middle of 1985 we had to move out of the Marquee because they needed the place for something else. When we loaded all of my stuff into a truck I suddenly realised just how much of it there was; there was almost everything there that you'd need to make technologically superb records, and there was hardly anything left in the studio because almost all the equipment was mine. The only thing we were missing was the heart of the operation, an SSL mixing desk.

I didn't want a studio so I'd had the idea of buying an SSL and taking it around to whichever studio we used in a flight case. A bit of a strange idea admittedly, but it seemed like a good plan. I met a lovely guy who worked for SSL called Pete Wandless and told him I wanted to buy one.

'Where do you want it?' he asked.

'In a flight case,' I said.

He tried to explain that you didn't have an SSL in a flight case, you had it in a studio. No one had ever suggested the concept of carrying one around with them before. When I'd convinced him I was serious he told me it would cost £210,000.

'I'll pay cash,' I said.

That completely floored him. He started telling me that you didn't pay for SSLs in cash, you leased them off the company. There were tax advantages and, anyway, it was just the way it was done.

I didn't want to lease an SSL. I wanted to buy one. But he said there were a couple of people I ought to meet.

He introduced me to two blokes called Peter Morton and Alan Shingleton from a company called Prime Leasing. They were staid businessmen who were unsurprisingly bewildered when I told them I wanted to buy an SSL and I was going to get a bank to give me the money.

'We've never heard of you,' they told me.

'I've never heard of you either,' I said.

They asked me what I'd done and I told them. Even by then it was a pretty impressive list. 'Musical Youth, Nik Kershaw, Tracey Ullman, Belle Stars . . . oh, and Dead Or Alive who've just sold three-quarters of a million singles.'

They were obviously impressed and told me they'd get back to me.

There were a lot of MCA records on my list and, unbeknown to me, the chairman of Prime Leasing lived in Maidenhead, next door to Brian Schofield, the head of accounting for MCA. They've told me since that the chairman asked his neighbour about me over the fence and Brian said he was about to pay me some royalties for Musical Youth and a couple of other acts. He'd said I was going places.

I got a phone call from Prime Leasing. They'd decided to do a deal with me. They wanted me to give them a cheque for £50,000 immediately as security, then pay off the cost of the SSL in instalments. It was what was called a front-loaded deal, meaning that the £50,000 was there in case the deal went wrong. I didn't have any money, but that seemed beside the point. I agreed.

Three weeks earlier, Willie Morrison, the Canadian producer I'd brought over to England, had found a property to rent at the Vine Yard, in Borough, South London. It was purportedly a studio that had never been finished and which was up for rent. So we went along to see it and, I tell you, it was a dump. But as we walked through the building, both Willie and I were reminded of the same thing: this was like Motown. The idea of having offices and studios all in the same place in this dilapidated building just brought to mind Motown's rickety old place in Detroit.

Back in 1985, no one wanted to live in Borough. Nowadays with the new Tate gallery and loads of development, it's become a really trendy place, but back then it was awful. It was so rough that even the dogs used to go round in threes. Yet there was something about the prospect of having a studio there that appealed to me. This was it: the place we could start something big. And of course we'd have space for the SSL. We decided to rent it.

I had to go down to the Allied Irish bank and tell them not only that we were renting a place, but that I'd also just written a cheque for £50,000 and that I expected them to honour it. I'd had a very good relationship with the Allied Irish in the past and they'd always been understanding, but admittedly this was pushing it.

For the first time I had to take on some engineers and get the whole operation up and running. One thing that had slipped my mind about having a studio was that it would need electricity, an easy thing to overlook. As has been typical throughout my life, I'd just leaped in without really thinking, and now I had to try and sort it out.

Spelt Like This were due in to do some recording, so a couple of us worked round the clock rewiring the whole place. We also went out and bought a Trident mixing desk to tide us over for the few months until the SSL arrived. And, as always, the main problem seemed to be cash flow. We were juggling debts all over the place. I had to do the Spelt Like This stuff because I needed the money from EMI to pay for all the things we were buying.

It was 15 January 1985, my birthday. I worked twenty-four hours to get the whole studio up and running for the Monday morning when Spelt Like This were due in. Come Monday morning I suddenly realised that I'd overlooked something. We didn't actually have any tape to record on . . . or a tape machine, for that matter. These things are fairly essential to the whole recording process! I was beginning to realise that I hadn't really thought it all through. My original intention was to get the SSL and use other people's facilities so I could just build the whole operation up slowly. Now I'd dived headfirst into renting a studio and suddenly I had all the realities of what that entailed to think about. I rang around and found out it would cost me four grand just for tape and I couldn't afford that. I went down to the Marquee studios and managed to get some tape on credit, but that still left the problem of the tape machine, and the band was due in that day.

Tape machines cost upwards of forty grand. They were expensive bits of equipment. Where on earth was that going to come from at nine o'clock on a Monday morning?

'I'm ruined,' I thought. And I had visions of all the dreams falling down around my ears.

But I am the luckiest man in the world and whenever it seems like there's no way forward, something comes along and saves me. It happened again. The phone rang. It was a guy from the bank.

'Hello Pete,' he said. 'Just to warn you that the bank's on strike. So whatever you do, don't write any cheques because we can't stop them.'

I thanked him for calling, and gingerly replaced the receiver. Then I almost punched the ceiling with happiness. This was the best thing in the world that could have happened, and just about the only way I was going to be able to pull the whole thing off. They'd gone on strike the day I needed some money and they couldn't stop any cheques I wrote! *Thank you God!*

I was on the phone to the tape machine suppliers in seconds and ordered a machine for sixty grand. Half an hour later it was at the studio and I'd written a cheque for it. Unbelievable.

I was writing cheques for tens of thousands of pounds at the drop of a hat. Anything I'd forgotten I just bought, so suddenly the whole studio came to life. The bank stayed on strike for four months, which was beyond anything I could have wished for. And the studio really started working.

What *wasn't* working was Spelt Like This. The project was the biggest travesty I've been involved in in my life. The talent was Tom Watkins more than anyone in the band and I never understood what EMI saw in them in the first place. I think that Tom felt that it was our fault, but it wasn't. We were doing everything we could to make something out of nothing, but it just wasn't happening.

The singer sang with a lisp for starters; it was like having Chris Eubank fronting a band. And he kept on going on about how he could sing like anyone from Prince to Bruce Springsteen, so he'd do his Prince or his Springsteen – and they all sounded exactly the same to me. Rubbish.

Because we were having all these problems we weren't getting paid by EMI. And horrifyingly, around this time we found ourselves in the position of not being able to pay employees some months, simply due to the cash-flow situation. It was good that it happened in a way, because it meant that the people who'd just joined the company to make money had left. And those who were prepared to skip mortgage payments and stick together were rewarded with a subsequent bond that made the company much stronger.

In the end we got in a new MD, Dave Howells, and introduced some real financial discipline. We cut down on the money we spent on couriers and cabs and stopped people taking lunches that lasted all afternoon. If we were going to make the business work, we had to be single-minded about it. What's more, we couldn't afford to waste the reputation as hitmakers that we were developing. Eventually, Tony and Eamon from the bank rang up to tell me they were coming down to see me. They said it was urgent.

I took them to a very pleasant lunch. I wasn't panicking, but I knew the money subject was going to crop up eventually. Back at the studio Eamon finally asked, 'So, Peter, how do you think you're going to pay us back?'

I told him about all the projects we were doing, but had to admit that we weren't actually getting paid immediately. Along the way, I mentioned a record we were thinking of putting out.

'Play me the record,' he said.

'What?'

'Play me the record.'

So I put it on. It was by Princess and it was called 'Say I'm Your Number One'.

'How much money do you need, exactly?' he asked.

I told him thirty grand ought to just about cover it.

'You've got it,' he said and shook hands on the loan there and then.

He loved the song and so the only reason the business survived at all was that my bank manager fancied himself as an A&R man.

11 Respectable

THE PRINCESS SINGLE WAS VITAL to our development, and the story behind its release was, like so many of the pivotal moments in my life, a mixture of instinct and accident.

The Spelt Like This sessions weren't working out and we really were just banging our heads against the wall trying to make something out of them. I'd had enough of it all and I remember driving along the motorway on Bank Holiday Monday in the spring of 1985, deciding that we had to scrap the project. I rang up Mike Stock and said, 'Look, we can't keep on doing this band any more. We're just wasting our time. Let's be men and accept that enough is enough. I'm going into EMI tomorrow to tell them they can have the tapes.'

A few weeks earlier I'd talked to my old mate Pete Robinson at RCA. He had Bucks Fizz and he was desperate to do something with them, so he'd asked us to come up with some songs for them. At the same time another friend, Jack Stevens at Epic Records, had asked us to write a song for a girl called D.C. Lee. We'd been wondering what to do, but were happy that there were at least a couple of people showing interest in us coming up with something ourselves. Sitting in the car that day, driving down the motorway, I decided we had to force ourselves to take a chance. And the first stage was abandoning the Spelt Like This débâcle.

After I'd told Mike we were going to give EMI their tapes and pull out of the project, I asked him and Matt to go to his house with Andy Stennett, a keyboardist we had.

'Write some songs,' I said.

The next day I went into EMI and had a huge argument with them, but eventually managed to extricate us from working with Spelt Like This. I knew that we were in a hugely precarious situation. The EMI money was something we really needed, and the Allied Irish bank were going to be questioning all the cheques I'd written any day soon. At the same time, the girl that I was going out with had been seriously ill and needed to get away, so we went on holiday to Mallorca together for a week. A German publisher had offered to lend me a villa for a week and it seemed too good an opportunity to miss, especially because I was skint.

Before I left, Mike played me a song he'd written called 'Say I'm Your Number One', a song that we thought we might be able to get D.C. Lee to use. The brief I'd given him for writing it had been to come up with a song that girls could mouth at guys they fancied in clubs and then, if they were rejected, they could pretend that they were just singing along to the lyrics. One of the session singers we used was a girl called Desiree Heslop and she sang on the demo of the song. Her brother had come to me and announced that he wanted to release the record himself because it was so good, but I'd said that Desiree was only a session singer and had just been paid to sing on something we were working on for D.C Lee.

I went on holiday for a week, spending all the time worrying about how we could make things work with the company, and when I got back, Willie said he had something to play me. But I had to promise I wouldn't fly off the handle.

'Why?' I asked.

'Well, it's something Matt, Mike and Andy have been working on. But you've got to give it a proper listen,' he said.

And he played a tape of Desiree singing 'Say I'm Your Number One'. They'd done a fantastic job with it; the arrangement was superb and the vocals were so brilliant, I remember actually seeing the hairs on my wrist stand up.

'YEEEESSSSS!' I shouted.

Later on I found out that all the other people in the office were either hiding or listening with their ears against the wall. When I shouted, they'd thought I'd hit Willie or something. But I loved it.

'There's bad news as well,' he said.

'What do you mean, "bad news"? How could there be bad news with a track like that?' I said.

'Well, the boys think we should release it ourselves.'

'Absolutely, categorically not,' I said.

Everyone was shocked. They knew that I liked the record, so the obvious move seemed to be for us to put it out. That was common sense. But it wasn't common sense to me. We were producers. I hadn't promoted a record myself for years and the other people around me hadn't promoted a record in their lives. We had a hard enough job as it was trying to persuade the bank that there was any justification for us writing all the cheques we'd written over the past few weeks. Me, Mike and Matt weren't going to suddenly start a record company on our own.

Then I had an idea. I decided to get back in touch with Nick East, the guy who'd done promotion for Barry at Proto.

I had a meeting with Nick and I said, 'Why don't you form your own record company.' And I played him Desiree's song.

'I haven't got a penny, Pete,' he said.

'That's OK,' I told him. 'I'll sort it out for you and to start off, I'll give you this record for free.' He loved the track, so he was interested.

'Here's the deal,' I said. 'You start a label and license the track from me for free. And you promote it. But you've got to deliver the record, to really make sure it sells. You've got to give me the enthusiasm and commitment you had when you were working for Barry. You've got six months before you have to pay me anything.'

He said he had a name for the label: Supreme Records. It sounded good to me. So he agreed; he somehow came up with a bit of money to get things started, then a few weeks later Eamon from Allied Irish Bank came in and gave me the thirty grand loan on the strength of hearing the track. That thirty grand was enough to start pressing copies.

Desiree's brother Don had become her manager and was determined to make sure that no one took advantage of his sister. He used to sit in the studio telling us that the aluminium in mixing desks was contributing to the exploitation of people in Africa, things like that; but he was a big bloke, so you never wanted to argue with him. He also felt he could come up with ideas for marketing her, and announced that he had a name that Desiree was going to use: Princess.

'But what's Prince going to think?' I asked him.

'It's going to be Princess,' he said. So we left it at that. Desiree became Princess.

At that time the whole dance scene was driven by pirate radio and the buzz you could build by having records played on pirate stations. We wanted to exploit that, so we pressed the record on a white label 12-inch and made it look like it had come in from New York. Nick promoted it to all the pirates, talking it up as this hot NY record. They all started playing it.

A couple of weeks later I got a phone call from Pete Robinson at RCA. He told me he'd spent the last fortnight trawling around New York trying to track down the people who'd made the record. He originally thought it must have been a Jam and Lewis record. It was only when he got back that he suspected it might have been me behind it. I admitted it was and he tried to buy it off me. He was surprised when I told him it had already been sold to Supreme Records, and so it wasn't for sale. In the past he'd known that he'd always have a chance of buying a track off me, but this time I was insistent that he couldn't.

Because of the promotion that Nick had done to the pirates, the record really started flying. Back then we used to have telex machines in the office and all of a sudden people were sending telexes offering huge amounts of money to put the record out in different territories. And I owned every-thing: I owned the production, the publishing *and* the master tapes.

The record went into the charts just outside the Top Forty, and we were ecstatic. We were a tiny little company, pitching ourselves against the whole record industry, and we'd made an impression. This wasn't like nowadays where you could just shoot into the charts for a week then straight out again. This was obviously going to start building into something.

But Don, Desiree's brother, came into the offices and started complaining. He seemed to believe that unless it had come straight into the Top Ten, we'd failed. I couldn't believe what he was saying; this was the most exciting thing that had happened to me! It was a dream come true. Matt, Mike and me; the team. And no one could take that away from us. We'd taken on the world and won. I had to tell Don that just because you didn't go straight into the charts at Number One, it didn't mean you weren't going to have a hit.

The next week the song had gone into the Top Twenty and we got *Top Of The Pops*. The day before the recording, Don came in with Desiree and said he had to see me about something urgent. He told me that he and Desiree were having a rough time. They couldn't pay their rent for the flat they were living in, and they needed a few grand to get their situation sorted out. By now Princess had sold something like 100,000 records, so they'd earn at least ten thousand pounds later down the line. I rang up Eamon at the bank and asked them to put ten thousand into Don's account.

I went out for the day and when I got back there was a blue BMW outside the office. I asked whose it was and I was told that it belonged to Don, Desiree's brother. He looked a bit sheepish, having dashed straight out and spent his cut on a motor, but I think he appreciated the immediate success we could bring about.

That record went on to really establish us. Wherever we went after that, all around the world, it became our calling card. It was the first independent Number One by a black artist in Germany, a country that Nick had given promotional copies to DJs in. No one had done that there before and it set a precedent. We sold loads and picked up awards all over Europe. It was the making of the company, because it was the first record that was just the team. There were no outside influences and suddenly we'd attracted a lot of people all over the world, who all saw that we were a team worth employing. In America, my old buddy Eddie O'Loughlin picked up on it and bought it to release over there.

So, not only did it make great money for us and bring together a core group of people at the company, it also established our credibility quite sensationally all over the world. Six months later I met Jam and Lewis face to face. They were with Janet Jackson, whom they were producing. Jimmy Jam pulled me over and introduced me to Janet; he said, 'This is Pete Waterman. Him and his guys are the only people who can compete with us. We know where they've stolen their ideas from, but they do it with style and take it into a whole new place.'

It was a great compliment from someone I really respected.

That one record was a statement that we were going to stand on our own and not worry about anyone else. It was the record that made Stock, Aitken and Waterman and we didn't care if we failed after that, because we'd proved to ourselves just what we were capable of.

We'd also got over the worst of the cash-flow problem. By August 1985 when the song was a Top Ten hit, the royalties started to flow in from things like Dead Or Alive. Supreme was Nick's label, but I owned the master tape to 'Say I'm Your Number One'. I controlled the artist, I owned the rights. Everyone involved got paid and it was a very equitable deal, but at the end of the day I took the risks and I called the shots. For the first time, no one could take advantage of me, because the money came directly to me. And serious money was starting to come in.

Early in 1986, we were approached to work with Bananarama. At that point the band was moderately successful, but hadn't done anything for a while. I was going out with their manager, Hilary Shaw, and she suggested we might be able to bring something to a track they were working on, a cover of the old song, 'Venus'. I was very keen to work with them because I was a fan of their music and loved the way that they were so obviously influenced by all those old sixties girl groups.

When I met Bananarama they reminded me of the Belle Stars. Siobhan, Sarah and Keren were three very opinionated, wild tomboy girls, with the same great image that Madonna adopted later on. They were very much part of the whole Soho scene and all their friends worked for the *Face* or ran clubs and stuff and they'd be out at every party going. They were the hardest drinking girls I ever met, and real maneaters – in the nicest possible way.

They came down to our studio and laid down the track. It was all right, but nothing out of the ordinary. We always went down to the pub at the end of work and just ended up getting drunk and talking nonsense, it was bit of a ritual. On the way down there one night I asked Bananarama what they thought of the track and one of them said that it was OK, 'But it's not "You Spin Me Round".' Now, they hadn't mentioned that that was what they wanted, but as soon as they did I knew what I could do. So I went into the pub with them, gave them the money for their drinks and came back to the studio.

'Give us an hour,' I said. 'Then come over.'

Back at the studio I got what we'd done of 'Venus' and underneath it I put a backing track similar to the sound we'd created on Dead Or Alive's 'You Spin Me Round'. An hour later the girls came back over and I played it to them. They loved it. And all it was basically was a Dead Or Alive song with them singing over the top of it.

I took it to Roger Ames, the boss of London Records, Bananarama's label. When I played him the tape he said he hated all the 'Ricky ticky drums.'

'That's just like the Dead Or Alive backing track, Roger,' I said. Suddenly he'd changed his opinion completely.

'Oh, man,' he said. 'Those ricky ticky drums are brilliant. That's a great record you've made there.'

'Venus' was released and went to Number Eight in Britain. In America the band's absence from the scene for fourteen months hadn't been so noticeable as in Britain because with America being so vast, careers work much more slowly. Bananarama were still fresh in their minds from the stuff they'd done before, much more so than over here. 'Venus' went on to be their first American Number One record.

We had a party for the single in the courtyard outside the studios. It went on all night and it was like a South London carnival. Where we were and what we were doing seemed to be just perfect.

Around early 1986, Nick East had been telling me about a pair of girls he'd heard whom he was interested in signing, but I'd not really taken much notice of him. Then one night I was at the Hippodrome in London for the Disco Mix Club Conference, an industry affair for the dance world. These two extraordinarily good looking girls came up and said they were singers and they wanted an audition. I was chatting away to them and I must have told them to come to the studio the next day, but by the end of the night I'd completely forgotten about it. The next day the bell rang: it was them and they'd come to audition. They had to remind me that I'd asked them to come up, but we let them in, and when Nick saw them he told me they were the two girls he'd been going on about. They were two sisters by the names of Mel and Kim Appleby.

As soon as I heard them, I knew they were really good. And the best thing about them was their personalities. They were sexy, but really cheeky and had lovely, in-your-face, exuberant personalities. They were stars without us even having to do anything. We knew we had to make a record with them.

They used to come round the studio all the time. I think half the people in the office fancied them, so no one minded them coming round. They were from a completely different world to Bananarama. Whereas Bananarama were part of the whole hip, Soho scene, Mel and Kim were socialising in South London, down the Old Kent Road. And they were well up for a good time. It was wonderful to just sit and listen to them talk about their escapades. One day they said they were going out that night, 'Showing out'. I asked them what that meant. They said, 'Oh, it's when you go out and kiss frogs, seeing if they turn into princes.'

I loved the phrase 'showing out'. And so we wrote a song for them and called it just that. 'Showin' Out (Get Fresh At The Weekend)' was a Top Three hit. Just before it came out, Mel said she had a confession to make to me. She said there were photos of her going round that the papers might pick up on.

'Oh my God,' I said. 'How bad are they? There aren't animals involved, are there?'

It turned out they were just some topless shots she'd done earlier when she needed the money. It was a bit of a scandal when the papers first used them, but it soon blew over. And besides, Mel and Kim were such natural pop stars and such fun to have in the charts that there wasn't much public interest in slagging them off.

Very, very quickly the two of them became like daughters to me. We had a fantastic rapport, and they were giving the company a really good, feisty image. Their follow-up single,

'Respectable', was an anthem, not just for them and their image, but also for the company itself. The lyrics came from an ad we took out in the trade press that used the lines, 'You can love or hate us, you ain't gonna change us . . . we ain't ever going to be respectable.' We definitely saw ourselves as renegades.

Mike Stock thought we needed a gimmick for the song, so he decided to put in the 'Tay, tay, tay, tay, t-tay . . .' sample at the beginning of the song. It was something hardly anyone had ever done before and was technically quite hard to do. He loved it, but Mel and Kim and their manager absolutely hated it. It was the only time I ever saw Mike really dig his heels in about anything to do with making a record, and he said that if they took it off the song he was never going to work with them again.

Mel and Kim took the track, complete with samples, away with them to a PA they were doing in Holland and later that night I got a phone call from the manager. He said, 'Whatever you do, don't take that bit off the beginning of the record, because I've got an audience here going absolutely wild to it!' We left it in and 'Respectable' became Mel and Kim's first Number One.

Mel and Kim were probably the first real *pop* stars we were involved with, in that we suddenly had to start dealing with them appearing on children's TV shows and things like that. We'd moved away from being underground dance producers to making records that were selling an extraordinary number of copies. But we were doing it without compromising our integrity. We were making records with very catchy tunes, but they were underpinned by technically brilliant production and great arrangements. We were using all sorts of effects and sounds that were genuinely innovative, but we never forgot that you don't succeed unless at the heart of it all you've got a great, strong song.

In 1986 I finally decided to deal with my illiteracy. Throughout my life, I'd always found a way to get around not being able to read and write, right back from when I was young and had to sign for my wages at the factory. I just used to stand at the back of the queue and look where everyone else signed, then sign where they had with a treble-clef symbol. It was more like a picture than a word. I'd picked up some basic words like 'cat' and 'dog' and by the time I started to get successful making records I'd learned a few more. 'Party' and 'invitation' were recognisable because I'd seen them so often!

The Allied Irish Bank was actually really good to me and had never made a big thing of it when I had to sign complicated forms. They just used to fill them in for me and show me where to sign and because we trusted each other there was never any problem. Other people weren't so sympathetic and I remember one record company who I was in court with over a contractual dispute got their barrister to make me read out the contract, knowing full well I wouldn't be able to. I just told the judge that I couldn't read and, although I didn't win the case, he said that I'd conducted myself with dignity. It's actually surprisingly easy to run a business when you can't read or write, if you have lawyers and accountants to deal with contracts and things on your behalf.

I do remember one particularly embarrassing moment. I used to either remember song lyrics that I'd come up with, or get them down on paper in this strange sort of hieroglyphics. It was a mixture of symbols that only I understood, and really it was basic childish writing. I was in the studio one day with Mel and Kim and they picked up this bit of paper saying it must be a fan letter from a five-year-old child. I had to tell them that it was in fact the lyrics I'd written for one of their songs and though they laughed about it and were sympathetic towards me, it did make me feel a bit foolish.

Then I went on holiday with my girlfriend Carol, who said that she wasn't going to go with me if I was going to keep talking all the time. She said she wanted a bit of peace and quiet, so I knew I'd have to take a book with me and decided to learn to read.

There are lots of books you might choose to learn from, but I chose the oddest one anyone has ever used: *Das Boot*, the story of German submarines in the Second World War. It was something I was interested in, so I figured I'd be more likely to work at understanding it and I spent the holiday learning words phonetically like a child. With submarine, for example, I knew that s-u-b spelt sub and 'marine' looked a bit like 'margarine', a word I knew from seeing on packets in the shops, so I thought it must sound a bit like it too.

It was a terribly laborious process, but eventually I began to pick up the basics. I'm still not a big reader and I can't do joined up writing, but just being able to get a grasp of it all is something I consider a major achievement. Mike Stock always said that you had to deal with whatever I wrote like you were communicating with someone who had English as a second language. While I'm not first in the queue when the library opens, the books I have read have shown me that there is great wisdom hidden in books, so much so that I've always told people that if I'd learned to read when I was a teenager, I would have made twice as much money as I have.

We mixed and produced a whole load of artists over 1986 and 1987, because we had so many projects on the go at once. People like Amazulu, Red Box, The Blow Monkeys, Pepsi & Shirley and Five Star. They all came and went and, without exception, the songs were hits.

We were also expanding the number of people working much more closely under the Stock, Aitken and Waterman banner. This involved writing, production and having far more involvement creatively. We did a couple of singles with people like Sinitta, and Sam Fox.

Sam was a lovely, sunny person, with a great sense of humour. She played the boys at their own game brilliantly, and handled the level of male interest in her, which in the mid-eighties was fanatical, with ease. Just how much of an icon she was was brought home to me on one of our regular trips to the local pub, the Gladstone, affectionately known as the Glad. The staff and regulars were used to me, Matt and Mike turning up in there with all sorts of celebrities, and never batted an eyelid. But when we brought Sam in for a drink, the place erupted. I'd never seen anything like it.

People like Sam Fox and Sinitta may not have been singers we saw as having twenty-year careers in the music industry, but we knew we were capable of giving them a few hits. And we did.

I had a friend up North who was always trying to get me interested in his acts. One weekend he invited me along to see a showcase he'd put on for a few groups. One of them was an awful country outfit called Poacher whom I had absolutely no interest in. I had a stinking cold and I was only there as a favour to my mate, so I wasn't particularly keen on staying around. I just wanted to get home, but I made the effort and went along.

I was glad I did. One of the other groups that were playing had an incredible singer. The band was completely ordinary and the songs were rubbish, but this kid had a fantastic voice. He reminded me of Van Morrison or something. So I told my mate, 'Great look, great voice, bad songs. I'm not interested in the band, but I want that singer.' His name was Rick Astley.

Rick came down to London and did an audition. He sang his version of Paul Young's 'Wherever I Lay My Hat', and it blew me away. So we got him working for us under the youth opportunities scheme. He'd get £40 a week, or whatever it was, from the government and we gave him a pretty non-specific job at the office. During the week, he'd live at my London flat, then go back up to the house I'd bought at Newton-Le-Willows, near Warrington, at the weekend.

Many different people just used to drop in at the office at the time, including DJs like Gary Crowley, Steve Walsh and Pete Tong. And of course Bananarama had a wide social circle, so all their mates used to pop round too. And I liked that; it made for a wonderful creative atmosphere. Because Rick was so friendly he used to offer to make cups of tea for everyone, so the myth has grown up that he was the office tea-boy who turned into a pop star. He wasn't at all. He was just a lovely, friendly kid who happened to make tea for people while we were working on making him successful.

I did have a vision for Rick, which was that he would be the new George Michael. I saw that George was going to be taking a sabbatical and knew that the kids would want a male singer. Rick could fill that gap perfectly. That's not to say that he was a puppet. I've always found that if you try to make a singer do a song that they don't want to do, then you're never going to have hits. We had to give him songs that he would be comfortable doing and because we got to know him so well, we knew exactly what those songs should sound like. What we did better than anyone else was get a feel for the personality of our artists and tailor what we did to those personalities.

We'd got a deal for Rick with RCA Records and started working on a track called 'Never Gonna Give You Up', but it was by no means finished. Somehow it found its way onto a Disco Mix compilation tape and people who heard it suddenly got really excited about it. A few radio stations made their own edit of the record and started playing it, even though it was still basically just a demo. Because there was no information other than the title of the song on the tape, everyone started wild rumours about who was actually singing. At one point the smart money was on Luther Vandross! Rick's voice sounded so good.

So already, and again by accident, we'd built up a buzz on a record before it had even been released. When it finally did come out it was Number One, and Rick went on to be very, very famous.

There was no fake public image. What you saw was what he really was. With 'Never Gonna Give You Up', we'd used the song to kind of show that he was just a shy kid, and it was a rarity for a song sung by a man, in that in the lyrics he took the weaker, traditionally female role of being the one who wasn't going to let their partner go. It was basically a rewrite of Dusty Springfield's 'You Don't Have To Say You Love Me', but with the roles reversed. It was a perfect example of how we always made the song fit the singer.

Over the next couple of years Rick Astley was just about the best-selling male performer in the country. He also became a bit of a heartthrob. Now, Rick was an incredible talent, but he had an underlying problem, which was a real lack of self-confidence. When I'd first seen him he was in a band, and ultimately he was happier in a band than being a solo performer. He didn't ever become entirely comfortable with the notion of having all the attention on him – which was something we were to find out later.

What I've discovered with all the acts I've worked with is that eventually the people you make famous abandon the discipline and the wise advice that made them famous in the first place. And things change.

That was starting to happen when Mel and Kim changed their management and got in new people. It seemed like the impetus began to be lost, but we carried on working with them anyway. Then, when they were playing abroad, we got news that Mel had collapsed on tour. And when they got back, it was revealed that she had cancer. It was something she'd had in the past, but we'd thought she'd got rid of it, and now it seemed it was back. And so all the recording and stuff with them was put on hold while she went through chemotherapy. I remember going to see her when she was being treated and it seemed such a tragedy that someone so young and full of life was being attacked by such a terrible disease. She fought it with great dignity and bravery.

Rumours had started to go round about her and she took the very brave decision to hold a press conference to say she had cancer. It would have been understandably easy for her to hide away, but she went out there with a bald head and admitted that she had the disease. It was an incredibly courageous thing to do and I've always respected her for that.

We knew she was very seriously ill, but she'd beaten the disease in the past and we all hoped she would again. And she even did some recording, even though it was obviously very difficult for her.

On 18 January 1990 I was in Tokyo with Kylie Minogue. I came back to the hotel and all the staff were lined up in the lobby. One of them presented me with a note and they all bowed their heads. The note said that Mel had died. She'd had a cold, which had turned into pneumonia, because she was so weak. She was only 23. It still tears me apart just remembering it. She really was like a daughter to me.

I don't know if Mel and Kim would have gone on to be bigger stars because with the new management there had definitely been suggestions that they had lost that initial sparkle, but as a person Mel made the world a richer place. I still miss her.

In 1987 I went to a party at the Toy Museum in Paddington and met a girl who I started going out with for a while. She was a Zimbabwean Jew who lived in Paris and worked at an art gallery. I used to go over to Paris every weekend to stay with her. While I was over there I started listening to a radio station called NRG, and I loved the records that they were playing, which were basically dance songs coming in from Rimini — things like Black Box and Spagna. They'd also play Mel and Kim and Bananarama, which fitted alongside perfectly. I realised that we were making peculiarly European dance music. It was 'whiter', if you like, than traditional r'n'b and while it was dance music it was also very pop. When I went over to Paris I'd go to dance record shops and find that they were selling white labels of stuff we'd done, pressed up even before the record companies we gave the tracks to had got them. So God knows where they got them from, but they did. We'd obviously tapped into a sound that they loved. That became an acid test for us: just how quickly there'd be white labels available in Paris.

We prided ourselves on the way that it was us against the world, but though we were having so many hits, record companies didn't copy us because they hated us. And most of the people we dealt with in the rest of the industry were either annoying or stupid or both. For example, we had one guy come over from Germany who was shocked to find that a record sounded really loud on big speakers, but weedier on little ones. And this was someone in charge of investing money in making music!

The A&R men from the big companies just seemed like amateurs to me, too. If we wanted to impress them when they came to the studio to see how a track was going, we'd just dim all the lights so that all the flashing lights on the desk seemed really bright. And, quite astoundingly, that reassured them. You just couldn't believe the idiots you were dealing with, but because we told them to get lost if they annoyed us, we got a reputation for being arrogant. We didn't care; to use a football analogy, if we were going to play against the giants then we were going to make sure the pitch sloped in our favour. And we'd shine the floodlights in their eyes while we were at it, too.

12 Roadblock

O
UR SUCCESS WAS PRETTY PHENOMENAL. Funnily enough, at the time we weren't really aware of what an impact we were having on the industry. We were just getting on with doing what we knew best. There were some suggestions in the media, though, that we were operating to a sort of self-serving agenda. For example a piece in *Record Mirror* had laid in to Mel and Kim and called me a 'Capitalist Svengali', basing most of their displeasure around the fact that we'd put out a Mel and Kim single called 'FLM' with the letters standing for Fun, Love and Money. In fact the 'fun, love and money' thing was only there for the public. The initials really stood for 'Fuckin' lovely, mate', which was Mel's catchphrase. She used to say it all the time; whenever she met you or she had something to do, it'd be, 'Fuckin' lovely, mate', so we thought we'd make a private joke out of it on a record. In the same way, because she was always giggling, we sampled her laughter all over their records. Just as with the Dead Or Alive record's TDF mix, a private joke was turned into something that would be acceptable to the public.

The person who wrote the *Record Mirror* feature thought there was something much more unpleasant behind it and had a go at us for writing about wealth. We were shocked, because if you listen to the song, it's quite obviously tongue in cheek and Mel and Kim were quite obviously playing up that tongue in cheek side of it.

The Times had picked up on the *Record Mirror* article and decided to do an interview with us portraying us as 'the acceptable face of Thatcherism', which turned out to be the headline of the feature, above a picture of the three of us standing in front of a guided missile that I have hanging up on my wall. The interviewer had decided to investigate whether we were really such a bunch of flash capitalist manipulators as the *Record Mirror* feature had claimed. The guy went away from the interview having realised that we quite obviously weren't. In fact we were anything *but* capitalists in the way that the company was run. The artists, writers and producers were all on an equal level, and the way we operated was much more like a co-op. It may have been a dictatorial democracy in terms of my right to ultimately decide what we did, but when the winnings came in they were shared equally. No other pop company has ever been run like that, and while we didn't have a problem with making money as a concept, we were determined that when the money was made, it would be shared equally between everybody. We managed to run the company in that way because, unlike any other company, we never gave big advances to anybody. The artists got five hundred pounds and the producers got five hundred pounds. If you failed then no one got paid, but if you succeeded, then everyone got much more than they would have got under a normal record company's standard deal. That was how we built up our company. My attitude was, and is, that I don't want a huge amount up front, but if I make a hit then I want a percentage of the money it makes.

We never really liked doing interviews and must have only done half a dozen in all. After *The Times* one, we waited a good two years before we did another broadsheet interview, this time for the *Observer*. They put up huge posters of a picture of the three of us all over London, including one right opposite the office, which nearly gave me a coronary when I first saw it. When you see yourself on a twenty-five foot poster, it's unreal. I'd expected the *Observer* feature writer to crucify us, but even she had to acknowledge that, while she didn't like our records, we weren't the ogres that we were generally perceived as. A few days later there was another phone call from the *Observer*. They said that they were getting a new arts editor who had made it one of the conditions of joining the paper that she be allowed to defend us. So this woman wrote an absolutely wonderful piece about us, saying that she had two teenage daughters and that they both loved the records we were making. She described what we were doing as candyfloss, but said that there was nothing wrong with candyfloss if you remembered to clean your teeth afterwards. I was astounded, not just to have an arts editor defending us, but one from the *Observer*. And she was spot on. She described what we were doing as 'frippery' and although it was the first time I'd ever heard the word, when I'd looked it up in a dictionary, I had to agree.

Matt and Mike were never comfortable with doing interviews and I used to try and keep them out of it as much as possible. They were far more intellectual than me and used to feel that they had to defend themselves by showing how clever they were. If the interviewer came up with a big word, they'd come up with a bigger one, which gave the wrong impression of why we were doing what we were doing.

For example, we wrote a song for the Reynolds Girls, called 'I'd Rather Jack Than Fleetwood Mac', which was inspired by a radio seminar I went to where everyone was banging on about demographics. I wanted to make a song that cocked a snook at that whole idea of the blanding out of youth culture, something that pricked the balloon of pomposity about having reverence for old rock bands. It was just a bit of fun, but Matt and Mike went on Simon Bates' radio show and turned it into a real in-depth intellectual argument, which made the whole thing seem really dour. Simon Bates wanted 'Sod the industry' soundbites, but instead he got a university thesis. Matt and Mike loved making the records and didn't feel any embarrassment about doing so, but when they were called upon to explain what they were doing to interviewers they tended to over-analyse everything purely as a defence mechanism. My attitude in interviews was always, Well, if it pisses you off that I'm making these records, I'll give you half a dozen more just to piss you off even more. The worst thing you can do to me is slag me, because it just makes me more determined to be successful.

Those years were like living in a dream, because everything we were touching was turning to gold. We didn't have any flops. Or if we had stuff that wasn't a major success, something good came out of the experience.

For instance, for a while we worked with a band called Brilliant, who included Jimmy Cauty who went on to be in KLF; we also met Youth who had been in Killing Joke and went on to make a name for himself as a producer. He said publicly that it was me who taught him to produce records. I think he underestimated the complexity of what we were doing, but it was flattering anyway.

KLF nicked the concept of what they were doing from our whole belief in achieving whatever you wanted. Of course with KLF, it became over-hyped and just too silly to be true. The records themselves were sensational, but they were basically just Stock, Aitken and Waterman records.

With Brilliant we did a cover version of James Brown's 'Man's World' and that was probably the most critically acclaimed record we ever made, at least by the music press. It never seemed that extraordinary to me, putting a reggae trombonist on a record, because it felt like quite an obvious thing to do. We were getting people from all over the world asking us to produce their records. Technology was in its infancy at the time and we were using it imaginatively. Plus we'd created this image of mystique and bravado; we'd started banning A&R men from the building and insisting that we only talked directly to the bands and their management. Also, we never let anyone have the disks from the programming, so no one could analyse how we were doing what we were doing. All this was simply for commercial reasons. We didn't want anyone else interfering with the process.

When bands came in with stuff that was all arty I'd take them aside and just beat the shit out of their ideas. I'd make them understand that they couldn't wrap their way of working in riddles, it all had to be common sense. They had to concentrate simply on doing what they had to do. Bullshit never sold records. I hated any pretence. And if you were going to make a career out of mystery and image, you couldn't introduce them until you'd got a decent song underneath.

In the summer of 1987 we made the first of a couple of singles under the name Stock, Aitken and Waterman, a song called 'Roadblock'. Around then there were rumblings from various people in the industry that we could only make one sort of record, a straightforward pop hit. This was rubbish of course; the reason we were making pop hits was because those sorts of songs suited the artists we were working with best. There wouldn't have been any point in making a record completely out of character for the people that were singing it. Bananarama, for example, were basically just three lairy girls who sang in harmony. That was what they did, and that was what they were good at. They were beginning to develop their sound towards making slightly trendier records, but the core of anything they did was still just them singing in harmony, and they were fully prepared to accept the limitations that imposed.

Bananarama were still hanging out with their hip, Soho crowd and a lot of them would come down to the studios, along with loads of the pirate radio DJs and movers and shakers on the club scene. One day the DJ Pete Tong popped in and started going on about Rare Groove, a style of music that was very popular at the time. He played me some Rare Groove records and to me they just sounded like old r'n'b records that hadn't been hits. They were very reminiscent of the sort of stuff that James Brown used to put out on his own label, People Records. Good songs and all that, but nothing particularly new or innovative. Still, everyone was raving about this supposedly brand new type of music and I was surprised when my old mate Tilly Rutherford, who was working as general manager for PWL, started telling me how good it was. He'd run the Soul Hole shop with me back in Coventry so I thought he, more than anyone else, would have realised that it was just a rehash of songs we'd been listening to all those years before. But he wouldn't stop banging on about it, so Matt, Mike and I decided to make a record that would shut Tilly Rutherford up, and also maybe prove to the doubters that we could make a record in a style completely different from what people were used to hearing from us.

The big buzzword at the time was 'Roadblock', the name given to illegal, impromptu parties that had originally been held in America, but which had now become fashionable on the underground London dance scene. Mike came up with calling a record 'Roadblock' and wrote a song that was basically a celebration of going to a roadblock party. Meanwhile Mark, one of our engineers, had brought in a 12-inch record that had a really nice reggae groove on it. It was a new record, but the groove sounded kind of old-fashioned and while in itself it wasn't a hit, it was exactly what we were looking for to put on our 'Roadblock' record. We combined the rhythm from the 12-inch with Mike's lyrics, fiddled around with it for a while and came up with a song.

We had strict rules about no one from the office being allowed to go into the studios, because it stopped the studio engineers from getting on with their work, and since the studios were soundproofed we could be doing anything inside without anyone else in the office knowing about it. So we set to work recording this 'Roadblock' single. We didn't know who to use as a vocalist on it, but Mike or Matt suggested we use Jimmy Ruffin, the old soul singer we happened to be working with in one of the other studios at the time. We got him down to have a go at it, but because it was exactly the sort of song he'd been used to singing for so long, it sounded too polished and too perfect. We decided instead to ask a girl called China, one of the session singers we regularly used, to try it. And her voice was just right. At the beginning of the recording she'd done this funny trill, running up and down the scales as a way of warming up and Matt and Mike had not only taped it, they'd also sampled it all over the song.

We wanted to make it sound live, like an old r'n'b record by Ramsey Lewis called 'Wading In The Water' which was recorded in a club and had the sound of all the people in the club in the background. Don't forget that this was just something we were doing in a day to take the piss out of Tilly.

Late that night, we asked a few boys from the office into the studio, along with all the contents of the dishwasher. And we taped them talking while they rattled all these dishes and forks and spoons and things, recording two tracks of this ambient noise. Next we got every single person from the office into a vocal booth to do this 'Roadblock, ooh ooh ooh!' chant. It was a right old racket. Finally Pete Hammond and I worked through the night to finish off the record, but instead of using the SSL as we always did, we turned the computers off and did all the mixing manually like they used to do in the old days. That again gave it much more of an authentic old feel. Then we chopped in a couple more samples from old records and edited it down to a 12-inch. I went and pressed up an acetate and took it outside and rubbed some dirt from the street all over the label so it looked genuinely old.

The next day I slipped it into a pile of old records in my office and invited Tilly to look through them. He picked out 'Roadblock', put it on and started raving about it.

'If only you could make record like this, Pete,' he said.

'You prat Tilly,' I said. 'I made that one.'

He didn't believe me, but I went and played him the master tape we'd done the day before. He was gobsmacked.

We decided to put 'Roadblock' out, pretending it was a bootleg, just to see what would happen. We vowed not to tell a soul who had made the record. We pressed a thousand copies and just put the word 'Roadblock' on the sleeve together with a New York number, which happened to be the number of my lawyer over there. Unfortunately when we got the thousand copies back from being pressed we saw that Malcolm Davies, who'd pressed them, had put PRT, the name of the pressing company, on the run-out of the record – which gave the game away, identifying its origin. We knew that once people saw that they'd be able to trace the record back to us, so I got a soldering iron and I sat there and scratched out every single matrix mark on every single record, making them completely anonymous. Anyone who has got one of the original copies will see that every bit of identifying information has been scratched out.

We took the record to the distributors who sold records to dance shops and let them get on with spreading them around. And then I went off on holiday to Sardinia for a fortnight, thinking that we'd pulled off a fun, low-key hoax. Everyone would think it was an American record and no one would know who it was by. While I was away I rang Tilly up, and he told me that everyone in London was going barmy for 'Roadblock'. There had been orders for something like 10,000 copies!

When I got back there was a phone call from my lawyer in New York. Of course, I'd forgotten to tell him that I'd put his number on the sleeve and people had been ringing him up every day asking about it!

My old mate Chris Hill, whom I'd first known as a Northern Soul DJ, was the first to rumble that the record was by us. He knew that it sounded like an old record, but was too well produced.

'It's very, very clever,' he said. 'You've got to put this out as Stock, Aitken and Waterman so that all those people who've said you can only make one sort of record will have to start eating humble pie.'

I'd been to see Alan Cowderoy at A&M Records before I went away. I'd told him he could have 'Roadblock' to release, but I wouldn't tell him anything about it at the time. Now I went in and revealed it was me, Matt and Mike and that we wanted to release it under the name Stock, Aitken and Waterman. He actually said to me, 'You can't put it out under your own names. It's too good!' And he wasn't the only one. Two or three other people told me it was *too good* for me to put my name to, then they seriously expected me to listen to them. The whole point of the exercise had been to make people listen to the record not look at whose name was on the label.

I wanted praise where praise was due, so we put it out under our names. At the same time we refused to play the song live or to appear on *Top Of The Pops* and by doing so, we stopped it getting to Number One, which it undoubtedly would have. We'd made our point by getting people to admit to liking what we'd done and acknowledging that we could make what they considered 'good' records, but we didn't want to pretend that we were anything other than producers. We weren't pop stars and we didn't want to pretend that we were. So it became the only massive record that we produced that never had a *Top Of The Pops* appearance. Still, 'Roadblock' went on to be sampled all over the place and still is, right up to this day. We even rewrote it ourselves to create 'Better The Devil You Know' which was a hit for Kylie Minogue and, later, Steps. Even Geri Halliwell's last single sounded basically like 'Roadblock', and it still gets played out at clubs now. We allowed Bananarama to put out a reworking of the track called 'Mr Sleaze', but they weren't supposed to credit us with it. Nevertheless, they went ahead and put 'Stock, Aitken and Waterman' on the writing credits. We didn't really mind, because Bananarama were family, but it would have been better to have left the mystery.

Bananarama were invariably up for anything and they were great fun to work with. They were also responsible for just about my favourite song I ever produced, 'Love In The First Degree'. They'd played me just the drums and bass from it one day and I knew just from that that it was going to be a smash. I'd woken up one morning with an old song by Bobby Freeman called 'Tossing And Turning' in my head, the tune of which became 'Love In The First Degree'. When the song was finished, the girls also did a wonderful video, which was a spoof of Elvis Presley's 'Jailhouse Rock'. So I loved everything about it. Then, just before it was due to come out, they decided they didn't want it released because it was too obviously commercial, so for the first and only time I had to put my foot down and say that if they didn't release it then I no longer wanted to work with them. That's not the sort of stance I usually take, but this song was far too good not to be released. I said to them that if it wasn't a hit then they need never approach me to do any work for them ever again.

When it came out, the midweek prediction for the first week's sales was Number 42, which was devastating for me. I couldn't understand how I could have been so wrong. This sounds daft, but I used to listen to the chart rundown on Radio One every Sunday, and I used to make sure that no one told me where our records were in the charts until I heard it on the radio. The next Sunday I was out in my garden mowing the lawn at my house near Newton-Le-Willows with the radio on. I listened to the DJ reading out the chart positions and playing the records and by the time he'd counted down to Number 20, Bananarama still hadn't been mentioned. By then I was convinced it was a flop, then 20 to 10 came and went, but still no sign of the record. Eventually the DJ announced, 'This week's highest new entry, Bananarama, in at Number Eight.' I'd been right after all! Jokingly I said to myself, 'There's the sound of a new Ferrari.'

I told this story a few years later to some people who were making a documentary for Radio One, and as the documentary was going out, my neighbour was sitting in his garden listening to it. At that very moment, a brand new Ferrari was delivered to my house. My neighbour nearly had a coronary, because it was such a coincidence. It was like a fairy story.

'Love In The First Degree' was Bananarama's biggest UK hit and went on to help them become, by the end of the eighties, the best selling British girl group of all time. They had their idiosyncrasies, like initially refusing to use the word 'love' in any of their songs, but I just went ahead and made them do it anyway. We'd spent six weeks trying to write songs without the word 'love' in the title and realised it was impossible. So we used to just play them bits and pieces of loads of different tracks and when it all came together we'd rush it through so there was no time for them to change their minds.

We had a great working relationship with Bananarama, because we pushed each other to achieve. There was a mutual respect and I still think they're one of the greatest groups this country has ever produced, although things didn't always go smoothly.

Siobhan had amazing talent, but could be difficult to work with. I got on with the other two in the band really well, but there always seemed to be conflict between Siobhan and me. I still think it was her fault, but then she'd probably say it was mine. It was just one of those things. My attitude to her was the attitude to everyone I've worked with, my job isn't to be Mr Popularity, it's to make the artists millionaires. If you don't like me as a person then I haven't got a problem with that. The record company pays me to return their investment and if that makes me unpopular, so be it. I used to have huge arguments with Siobhan, but that was only because I respected her and knew that you had to fight with her to bring the best out in her.

When we'd been finishing the Bananarama album, we'd got stuck on one final song and couldn't think what to write. Then one day I was walking past the TV and I saw a preview of a programme called *Strike It Rich*. It triggered off the idea for a lyric and I came up with 'Ain't life a bitch, you gotta keep on working 'til you strike it rich.' We used that as the hook for the final song.

Siobhan exploded. 'I can't possibly sing that,' she said. 'It's a capitalist song.' She just hated the idea of singing the phrase 'strike it rich' and refused to sing it. We recorded it, but when it came to the chorus, Siobhan refused to sing the phrase 'strike it rich'. We used it anyway.

Then Siobhan announced she was getting married to Dave Stewart. There were fantastic ornate invites and the two of them chartered their own jumbo jet down to the wedding reception in the South of France with people like Bob Dylan appearing. They'd spent thousands and thousands on it all. I said to Siobhan, 'That's a bit gauche for a socialist, isn't it?'

There was no way Siobhan wanted me to come to her wedding, but I was still going out with Hilary, their manager, and so obviously they wanted her at the wedding, but they didn't want me there. I got a grudging invite, but I was busy anyway, so I didn't go. It was probably just as well.

One day I was in the studio and the girls came in. Siobhan had the most fantastic, expensive bracelet I've ever seen. It was a beautiful piece of jewellery, which must have cost an awful lot of money. Someone asked her where it was from and she said, 'It's from Dave. It's his atonement present.'

'What on earth is an atonement present?' I asked.

'It's because he was rude to me in a previous life,' she said.

It's sad that we didn't get on, because she was supremely talented, but it didn't stop us making some great records with the band. And I'm sure that they were one of the few bands I ever worked with who would have challenged and interested me for a lot longer than our professional relationship actually lasted. We did have some fun together now and then. Like one time when I went to America with them and we ended up hanging out with a mobster who was a huge Bananarama fan. Then another time when they set off the fire alarms in a hotel in Boston, and I got arrested because the people at the hotel thought they were my daughters! They may not always have been the easiest people to work with, but they were certainly dynamic.

While all this was going on in 1988, RCA had been approached for Rick Astley to make the fastest record in history for the *Guinness Book Of Records*. He was going to sing it live in the afternoon on Radio One, then it would be pressed in the evening and out in the shops within 24 hours. We got roped in on it. It had all been sorted out already with Rick's manager, so although, to be honest, we weren't particularly keen on doing it, it was a done deal that we had to play along with. We found ourselves caught up in the complicated logistics of the scheme, desperately planning how to achieve it.

Come the rehearsals, there was no Rick Astley. He'd disappeared. His manager didn't know where he was and neither did his record company. He wasn't at home and we were told that he hadn't been in touch with anybody. This went on for three or four days. Then on the grapevine we heard that he didn't want to do the record, and that, apparently, we'd tried to force him into it. I was put into the position where I felt I was being branded an ogre when in reality I was the innocent party. The record never got made.

From then on, the relationship between Rick and us started to change. He and his management started to suggest more and more that we were bullying him into doing things and trying to use him as a vehicle for ourselves. But if you look at Rick's debut album, which came out in 1988, you'll see that there are only four Stock, Aitken and Waterman songs on it. Rick wrote the rest. I do actually believe, and I've believed this throughout my career, that in the pop world, you can't always do what the artist wants to do. You have to have someone who has a detached, commercial viewpoint on what you are going to sell. The artist *can't* be objective. It's impossible for them to make any critical judgement of themselves and they'll always duck the major questions about what they're doing.

I'd nurtured Rick Astley and brought him through. I'd had a lot of fun with him and, more than anything, I'd liked him tremendously. Suddenly, as far as I was concerned, he'd gone mad, and it was like I was a stranger to him. What I didn't know then was that he had a problem with his own success. We found out later that he just could not stand being famous. He hated the pressures that fame brought and he was genuinely petrified of failure. So he looked at us as an operation that had forced him into a position that he couldn't sustain.

To me it was obvious what to do. If he wanted to go off and do his own thing, then fine, let him go off and do it. People told me I was being stupid, because he was bringing in a lot of money, but as far as I was concerned Rick was a mate. And if he didn't want to work with me then what was the point of trying to force him? Nothing good was going to come out of it.

We did a deal whereby BMG Records would buy out his contract from us. It was Christmas 1988, and it was horrible. David Howells and I had to go to BMG's offices in Tottenham Court Road to sign the papers. Rick was up on the second floor and we weren't allowed past reception. They were having a big party to celebrate the signing and we weren't allowed anywhere near him. So we had to wait downstairs, then they brought down the papers for us to sign and we walked off into the street with a very, very large cheque. It was bizarre. I caught a train home to Warrington where I was living and David went back to the office. That was it. End of connection between Rick and us.

It was sad because here was a kid we'd been with since the beginning. I was so disappointed that people had fed Rick Astley lies about me. If he was fed up, it was time to move on. Some people hated him for what he'd done, started calling him ungrateful, but I wasn't angry with him, just disappointed. I thought he'd made the wrong decision, but it was his right to make it.

You've got to understand that there hadn't been a phenomenon like Rick before, and some would say that there hasn't been one like him since. This boy sold 15.2 million copies of his debut album. He was huge all over the world – probably only George Michael has achieved a comparable level of success – so the pressures on Rick were enormous. What was worse, BMG, which RCA was part of, saw Rick Astley, even when we were working with him, as the new Elvis Presley. This was perhaps the strangest marketing concept that anyone had come up with. Rick was a lot of things, but Elvis Presley wasn't one of them. He saw himself as part of a band, rather than as a solo artist. He surrounded himself with musicians because he felt vulnerable on his own.

Rick is the most fabulous singer I have ever worked with, and that includes people like Luther Vandross. He has a marvellous voice and I rate him as one of the greatest British singers of all time. But he's a singer rather than a pop star; he's Frank Sinatra rather than Elvis Presley, if you like. People who had no idea about Rick kept on shoving their oars in with ideas for a kid they knew nothing about.

When we were still working with him we'd been to a party to celebrate the success of his album at a private club round the back of the Ritz. All these Americans flew in with awards. David Howells and Matt, Mike and I were there and we weren't even acknowledged; we got given our award in a box as we were leaving. I spoke to some of the business affairs people at BMG and told them they should go and point out to their American bosses that BMG didn't own the Rick Astley masters, I did. They were giving the medal to the striker, but they'd severely pissed off the midfield and the defenders and the goalkeeper.

Then we got a letter from BMG saying that the contract we'd originally signed with Rick was unfair. I knew it wasn't. So I spoke to a barrister and he told me that no judge would ever see it as an unfair contract. We'd signed Rick all those years ago and he was just helping out around the place. And since then we'd paid him cheques for huge sums of money. What was unfair about that? We never heard anything more from BMG about that one.

The deal that we'd given Rick actually meant he got fifty per cent of everything. It's the sort of deal no one does any more, because basically the artist gets too much money as far as the major corporations are concerned. It was a deal that only worked really well at PWL, because we were such a tight-knit family. We all made great money from the Rick Astley thing, but Rick got more than he would have got anywhere else.

I don't understand why people get precious about pop music. My advice to bands is just, 'It ain't rocket science, so just enjoy the ride and it'll be over by Christmas. Or, if you're lucky, next Christmas.'

After Rick left, a lot of friendships fell apart. So many people who were connected with Rick had been lying to us. And it was all so unnecessary. It was just greed. We had a song for

Rick called 'Nothing Can Divide Us', but of course he could no longer do it. So a few months later we decided to give it to Jason Donovan, whom we'd signed. That was the only time we ever wrote a song for one person on the roster and gave it to another. Yet because we did that just the one time, this myth grew up that we just sat churning out songs and handed them out randomly to our latest puppets. A suggestion like that is ridiculous, and completely insulting.

Over the years one of the questions that people have always asked me is, 'How do you make a Stock, Aitken and Waterman record?' And the simple answer is that you have to be Stock, Aitken and Waterman. There was no magic formula and it would be dishonest to pretend that there was. If there was any kind of conscious impulse behind any record we made it was to maintain integrity and never try to come up with something that didn't come from the heart. That might sound odd if you believe that we were 'just' making pop records, but then songs like 'I Second That Emotion' and 'You Just Keep Me Hanging On' are 'just' pop records, too. There is nothing wrong with simplicity, and I believe that there has been as much genuine feeling behind the records that we've made as behind any rock catalogue.

People talk about commercialism as a dirty word. That's bullshit. Travis are one of the finest commercial pop bands around, but because it's disguised within the rock genre it's respected. When you're in a rock band you're invariably writing songs for yourself, whereas we have spent our careers making records for other people; but that doesn't mean that we just pinned songs onto our artists like pinning the tail on the donkey. You have to consider who is going to be singing the song and what you want the audience to feel when they hear it, but that is as far as any conscious decisions go.

When I think about what I look for in a song, then I go back to the people I consider classic songwriters, people like Cole Porter, the Beatles and Holland/Dozier/Holland, but I couldn't explain what unifies those people other than the ability to write songs that can make the hairs on the back of your neck stand on end. My one intention in making records has always been to make people happy and I won't deny that. Because I had a tough childhood and because I'm not a terribly confident person in social situations, the music I've produced has perhaps been the only outlet I know for communicating sociability. On the other hand, maybe it's completely natural to acknowledge that the one thing that's universal in this world is that people like things that make them happy. I've been in the business for so long that I've realised that my real strength comes from being able to gauge what the public will respond to most positively. It is an instinct, but one that's taken thirty years to hone. And ultimately, those thirty years are the only explanation I can offer as to the 'secret' of writing Stock, Aitken and Waterman songs. The secret is that there *is* no secret, just integrity and belief in the power of pop music.

Making a record doesn't happen on its own. There's a team involved: you've got the artist, the songwriter, the producer, the record company, the promotions person, the guy who goes on the road and sells it to shops and a lot of other people. And when that whole team works together, you've got a smash. Just because you're the person up on stage warbling it doesn't mean you'd be there without the others who did so much work. People never have the guts to tell the pop stars that they're only one of eighteen people in a very long and involved process, and that the other seventeen people's contribution is just as important. They don't tell them because they know the artist will sack them so, because they're on their percentage of a million pounds, they keep quiet. And the artist gets more and more detached from reality.

We were beginning to realise that we were making rods for our own backs by our very success. We were the ones showing the artists how to make money and the first person they wanted to take out of the equation as soon as they made the money was the person who showed them how to do it in the first place.

Nowadays I've actually accepted it's going to happen and that as soon as I've made someone famous and rich, I'll be the first to get knocked out of the loop. It happens again and again. I've even got a sign up in my office which reads, 'If you pick up a starving dog and give him food he will not bite you – this is the principal difference between a man and a dog.'

At the same time I can categorically say that after an artist leaves me, there is no way I want to see them go on and fail. There would be nothing to be gained from crowing at their failure. If they go on and are successful, it shows I told them how to do it right. If they fail it shows they didn't listen.

I was always brutally honest to the performers. If they made a bad record, I'd tell them it was a bad record. I'd maybe defend it in the press or in public, but I'd tell them what I really thought to their face. I don't lie to myself, I don't lie to the people I work with and I don't lie to the artists. So the people who work here might call me a bastard to work with, but they know it's because I won't tell them something that is shit is good just so as not to rock the boat. Ultimately I'm the one who has to take that record and sell it to the other seventeen people who make up the line between them and the public. Someone has to be blunt enough to say, 'I can't sell it. Do it again.' And it's that attitude, that bull-headedness that gets me disliked. I don't care. Someone's got to have the balls to be honest.

After Rick Astley I wondered whether I ought to be more mellow, more user-friendly. Maybe that would be the way to behave. It was certainly the way people were telling me to be. Then I thought, 'No, I'm not changing.' It was my name on the rent book, my name over the door, my name on the cheques. And while it was my name there, I was going to be the one calling the shots. None of the kids could go along to the bank and get a four hundred thousand pound loan based on nothing but a singing voice, but when they came to me that was exactly what they expected. I was their bank manager and while I was owed money, I said what went. I didn't care what happened when they had made the money back. If they wanted to go off and do their own thing, that was perfectly all right by me. I made the decision that no matter how unpopular it made me, I wasn't going to be a yes man. I had set the company up to be a unique operation. It was going to be a company where the artist got paid what he was due, where the producers and writers were looked after, where no one got ripped off.

By 1988 I'd achieved that. We'd got fabulous equipment for the producers to use, we were giving the artists higher percentages than anyone else. No one had anything to worry about other than the job of getting on with making great records, just like Philadelphia. It was just what I'd intended. Call it a workshop, a factory or whatever. If it was a factory, it was one where the wealth was shared with the people on the shop floor. To keep it running there could only be one boss and that was me. And to maintain that was more important than being liked.

At the time I thought that Matt and Mike were perfectly happy with the situation. It was only later that I found out otherwise.

I say that we were making a lot of money at this time, but you have to realise that getting that cheque from BMG for Rick Astley was a rarity. Most of the time we were dictated to by the schedule of royalty payments – they were inflexible – so we were constantly having cash-flow problems. A year or two earlier I'd even had to sell shares in PWL to Dave Howells to keep the company going. Banks, you see, apart from the good relationship I'd had with Allied Irish, were completely ignorant of the workings of the music business. And because of that, they weren't prepared to give us any breathing room. We had money due from all around the world on Rick Astley and the banks were prepared to pull the plug on us.

I remember at one point sitting in a hotel suite with people offering us millions for some deal and at the same time there was a phone call from Barclays saying if we didn't deposit a cheque for £50,000 in the next fourteen hours, they were going to stop all the cheques and we wouldn't be able to pay any salaries. I had to sell David ten per cent of the company just so we could last through the month. Everything we were touching was gold dust, but the banks couldn't see the bigger picture. They were quibbling over £50,000 when we had, conservatively, twelve to fourteen million quid coming in a few months later. It's only in the last three years that things have begun to change, but before that banks were entirely ignorant of an industry that could have made them a lot of money.

I've always invested my money in things I know about, whether it is motor cars or something music related. A few months further down the line I'd bought a Jaguar. Barclays said I should invest in stocks and shares and persuaded us to give them £30,000 to invest. The next day was Black Wednesday and the stock exchange was wiped out. That Jaguar is still sitting in my garage and it's worth a lot more.

At MIDEM in 1987 we had been talking to Mushroom Records from Australia about our All Boys Music back catalogue, and they mentioned they'd signed someone called Kylie Minogue to their label. Gary Ashley from Mushroom, who had become a rich man from handling our publishing in Australia, suggested that we go into a joint venture with us having our own label. Now this was the first time that anyone had ever approached us with the idea of giving us our own label to work an act. I couldn't agree to doing a label deal with Mushroom simply because Australia is so far away. Who wants to have to get on a plane for 24 hours to have meetings? So I said no. And besides, I didn't have a clue who Kylie Minogue was.

In early March 1987, we got a call from Mushroom. They wanted us to send one of our engineers down to Australia on a kind of sabbatical, to help them work the SSL decks in their studios. We'd made the SSL desks very famous by then, so even in Australia they'd become popular. And what they wanted was one of our engineers to 'Show them how it worked'. Now, if you had a suspicious mind you might think that what they really wanted was to get one of Stock, Aitken and Waterman's engineers over there so they could pinch our sound. However, we were proud of the fact that we could help out the British industry by promoting SSL desks, a British product, so we agreed.

We had a Canadian guy, Mike Duffy, working for us, who somehow had a British passport, so we agreed to send him. He was on loan and Mushroom paid his wages and paid us a small fee for him being down there.

Mike loved it there. He rang me up a week later and said, 'You've got to come down here, boss, you'd love it! Everyone wants to make records that sound like yours. That's why they wanted me here. They want me to make one of your records. Kylie Minogue doing a cover version of "The Locomotion".'

'Well, go on then Duffy,' I said. 'Go ahead and do it.'

'I can't, boss,' he said. 'I don't know how to do it. You're the only one who knows how to make your records.'

'Duffy,' I said, 'you've seen me do it enough times. Just copy that. And make yourself a hero.'

'Are you sure?' he asked.

'Yeah, no problem. Just do it.'

I didn't hear from him for three weeks, then he rang up and said he'd done the record. He played it me over the phone and it wasn't great, but it was passable. 'I told you I couldn't make records like you,' he said.

'Don't worry son', I said. 'It's good enough. Just go with it.'

And I didn't really think any more about it. We had a lad down in Australia and he'd made himself a little record that sounded roughly, *very* roughly like one of ours, and he was making a name for himself. I was happy for the boy. He knew his limitations, but he'd done his best and he'd rung up for my blessing. Good for him.

Six or seven weeks went by and I got a phone call from Duffy.

'Pete,' he said, 'I'm Number One in Australia.' It wasn't 'boss' any more. It was 'Pete'.

'What with, Duff?'

'With "The Locomotion".'

I thought he was joking, but they'd sold something like forty thousand records; the biggest hit Australia had ever had. And all of a sudden, he wasn't one of my engineers any more, he was one of my producers.

He'd sent a copy of the record over a few days earlier, but I'd never listened to it, so, right there, at three in the morning, I got up and put it on. It was rubbish. So I put it back and went back to bed.

A couple more weeks went by and Duffy rang again. He said it was still Number One out there, and that he thought I really ought to produce Kylie Minogue.

Mushroom wanted more records and he'd only been able to make 'The Locomotion' by swaggering in with self-confidence. He said he couldn't take Kylie Minogue to the next stage because he'd used his one trick. It was simple because it was somebody else's song. Now they wanted him to write for her and he couldn't do that. And all the other potential songs that they were playing him were no good. He just couldn't do it.

This was my boy and he was in trouble and calling for help. 'OK,' I said. 'We'll sort something out.'

Dave Howells talked to Gary at Mushroom and agreed on a joint venture. We had to set up a company to do it all under so, remembering how my old mate Tilly Rutherford called everyone 'Pal', I decided to call it 'Pal Productions'. I still didn't have a clue who Kylie Minogue was. I hardly ever watched TV because I was too busy making records. I'd never seen *Neighbours*.

We were so hot at the time that we could have rung anyone we wanted and got them to come into the studio and record for us. We didn't need any more work and I didn't need any more hassle or any more grief. But we had to help Duffy out. I must have agreed for her to come and record at our studios, though to be honest I don't remember actually doing so, because we were just so busy at the time.

I was at home in Newton-Le-Willows one Friday afternoon when I got a phone call from Mike Stock, at the office.

'Pete,' he said, 'is there anything you've forgotten to tell us?'

'Don't think so,' I said.

'Small Antipodeans ring any bells?'

'No, they don't,' I replied.

'Small Antipodean called Kylie Minogue?'

'Oh yes,' I said. 'I forgot to tell you. She's in town.'

'No, she's bloody not,' said Mike, 'she's in reception, and she's on her way back to the airport in a couple of hours!'

I told him I was sorry I'd messed up, but we'd just have to drop the whole project.

'We can't,' he said. 'She's expecting to do something with us, now!'

'She should be so lucky,' I said.

'What did you say?'

'She should be so lucky.'

'Great,' he said, 'that'll do. "I should be so lucky". Can we write some lyrics?'

So over the next half-hour we faxed lyrics back and forth to each other and then I got on with my life.

I rang Matt and Mike a few hours later and asked how it was going. Matt said, and I clearly remember this, 'Actually, I've got to tell you, this girl's got a really good voice.'

It was just about the first time I'd ever heard Matt express an opinion on any of our artists. He never used to comment at all, so I knew she must be pretty special. The session had gone really well, and she'd given them lots back. A pleasure to work with, they said.

'Fine,' I said, but still none of this had really sunk in.

A week later Gary rang up from Australia asking how it had gone. I told him it had been great, even though I hadn't actually heard the song. It was nowhere near complete. We were just so busy that I hadn't had the time. Next time he rang, I couldn't even remember the title of the song. I had to ask someone else in the office.

By November he said he was going to come over and listen to the track if we didn't send it to him. And we'd really done fuck-all on it. Matt and Mike had stuck the vocals down and put a bit of a backing track on it, then forgotten about it. We all had.

I used to work at nights on stuff then, so I got Pete Hammond, who was working with me, into the studio at four in the morning and we put 'I Should Be So Lucky' on. This great little tune bounced round the place.

'Hey,' I said to Pete. 'I quite like this. It's not bad, is it?' It was the first time I'd heard it.

We fiddled around with it a bit, changed the drums and by seven, eight o'clock we'd done a 12-inch mix, and pretty much finished it. I went off to bed and Matt and Mike checked the music, then we sent it off. We were so caught up in other stuff that we didn't think it was any big thing. It was just another job completed.

We'd always had great Christmas parties for our staff right from the beginning. That Christmas we had our company party at the National History Museum. This one was fantastic, with candles all around the dinosaurs. We had the comedian Lenny Henry as the DJ, doing his Theophilus P. Wildebeest character, and at one point he played a record that I thought was really good. I had to have it! I went up and asked him what it was and he thought I was joking. It was our record, 'I Should Be So Lucky'. I grabbed it off him and hung on to it for the rest of the night.

I'd started doing a radio show for Radio City in Liverpool on a Saturday. I like to keep my hand in playing records, and with us making so many hits, we'd obviously built ourselves quite a pop profile. I was still living in Newton-Le-Willows, so I'd be at the studio all week, then go back up North at weekends. It was easy for me to get to Liverpool each week to do this show and people listened to it because they knew they'd always hear the latest records first. The whole show had been about building a rapport with the kids who listened, letting them hear the hits before they happened. I did the show under the name 'The Hitman'.

After the party at the National History Museum, I was driven back up North and went in on the Saturday to do my radio show. I had the white label with me, with just 'Kylie Minogue' scrawled on it. And when the producer, Steve, saw it, he went bonkers.

'Kylie Minogue!!!'

'Yes,' I said. 'Kylie Minogue. What about it?'

'THE Kylie Minogue! From *Neighbours!* A record!'

'Yeah,' I answered, slightly bemused.

'Look,' he said. 'Just open the mic now and tell people you're going to play the Kylie Minogue record. Do it now.'

I thought he'd lost his senses. He hadn't even heard the record. And who was this Charlene from *Neighbours* that he was going on about? I was totally perplexed by his enthusiasm. I really didn't have a clue why he was so excited. But, anyway, I did what he asked, and announced we'd play the record. We played the first few bars of it, then Steve made me stop it and say that we weren't going to play it in full unless people rang in to request it. Within seconds the switchboard had almost melted.

Steve had to explain just how popular *Neighbours* was. It was just about the biggest programme on TV for the teen audience; the reason radio stations all over the country lost listeners at quarter to two in the afternoon when *Neighbours* was on. It was the reason education authorities all over Britain were going barmy about kids wagging school to watch TV.

Without warning me, Steve went off and set up a satellite link to Capital Radio in London. He asked me to play 'I Should Be So Lucky' without talking over any of it. No jingles, just the whole record from start to finish. He'd rung up the Radio City boss, too, who seemed just as excited.

Capital rang up and they were raving as well; they'd taped what we'd played them down the line and they were just about to play it in full. Both Radio City and Capital were shouting from the rooftops about the world exclusive of the Kylie Minogue record, and I'd begun to realise that it must be quite a big deal.

Steve said to me, 'Do you know what you've got here?'

I said, 'Well, it's a great little record.'

'It's more than that,' he told me. 'You won't be able to spend the amount of money you're going to make on this. It's going to be the biggest thing you've ever done.'

By the end of the two-hour show I'd had to play the record four times. And there were six hundred kids in the street outside thinking that Kylie was actually in the studio with me. They had to call the police!

It was astounding. I had absolutely no idea of the power of Kylie's presence in the market place. I was about to find out.

13 I Should Be So Lucky

I N DECEMBER 1987 I GOT A PHONE CALL from the BBC. Noel Edmonds did a programme called *The Late, Late Breakfast Show* and they were doing a Christmas Day special. They wanted to fly to Australia to film Kylie Minogue doing 'I Should Be So Lucky'.

We couldn't get better publicity if we tried, but I didn't know how we were going to be able to arrange to fly a crew over. Then they explained that they'd be paying to send their own crew. This was getting better and better.

The BBC was moving *Neighbours* to a new time slot at 5.30 and would be showing it at lunchtime as well. The first show in the new slot was going to be on Boxing Day, so getting Kylie on Noel Edmonds' show was good publicity for their *Neighbours* rescheduling. It wasn't just them doing us a favour out of the goodness of their own hearts, they were also getting a plug for their own programme out of it.

You could have knocked me down with a wet kipper. I had to be the luckiest man in the world! I'd accidentally got this Australian girl who turned out to be in the most talked-about show on TV and, what's more, it was just about to be moved to peak time which would add another three million viewers! This was unbelievable.

The record came out in early January and whereas I'd been expecting it to come in at Number 30 or something, it went straight in at 14. She did *Top Of The Pops* and the next week she was Number One. It was an absolutely amazing success and I don't know if any pop star will ever be as popular as Kylie was back then. She was being watched by fourteen million viewers a day. I never watched a single episode all the way through though; anytime I watched bits of it, it was usually with Kylie sitting next to me.

'I Should Be So Lucky' exploded, and with it, we exploded as well. I'd actually tried to license Kylie to three separate record companies, because I didn't want my own label, but they'd all turned her down. At the time we had offered her to record companies, we were used to being involved in five of the top ten records in the charts some weeks. And Stock, Aitken and Waterman were the most successful songwriters and producers in the business because we hadn't had any misses at all. We were offering record companies the ultimate pop record by the most famous TV star in the country; it was a guaranteed Number One record and we were only asking for £2,500 for it. If them turning that down isn't the most stupid decision in the history of the music business then it must be pretty close. If someone had offered me something like that I'd have chucked a hundred grand at it just to have a go. What would there be to lose?

And so, for the Kylie Minogue single, 'I Should Be So Lucky', I formed PWL Records. She made PWL the most successful independent record company in the world. All because those record companies wouldn't give me two and a half grand.

'I Should Be So Lucky' marked the beginning of a time when we had to reconsider even our own benchmarks of what constituted success. Over the next two years we must have sold forty million records. Anything I did with Kylie automatically sold half a million. When I'd started PWL Records, I'd been wary because I really didn't want to be in the business of being a record company, but here we were becoming the largest independent label around and virtually the most successful record company anywhere. And people were still saying it was a fluke, that this was all somehow one great big slice of luck. Sure, there had been moments of luck along the line, but we maintained our success and that took hard work and self-belief. We were always open to ideas.

After 'I Should Be So Lucky' went to Number One we suddenly found out that the deal with Mushroom Records was completely different from the one we thought we'd made in the first place. As so often happens in the music business, we'd never signed anything in the beginning. Because we thought we were mates, we didn't work things out fully in advance, and so we ended up making about half of the amount we thought we would. We didn't fight it, because Mushroom took the opposite view of the deal we thought we'd made. We had the choice of just putting it down to experience and carrying on working with Kylie, or giving up on the whole project. We'd just sold a million records, so we gritted our teeth and continued. I'm not the sort of person who bears grudges, but I know that Mike Stock in particular was very angry and disappointed at the way that things panned out with Mushroom.

Kylie was a lovely girl, but I think she was as surprised as any of us at the level of fame she was enjoying. She'd been on TV in Australia since she was 12, so she was used to celebrity, but this was getting ridiculous. And although Kylie is quite the sophisticated pop star these days, back then she was just a completely innocent little girl who, if anything, looked even younger than she actually was. She used to come over to the studios with her mother and sit in the reception doing basket weaving, or curl up on the sofa and go to sleep. Sometimes people wouldn't even realise it was her when they walked past because she really was like a little child.

When she came over to record for us, we moved her and her mum into my flat above the studio and I moved out to the Hilton, which was a nice adventure for me and also allowed her and her mum to have a domestic base while she was working. Her mum and dad were nice, genuine people, not at all pushy, so the fame was certainly not something for which she'd been relentlessly groomed.

Because of the weight of filming for *Neighbours*, we only ever had small windows of time for her to record, but she was very efficient. As soon as she went in front of a microphone or a camera, she just transformed from this innocent, completely non-worldly-wise little girl to a star. It was uncanny the way that she could be a completely different person instantly. She was a tiny eighteen-year-old girl and obviously had a huge workload, so she'd be exhausted half the time, but as soon as she had to work her whole personality would transform and she would just light up. We would literally only get an hour at a time to work with her, but we always got things done.

A few years ago she seemed to be going through a denial period and accused us of never giving her a chance to do what she wanted to do, but I think that now she's come to terms with the fact that there simply wasn't time for any indulgence. She was physically in and out in an hour and that meant our work had to be incredibly focussed. For her debut album we had three weeks to record twelve tracks, and on top of that she had thirty TV appearances that had to be fitted in. It was a whistlestop way of working.

One of the problems that Kylie always had was that she felt she lived in the shadow of her sister Dannii. Dannii was also a soap star, appearing in *Home And Away*, and in Australia she was a much bigger celebrity than Kylie. Dannii already had her own clothing range and you could sense that Kylie always felt she had a lot to live up to. Some of the more outrageous images that Kylie came up with later on in her career were, I think, a result of trying to emulate the wild, rebellious personality of her sister.

I never had any say in the public image of our artists, although David Howells did have a vision of PWL appealing to a young audience and so he did promote the clean-cut image of the acts on the label to some extent. I'd come up with the slogan 'The Sound of a Bright Young Britain' to sum up what we were about, and so there was some sort of responsibility to put across the notion of clean-cut, well behaved, innocent stars. But it was something that came about naturally, rather than being a calculated exercise.

David had worked on the *Album Covers* books, two successful compilations of album sleeves throughout rock and pop history, and I think he was very interested in the actual iconography of pop, so he tended to see a picture somewhere and then say that that was what he wanted the record sleeve to look like. He didn't come up with images for the artists out of his own head, but he did have a general idea of how he wanted the records to be presented.

You've got to remember that the whole concept of image and marketing was far less sophisticated back then than it is

now, so we didn't have any such thing as an image department or anything. We had one girl called Kelly, a friend of
George Michael's, who used to choose clothes for our acts, but
they weren't chosen to fit any particular image, they were
just things that were fashionable at the time. Kylie might
have objected to wearing certain clothes that were picked, but
that was simply because she was a girl becoming a woman,
growing up in public. As she grew up she obviously decided
she wanted to wear more 'womanly' clothes, but that's
something that would have happened whether she had been
famous or not. It's a stage that every girl goes through and
Kylie was no exception, but there was certainly no image
manipulation going on at the company. If anyone was
responsible for the public face of PWL, it was Smash Hits, who
consistently publicised our artists.

The Smash Hits editor, Mary Calderwood, had been into
the stuff we were doing from very early on, and she came to
me to ask if we would keep her informed of everything we
were doing. Each Monday she'd come down and take us out
for a curry and we'd all just chat about what was going on.
Pretty quickly the people at Smash Hits realised that by
tapping into the stuff we were putting out, they'd found
something that was fresh, new and had a huge ready-made
audience. When we had a photo of one of our artists on the
cover of Smash Hits they sold a million copies, and one issue
with Kylie on the cover still holds the record for the most
copies of a single issue that they've ever sold. If you want to
know who had the strongest vision for the way that the artists
were presented to the public, it was Mary Calderwood at
Smash Hits. We never had anything to do with any of that, but
Smash Hits knew that if they created this movement then
they could sell a lot of copies of their magazine. And,
similarly, Capital Radio made a conscious decision to put
Stock, Aitken and Waterman records at the heart of their
programming, because they knew it would get them a huge
share of the listeners. This was nothing to do with us – other
than that it was us who made the records in the first place –
and it would be wrong to try and pretend that there was a
masterplan behind how the public came to perceive us. We
wanted to make hit records and that was all.

I remember being up in Dundee at the D.C. Thomson building, meeting the people who did *Beano* and *Dandy*. They were doing an interview there with some of our artists and Mary Calderwood from *Smash Hits* had gone along to do a feature on it all. As we were walking out she said that it was strange that the PWL acts had become bigger cartoon characters than any of those featured in either *Beano* or *Dandy* and when she said it, I knew what she meant. Our audience, through *Smash Hits*, had made Jason and Kylie and Rick Astley and whoever we were producing at the time into Lord Snooty or the Bash Street Kids. They had become like a cartoon series and turned PWL into a weekly pop serial. At the time I'd never seen that, even though it seems obvious now in hindsight. So there was a quirky editor at *Smash Hits* who adored what we did and she was as responsible as anyone for what it all became. She seemed only to employ people who liked our records, and was adamant that there would be no negatives about us anywhere in the magazine, a reflection of our policy not to have any negative lyrics in our songs. And that helped us enormously to maintain our impetus.

All that public perception of the label was therefore filtered through *Smash Hits*' pieces on us, but there was only one element of calculation within the company itself and that was to make Number One records. We cared about nothing other than having hit records and we did it better than anyone else.

We released three more Kylie singles that year – 'Got To Be Certain', 'The Locomotion' (we'd worked on a new version from the one Duffy had engineered in Australia) and 'Je Ne Sais Pas Pourquoi', all of which went to Number Two, so within twelve months we'd made her a millionaire. And it wasn't the first or last time I've done that for someone; in fact, in terms of success I'm second only to the National Lottery in creating millionaires.

At Christmas 1988, we took a gamble and did something no one else had ever done. We'd noticed that at Christmas on TV the ads were really cheap, and tended just to be for things like holidays or DIY. People were stuck in front of the TV and there were never any ads for pop records. Tilly Rutherford, who was general manager at PWL, came up with the idea of booking TV ads all over Christmas for Kylie's debut album. You could get the slots cheaper than at any other time of the year and because everyone was used to seeing the same cheap ads, over and over, the Kylie ones would really stand out. It was a bizarre idea, but the more you thought about it, the more sense it made.

That was the worst Christmas of my life. I was going out with Denise, who was to become my third wife when we married in 1991, and I took her back to my house near Warrington. Her mum and dad had a pub just off the M25 and we went to her see her parents on the way. Driving there took us near Orpington and Steve Mason had told me that was where the warehouse was where we kept the PWL records that had been pressed up. You must remember that this was the days of vinyl, so records took up a lot of space. And these ones certainly did. The entire building was piled to the rafters with copies of *Kylie: The Album*, her first LP. As far as the eye could see there were just copies of her record. My bottle went completely and I was convinced that I was out of business. I'd spent all the money on TV advertising and now here was a small country's worth of records just lying around. In the period leading up to Christmas we'd sold something like a quarter of a million copies of the album and just to do that had been beyond our wildest dreams. Now there were at least another 100,000 piled up in front of me, which meant that any profit we'd made from the earlier sales was going to be wiped out.

I hardly slept that whole Christmas because I just kept on thinking of all these albums sitting in the warehouse. And I couldn't bear to watch any of the adverts on the television because that just seemed to reiterate what a bad decision I'd authorised.

On Boxing Day I got a phone call from Tilly Rutherford. He was burbling with excitement.

'I've just had a phone call from Woolworths. They've ordered another 80,000 copies of the Kylie album. Can you press them up?'

'What about the 100,000 in the warehouse?' I asked.

'Oh, they've gone already,' he said. 'We got orders for those by eleven o'clock this morning.'

The TV campaign had been a phenomenal success. The people from the big record chains had been sitting around watching TV and realised that every kid was going to be wanting a Kylie album. And all the mothers and fathers were going to want to buy one for their kids too. This was a record that had four hit singles on it already, so it was shaping up to be a *Greatest Hits* before it had even got started.

In January 1989 that record went from 250,000 sales to 2.7 million sales. No one had sold so many albums over Christmas in the history of the record industry before that. It was a Kylie Christmas and it was staggering.

People were coming up to me and saying that it had been an audacious, brave move, but it had been Tilly's idea and, thanks to him, I'd had a horrible Christmas. If I'd been able to take credit for it, at least I would have been able to enjoy those three days, but instead I was more worried than anyone.

In retrospect I can see that Kylie was always going to be a success simply because with her we had the perfect embodiment of what it takes to have a hit. You have to have a great song, a great production and a great performer and if one of those elements is missing, you're never going to succeed. The thing that most people, the stars included, forget is that all three of those elements are equally important. That's not to do disservice to Kylie's enormous talent, because I can categorically say that something like 'Je Ne Sais Pas Pourquoi' would not have been a hit if she hadn't sung it. At the same time it took the song itself and the production to give her something to have a hit with.

Kylie's character Charlene on *Neighbours* had a boyfriend called Scott who was played by Jason Donovan, and by then we'd also started working with him, too. It was Mushroom who approached us originally about him recording some songs, and our first reaction was to have nothing to do with him, because the whole idea seemed too tacky, but we eventually helped him out by suggesting that he go into the studio with Pete Hammond. At that point we had no intention of producing him. For some reason though, he just couldn't get anything that he was happy with done by working with Pete, so he came to us and insisted that we do something with him instead. I went out for a Chinese meal with Kylie and Jason and asked Kylie whether she wanted me to work with Jason. I told her that if she wanted me to, I'd do it. She said she wanted me to.

It just so happened that we had lost Rick Astley and had the song 'Nothing Can Divide Us' which we thought would be perfect for Jason. He went in and recorded it and we realised that it was far too good to ignore so we put it out. And having met Jason, I immediately hit it off with him. He was quite a lad, which was unusual among the acts we were working with, and he and I used to go to motor races all over the country. He'd driven sports cars in Australia and was really into it all so when we had a bit of spare time, we used to go to Silverstone together and drive around the track for a morning. He was a fun-loving guy and always up for a laugh, and I got on very well with him.

While he was working with us, Jason was embroiled in a court case where he was forced to sue the *Face* magazine for accusations about his sexuality. They were completely unfounded and he won the case, but the whole thing had only come about in the first place because of an argument I'd had at a PWL Christmas party a year earlier with someone at the magazine. In my opinion, one of the reasons for the whole case came from the *Face* trying to get at me and at the squeaky clean image of Stock, Aitken and Waterman, with Jason just being the easiest target. I don't think he even ever knew that he'd been caught up in the crossfire, but it seemed to me that what they said about him was motivated by trying to attack us.

It was almost funny that we were so successful, but disliked by so many people. In August 1989, Cliff Richard, who is an old friend of mine, asked us to produce his hundredth single, 'Just Don't Have The Heart', which we did and it got to Number Three in the charts. It was just something I was pleased to do for a friend and someone who had been in the record industry for so long. I met him afterwards, though, and he told me that he had had more problems justifying working with me to people than he had had justifying his faith in God! All we were doing was making pop records and somehow we were being seen as despicable. That was something I always found quite extraordinary.

* * *

Because we were working with both Kylie and Jason, who were romantically linked, there was inevitably a feeling amongst the public that we'd have them do a romantic duet together. We'd known right from the beginning that they were going out together, but the idea of a duet seemed a sickly proposition. Still we kept on getting kids coming up to us in the streets asking about this mythical record and grudgingly we decided we had to do it, even though Kylie and Jason had gone back to Australia. I was working in Sheffield, so I flew by helicopter to Heathrow, met Matt and we flew out to Sydney where we sat up all night doing vocals with Jason and Kylie before flying straight back to Britain. It was madness, but that was pretty much par for the course for the way we were working then. We mixed the track and once we'd revealed that we were doing it, we'd immediately had orders at the depot for a quarter of a million copies.

When I heard the finished version I hated it. It had absolutely no passion and, to be honest, sounded just like the calculated cash-in that we'd originally been wary of putting our names to. I hated it, Mike hated it and everyone I played it to in the office hated it. It was going to be a smash, simply because of who was singing it, but we didn't feel any pride in making it. I was quite prepared to pull it and just abandon the song altogether, but Mike went into the studio and remixed it in four hours. It still wasn't wonderful, so I thought I'd have a go. Somehow it all came together at the last moment; so we rushed it to the pressing plant and got it out. It went straight to Number One and sold a million copies.

My radio show in Liverpool had really taken off by now. It was based around the idea of me playfully antagonising the listeners and preaching to them that the songs I played would be hits because I told them they would, which was just a slightly exaggerated version of me being myself. It had been rough around the edges to begin with, but its strength came from its uncompromising, larger-than-life attitude. If you think of Robin Williams' character in *Good Morning Vietnam*, that was what it was like. It didn't matter that I kept taking the piss out of the listeners, that just meant that they could ring me up and tell me off and we could have a banter over the air.

Within the first few weeks of starting the show, I was playing records that no one else had heard and we began to build a real hardcore audience. All the dance music shops in Liverpool used to tune in. They hated me, but they knew that the records I was playing were spot on. And I got myself a little posse of four or five kids who manned the phones and stuff so it became, well, a Tufty Club is the closest way of describing it. Three or four months in and it had really established itself and I used to do things like live mixes on the air, or take off a record half way through if I was bored with it. One week I'd mixed a new Kylie record in London on the Friday night and played it on my show on the Saturday. After I'd finished playing it I gave Radio One's phone number out and told all the kids to ring up Radio One and ask how, if they were supposed to be the hippest radio station, they weren't playing the Kylie record that had just been played in Liverpool. The fact that I had the only copy was beside the point – it was just a great wind-up. And that was what I wanted. I wanted jarring, in-your-face radio that would be better than anything you heard anywhere else.

I used to try to do the show every week, no matter what other engagements I had. For instance, for a while I was working in Tokyo and was commuting back each week to do the show. One day I'd been diverted via the North Pole and literally got into the studio as my theme music was playing. I'd been delayed by polar bears on the runway at the Arctic Circle, so I told the listeners and asked them to ring in if they'd seen any polar bears round Liverpool. Kids were ringing in from all over the place looking for polar bears. It went on for weeks.

The radio show became part of youth culture in Liverpool and at this time I decided to do a roadshow based on the old idea of the Motown Revue. We took 2,000 kids on a ferry across the Mersey for a quid each, so that they could dance the afternoon away. It wasn't entirely successful, because the records kept jumping all over the place, but the fact that we'd attracted so many people meant that we decided to do the same thing in a proper club. We booked different clubs around Liverpool between 6.30 and 9 and hired a couple of acts from London to do a PA. We got down the art of running it to perfection very quickly and the venues used to be crammed.

From doing the shows in Liverpool, we expanded, still taking our lead from the old Motown Revue, until at one point we booked eleven acts and took them to 37 venues, going all round the country and living, eating and sleeping on the tour bus. We'd also got Coca-Cola and Iceland frozen foods in as sponsors and ran it as a non-commercial exercise. I put in £50,000, Iceland put in £50,000 and Coca-Cola put in £100,000. The kids would pay a quid to watch the acts and listen to records with a free Coke and an Iceland beefburger thrown in. It was unlike anything anyone had ever done before, and on any night there'd be at least five acts on stage that the kids had seen on *Top Of The Pops* the week before. People were saying that rock'n'roll was dead, but what we were creating was a new kind of rock'n'roll. It was a young audience who had a scene of their own that other people resented them liking, but to which they were fiercely loyal. It was the height of Stock, Aitken and Waterman mania, and it had just as much energy as any other more credible rock movement. Back in 1957 it was kids deliberately adopting a lifestyle alien to the mainstream culture they were told they should like that made rock'n'roll so strong. This was just the same, but instead of Little Richard, it was Jason Donovan. The music may have been different, but the commitment from the kids was just as strong.

Kylie was the focus for the whole movement and she was just as important an iconic figure as the rockers or the punks or whoever had been in the past. *Smash Hits* supported us to the hilt, because they could see that what we were doing was, in its own way, revolutionary. We had the radio show, *Smash Hits* and the kids at the roadshows all championing PWL Records and Stock, Aitken and Waterman, while the rest of the industry and the media were saying it was all rubbish. And by criticising it, they just made it stronger, because the kids were always going to support something that old people were telling them they shouldn't like.

We saw ourselves as a breath of fresh air in an increasingly staid music industry and we redefined what it meant for kids to go and see acts they liked. Other people would charge them a tenner to go and see someone at a venue like the NEC in Birmingham where they'd be stuck half a mile away from the stage. We'd charge them a quid, give them a free burger and Coke and they'd be so close to the acts that they'd practically be able to touch them. We only ever booked 2,000 or 3,000 capacity venues so it was always small enough for the kids to feel like they could really connect with the acts. And we went to places like Barnsley, Wigan and Leicester where no one else had ever played before.

Out of those shows came a whole new roster of acts that we worked with: people like Big Fun, London Boys and one girl called Sonia who had a Number One with a song called 'You'll Never Stop Me From Loving You'. She was a bubbly Scouser who really wasn't so different from the audience she was playing to. She could easily have been one of the kids listening to the Radio City show and in fact we found her when she talked her way into the radio station one day. Big Fun and Sonia's careers didn't really pan out, because when we signed them we probably weren't conscious enough of our own insistence on all three elements – the song, the producer and the artist – all being right. Big Fun looked too anonymous and quite frankly could have been anybody, so the audience just didn't take them to their hearts. They were nice lads and they went down well on the tour, but you could soon see that they weren't completely serious about what they were doing. I've never been able to work with people who really didn't want to be the best at what they did. Sonia did have personality, and in fact came across like Cilla Black or someone, but she just didn't have enough scope in terms of different facets to her personality for us to be able to do much else with her. There was no mystery or light and shade to her, there was just that perky Scouser routine.

As a company we seemed incapable of failing, even when the gambles initially looked so ridiculous. In the previous year, not only had we been responsible for the Kylie phenomenon, we'd also had more hits with Bananarama, Sabrina, Sinitta and Hazell Dean, among many others. There was still a family, but it was growing faster than we had ever imagined. It was literally a blur of writing and recording.

And we were making money. Christ, we were making money. It's probably not unreasonable to say that at the height of our success we were earning something like a million pounds a day.

A million pounds a day and we were still having problems with the bank. What we hadn't woken up to at the time was the balance sheets. The company was starting to creak. Without knowing it we just couldn't cope with the enormity of what was happening. All of a sudden there were lawyers and accountants costing us a fortune, as well as a whole load of spending that came purely from an illusion of invincibility.

To the outside world, and to a lot of people in the company, it looked like we couldn't move for cash. Yet I still lived in a comparatively modest house and though I'd bought some cars as investments, I hadn't taken a penny out of the company as a salary or a director's bonus. Matt and Mike, Phil Hammond, Pete Harding, the artists, they had all become materially wealthy, but while I was living a comfortable lifestyle, I hadn't taken anything that would give me independent security. Certain people in the company had earned three or four million pounds, but almost everything I had was reinvested in the company. I owned the company, which was probably worth 120 million pounds, but it was only worth that if I was going to sell it. And I had no intention of selling it. I had a nice life compared to the average person on the street, but as far as actual wealth, I had made nothing from it all. I hadn't taken what a director would normally take in terms of salary or bonuses which, with the turnover of the company, would have been at least a million pounds a year. On top of that I could have taken another two million as a producer and writer, but I didn't. I could do what I wanted to do in terms of making records and that was what I'd always wanted. I was happy with that and far more concerned with the idea of building a company. It was important that any money I made went straight back into the company.

It's a bloody good job I did put so much of it back into the company, because we were later to find out that the whole thing was falling apart. The money influx became just about the worst thing that ever happened to the company. So many people in the company had lost sight of why we were doing what we were doing the money became more important than anything else. I found myself surrounded by people on huge salaries, and I was supposed to make decisions based on the enormity of the overheads and the enormity of the salaries rather than the quality of the artists and the quality of the records. There was a sense among certain people that they were infallible. It was taking power away from my dream and turning it, not into a nightmare, it was never a nightmare, but it was someone else's dream.

I have to say that the worst thing that ever happened to PWL was Kylie Minogue. That might sound silly, considering the amount of money she made us, but it was her success that changed the company completely. Plus the Kylie phenomenon had completely polarised public opinion, and constricted how people saw us. We could no longer be underground dance producers with any sort of credibility, we were just identified with Kylie's pop records simply because she'd become so huge. If I had the chance to do it all again I would have sold Kylie to EMI immediately after the first album, which had been an option, and the company would have gone on to be twice as successful. She put so much money into the economy of the company that it spoiled the team. Mike Stock and I both agreed later that it would have been far better to have stopped working with Kylie after her debut album and taken a step back towards working on the sort of stuff we were doing before, because then we wouldn't have had nearly as many pot-shots taken at us by the critics, and we would have had the time and money to have developed something that wasn't going to completely take over our lives.

As it was, we worked with Kylie from 1988 until 1992, and I always found her to be a very bright, very intelligent girl and I always liked her. I never had the same sort of social relationship with her as I did with Bananarama, so the time I spent with her tended to be in a professional capacity. It *had* to be a very professional relationship because we were talking about millions of pounds being involved in her career. She kept herself pretty much to herself, but one thing I noticed about her was that because she'd started in the business so young, it was as if she'd never had a chance to be a teenager. Once she met Michael Hutchence from INXS and started going out with him, she started acting like a teenager, as if she was making up for all the things she'd missed in the past, and she started to behave a lot more wildly.

'Better The Devil You Know' was actually inspired by Kylie's relationship with Hutchence, although he never actually hung around the studio with her or anything. She rang me up at this time and asked if I'd help shield her from the press so she came up and stayed with me in Cheshire and we went horse riding and stuff together. Of course, the paparazzi wouldn't give up and we had to put up with photographers falling out of trees and falling through hedges left, right and centre.

Towards the end of the time she was working with us she was discovering a whole load of new ambitions, setting her sights at becoming the new Prince or Madonna. What I found amazing was that she was outselling Madonna four to one, but still wanted to be her. Everyone wanted to be Kylie Minogue except Kylie Minogue, who wanted to be Madonna. On top of that, I think Kylie was getting embarrassed by her past because it was part of her growing up. She had to reject her past so that she could find her own identity. I was fine about that, but it just meant that if she wanted to do something else she'd have to do it with someone else.

By the third Kylie album I really don't think Mike, Matt and I had our hearts in it any more and while we still made some good singles with her it was obvious that she wasn't primarily interested in making pop records for her public, but for herself instead. The epitome of that was 'Word Is Out' which was a good little song, but which was accompanied by a video shot outside the PWL studios where she portrayed herself as a prostitute. We only involved ourselves in any way in the videos she made for her first five singles or so, and after that it was completely up to her what she wanted to do. Dressing as a prostitute wouldn't have been my choice and the public seemed to understand that as well, because once they saw it her popularity just fell away.

I've found throughout my career that acts do what the public wants and then there comes a point when they decide to do what they want and the public doesn't like them any more. I'm not saying acts shouldn't develop, but as I tell almost everyone I work with, the Beatles didn't write *Sergeant Pepper* immediately after 'Love Me Do'.

One band or singer can't go on making hit singles forever, but as a producer I can. And that means it's going to be inevitable that I only work with artists for a certain length of time, for as long as I'm still interested in what they're doing. Inside I'm fourteen years old forever, and all I want from my acts is someone who keeps that fourteen-year-old interested. Every time I go into the studio I'm under the self-imposed pressure of making hit singles, because that's what I've done for 25 years of my life. I don't know any artists who could keep that pressure on themselves so they end up getting bored and, to me, boring. It's always obvious when a working relationship has to end, and when it does I'm never bitter about it, because if I've given them a lot of hits then I've done my job. Whatever they do next is up to them. All I hope is that they've learned something from their experience with me.

Kylie had one supreme strength and that was her amazing natural talent. She was a great performer. She could sell snow to Eskimos. Over the years since she's created a persona for herself that's proved to be enduringly successful, meaning that she's now ready to admit to her past. I heard that she even did 'I Should Be So Lucky' at a show with Nick Cave recently, so maybe she has come to terms with it. I wish her well, but I haven't spoken to her in years.

Jason also seemed to find it hard to deal with the public persona that had grown up around him and he made what was to be his last single for us in August 1991, a Beatles-y take on the song 'Happy Together'. He'd made a very successful career for himself and had sold millions of records, but apparently it wasn't enough.

I'd received a phone call from his manager in Australia earlier in the year, who told me that Jason wouldn't be coming back to England for a few weeks because he (Jason) felt that he was 'overexposed'. Sure enough, he stayed away for a few weeks, then turned up at the office with a beard and long hair, announcing that he was really into Happy Mondays. He said that he'd got a group together and they were going on a world tour, because there were just too many pictures of him everywhere.

I pulled out a fifty-pound note and pointed to the picture of the Queen.

'Jason,' I said, 'I wish I had ten million pictures of her like that and that would really be overexposure!'

Still, he wasn't to be dissuaded and insisted that he had to drop out of the limelight for a bit or at least make some records that sounded like Happy Mondays. It was too bizarre to even contemplate.

In early May, his manager Richard East rang me up again and said that Jason had got an offer to play the lead part in the stage production of *Joseph And His Technicolor Dreamcoat* and that Andrew Lloyd Webber, whose musical it was, wanted me to write five more songs for a reworked score. They were going to put a whole new show on produced by Cameron Mackintosh and they wanted me to write the new songs as well as releasing Jason from his contract.

Well, you never say no because life is full of mysteries and, to be honest, I'd got used to strange offers throughout my life. Still, the concept of a teen pop star turned Happy Mondays fan who was worried about overexposure playing the lead in an Andrew Lloyd Webber musical was one of the oddest yet! I'd never met Lloyd Webber, but I thought it might be a bit of an adventure so I agreed to discuss the project.

Jason, his manager Richard East and I got in the car a few weeks later and drove down to Lloyd Webber's house at Watership Down in Hampshire, the place where the book about the rabbits was set. It's a really hard place to find and he's got a front drive that goes on for so many miles you sort of think you might just run out of petrol before you even reach the house, but we eventually made it down, by which time it was dark.

He's got an enormous house because he's not exactly subtle. It's like Versailles or something. The butler who inevitably opened the door announced that Mr Lloyd Webber was currently doing an interview with an American television station, and ushered us into this huge room with a roaring log fire to wait for him. He offered us a drink and Jason had water while I had a gin and tonic. Ten minutes later Lloyd Webber still hadn't arrived so we were offered another drink and I had the same again, while we waited like schoolboys about to see the headmaster. This went on for about an hour and a half, by which time I'd had something like eleven gin and tonics and was starting to feel very drunk, but kind of confident. I even had my feet up on the table as far as I can remember. His wife, Madeline, eventually came in and we got on like a house on fire. We had a few more drinks, by which time I was so pissed that I couldn't see the end of my arms, but then Andrew finally turned up and it seemed a good idea when he suggested we go off for a drive to his local pub. Jason could see how drunk I was and quietly told me that I should calm down, but I was well away and told him, 'Don't worry Jase mate, I can handle this.'

So we all piled into a Range Rover, with me in a leather coat I'd bought that day from Jones' for five grand, and we set off across Watership Down. I was sitting in the back with Jason, and Andrew and Madeline were in the front with their Jack Russell. Every fifty yards or so they stopped the car and chucked the dog out. It would run about for a bit and then get back in the car before they drove on another fifty yards and did the whole thing again. I hadn't a clue what that was all about, but I was so drunk I didn't really question it.

We got to the pub, where we carried on drinking and quite possibly discussed business, although I was too far gone to remember what on earth Andrew said, and eventually we all piled back into the car to go back to the house. Yet again they kept lobbing the dog out every fifty yards and they finally explained to me that it was because there were so many rabbits on Watership Down that they were trying to teach the dog to catch them. The only thing was that the dog was so hopeless that it never got near any of them.

I was starting to feel really sick with all the stopping and starting and Jason kept kicking me in the back of the leg telling me to 'keep it together', while his manager just looked sort of embarrassed, so the next time they jerked to a halt I told them I was going off for a wee, while the dog ran about.

I got out of the car and jumped into a bramble bush with the dog in my brand new coat. Once there, I reached out and grabbed a rabbit and wrung its neck then shoved the dead rabbit in the dog's mouth, whacked its arse and pushed it back towards the car. Andrew was so excited that his dog had finally caught a rabbit that he cheered like it had scored the winning goal in a cup final. I killed another rabbit and shoved it under my coat, then put that in the dog's mouth as well and Andrew was ecstatic. I think he was convinced that he'd got the best rabbit-killing dog in the world. And when we got back to the house he got his French chef down and made him cook rabbit fricassee. To this day I haven't a clue whether we even mentioned Jason being in *Technicolor Dreamcoat*.

The next morning I had a meeting with Bill McAlpine about some railway business and I felt really, really hung-over, vowing I was never going to drink again, but when I turned up at his house in Henley he insisted that I join him and his guests in an enormous goblet of white wine from his own chateau. Just as I put the glass to my mouth and took the first sip, a wallaby came in and bounced across the front room. I was convinced that I was hallucinating, but when I rubbed my eyes it was still there, just bouncing around. Everyone at the table burst out laughing and Bill McAlpine told me it was a wallaby he got in specially to play a trick on guests with hangovers. It was known in their house as The Wallaby Joke, and the last person they'd done it on had gone to bed for three days. I was pretty much prepared to do the same.

A few weeks later we decided against writing any songs for Jason for *Technicolor Dreamcoat*, because they seemed even simpler songs than S.A.W. ones and there certainly wasn't any sort of Happy Mondays element. It seemed to me that one of the main attractions for Jason was that he was getting paid a lot of money. We'd been to a meeting at Andrew's London house and had bizarre discussions about camels while Andrew played us some prospective tunes that really didn't impress Mike and me. It just wasn't a project that we felt excited about, so we let Polydor Records, who were behind the whole thing, buy Jason out of his contract. But those were certainly some of the most peculiar weeks I've ever spent in my life.

Later that year we put out Jason Donovan's *Greatest Hits* album and the only tracks not on it were the hits he had from *Technicolor Dreamcoat*. As far as I'm concerned, when you put children on records, you're not Happy Mondays. Still, I had some good times with Jason and he brought us a lot of success. Even his projects outside the record business could work to our advantage because he was just a hugely popular iconic figure. I remember he was in a mini-series on TV called *Commandos* and I was immensely pleased when Jason got killed in the third episode because the next day the sales of his 'Sealed With A Kiss' single and the accompanying album went straight through the roof. We couldn't have bought better publicity.

The best thing about the whole period in the late eighties and early nineties was that the other record companies hated us. I mean, *really* hated us. What we had done was say to the American bosses that most of their European employees were idiots. They'd allowed us to take a huge chunk of the record industry from right under their noses. And we loved winding them up.

Because of that, they tried to get their own back. For example, we won a Best Producer Award from the BPI for 'Never Gonna Give You Up', but they wouldn't let us go up on stage to collect it at the filmed ceremony because they said it wouldn't make good television – this despite the fact that they'd always thought the producer's awards were good television in the past. And then the next year, when it was obvious that we were easily the most influential producers around, they completely dropped the category for the awards. I believe that they knew that the only way they could stop us winning was by actually dropping the category, which I thought was mean-spirited but typical of the sort of thing that was going on then.

We took an advert out in the trade press with a photo of me and Dave putting up a whole wall of platinum discs and accompanied it with the caption, 'No S.A.W. No comment', a parody of the *Financial Times*' 'No FT. No comment.' If they weren't going to give us an award we were at least going to show them just how successful we were.

We got support from radio DJs like John Peel and the journalists from *Melody Maker* and *NME*, people from within the industry who understood integrity and injustice. In theory, to them, we were the antichrists of the record industry because we made pop music, but they saw that the record industry, which had ostensibly been a commercial venture, had suddenly turned on pure commercialism. We were the antithesis of what they stood for, because we were just peddling pop music, but they understood that we were being persecuted for what the big companies were getting paid to do in the first place. The journalists had to start defending us and John Peel decided to champion us on his radio programme. It was bizarre, but that was how far the industry had got out of touch with its roots. The record industry by the mid-eighties had completely lost touch with its customers. The accountants and the lawyers had got it completely wrong. American companies had tried to make their operation something global, but punk had come along and destroyed that, brought British record buyers in to an insular vision. However, the record companies over here had managed to sanitise and ultimately destroy even that concept. Then we'd come in – a bunch of guys making gay disco records – and we'd blown them out of the water.

Tony Wilson from Factory Records once said that we had an A&R department in every school in the country, and he was right in that we were picking up what the kids wanted faster and more perceptively than anyone else around.

When I look back with any sense of personal gratification at what I've done in my career, I will treasure the Ivor Novello awards that Mike, Matt and I received in 1987, 1988 and 1989 when we were voted Songwriters Of The Year by our songwriting peers. The BPI and the majors may have done their best to try and ignore our achievements, but these awards were from fellow songwriters and that meant a lot.

When I was first starting off in the music business, it was a dream just to win one Ivor Novello Songwriter Of The Year award, because so few people are ever given that accolade. When we won one for the second time the following year we were in hallowed company, since only the Beatles had previously won the award in consecutive years. Then came 1989, which was our most successful year yet, and in the other categories (awards based purely on statistics such as Best Selling Single, Most Performed A-Side, Most Played Song and the like) we swept the nominations and won so many awards that we couldn't even carry them all home. When it came to Songwriter Of The Year, the academy announced that because of our total domination that year they hadn't even asked the members to vote and as a special recognition of our contribution, they'd given the award to us. That meant we'd won the Ivor Novello Songwriter Of The Year award three years running, which was something not even the Beatles ever did! It was an awesome achievement for us.

And it was hard to argue with our domination of the industry that year. In 1989 we were the Number One independent publishing company in Britain and the Number Two corporate publishing company, second only to EMI and only beaten by them by 2 per cent of the share of the market. EMI had 16,000 writers and bought songs in from all over the place, whereas we had three writers and did it all ourselves. So you can see just how dominant we were. We were breaking records all over the place; there was a record produced by me in the Top 100 every single week from March 1986 to October 1990, so I think we proved our powers of endurance, too.

Those Ivor Novello awards are the awards that I'll treasure most for the rest of my life, and if I went bust tomorrow I know that I'll always be able to look back on them and know how important we were. I'd also like to think that we did something to resurrect the importance of songwriting, an art that the industry itself had increasingly done its best to devalue up until 1987.

Of course, although we had won more times than the Beatles, I would never dream to even countenance the thought that we in any way wrote better songs than Lennon and McCartney and there is no way that I would put anything we wrote alongside 'Yesterday', 'She Loves You', 'Hey Jude' or 'Happiness Is A Warm Gun', but I'd like to think that we made a contribution towards acknowledging the power of great pop songwriting.

We'd been doing it for five years by 1989, but the majors still disapproved of us and by keeping us outside their blueprint for what constituted the mainstream of pop, they allowed us to become more successful than we really should have been. If they'd played us at our own game, every major record company would have annihilated us. We couldn't have competed. But because they were so snobbish, so arrogant about pop music, so dismissive of it all, they allowed us to create the greatest, purest period of pop music since the Beatles.

They ended up making us heroes. We always had the same attitude when we were working with pop stars as when we were working with gay disco artists, but the record industry couldn't cope with the fact that we were doing it so well, doing what they should have been doing all along.

For example, we were the biggest independent label in Europe, and suddenly we were not allowed to be in the independent chart. 'Independent' was changed overnight from an economic definition to a description of a type of music, and that music was anything but pop. I could have taken them to the European Courts for restraint of trade or discrimination, but it just seemed an admission of defeat by the big companies to have been so transparent in their attacks on us that I knew we'd beaten them.

There wasn't even any panache behind the major companies' attempts to destroy us and we saw people rig charts, fake sales, give away records, anything to put us out of business. Yet not one person did the thing that could have stopped us – which was to compete.

During the eighties, the more the big companies ganged up on us, the more we stuck our fingers up at them, knowing they just didn't have the guts to take us on. We paid better royalties to our artists than anyone else, and broke the monopoly of the strictures that the industry had set up. We changed the way that people did business: the deals we did were based on what we thought was fair, and we found that other acts had their lawyers going to big companies and threatening that if they didn't do an equitable deal, they'd come to us, because they knew they could trust us.

We were being kicked from every single side, but we didn't care. The more they shouted the more we dug in and did what we wanted to do.

One Friday night in 1989, I was at home up North and I'd just been for a curry. I got back late at night and put the television on ready to watch something that might entertain me. And what came on but Elvis Costello moaning about politics. It was the last thing I wanted to hear and I knew I couldn't be the only person who felt that way. I realised that there ought to be some sort of programme that would be perfect for when you came back late from the pub or wherever, and just wanted a bit of escapism. At that time there was nothing on late night TV that fitted the bill, so I decided to do something about it.

Rick Astley's manager was the agent for a lot of actors appearing in *Coronation Street*, which was made by Granada. A new guy had just taken over as head of light entertainment at Granada, called David Liddiment, and he was a massive Stock, Aitken and Waterman fan, so I arranged to have lunch with him. I told him that I wanted to make a TV version of my radio show, filmed in a nightclub, for people to watch late at night and he agreed that it might be a good idea. So he commissioned a pilot.

I wasn't a young man and there was no point me pretending I was, so I looked for a blueprint for the show to a pop TV programme from the sixties called *Ready, Steady, Go*. That was presented by an old bloke called Keith Fordyce, and he had a younger foil on the show in the shape of Cathy McGowan. I knew that if my idea was going to work, I'd need a younger co-presenter too. Someone came up with the idea of a girl called Michaela Strachan so we asked her to try out.

I went along for the first rehearsal and one of the producers handed me a load of paper.

'What's this?' I asked.

'Oh, it's your script,' they said.

I could hardly read, so what use was a script to me? Then they gave me another piece of paper with a list of songs on it and told me that was going to be my playlist.

'Wait a minute,' I said. 'There is *no way* you're choosing the playlist. This is going to be like my radio show. I choose the records and it's my job to pull in the audience through the music. I don't care if the researchers want to book the novelty acts [the novelty acts were supposed to be a feature of the shows for some reason] but *I* pick the music.'

Michaela was just standing there, bamboozled by the whole thing and wondering what she had let herself in for.

We decided that because Warrington was near where I lived, we'd use a club in the town called Mr Smith's as the venue. One Saturday afternoon we went along to film the pilot.

Saturday afternoon is not the best time to film a programme that's supposed to look like it's capturing the club scene. The researchers had literally pulled about twenty people off the street, dragged them away from their shopping and told them to look like they were having a good night out. Half of them were still holding their carrier bags. They bounced about for a bit while I sat at some decks and introduced the records from one side of the club while Michaela was over the other side talking to the camera. It was quite possibly the worst programme anyone has ever attempted to make, and when it finished Michaela and I were just so embarrassed we were ready to run straight out of the building. David Liddiment came over.

'Actually, I quite like this,' he said. And so *The Hitman and Her* was born.

To get the show bedded down, we decided to do the first six programmes from Mr Smith's in Warrington. It was a local venue, and because of my reputation I knew that I could ram it. In fact it used to get so full that they had to close the doors at 8.30 p.m., and it wasn't going out until two in the morning. The whole thing was filmed absolutely live with a British telecom engineer stuck down a manhole outside doing the phone line feed. Can you imagine, we used to have phone calls live to the show? Phone calls to a nightclub! It was chaos, but gradually we started to hone the whole thing into something worth watching. We got someone else to take over the decks, then put all the records on cartridges so they wouldn't jump while everyone was leaping about, and we built up the relationship between Michaela and me, making it funnier and camper. It really started to take off and ultimately became something of an icon for the eighties. I used to meet Princess Di occasionally at functions and she once told me that she used to come down in the night to feed her children and watch the programme. 'Are people really like that?' she asked me. I told her that they really were.

That was the beauty of the programme; it was real people in a real setting doing what they really do at nightclubs. In the years since, there have been so many programmes ripping off the look of that show. All that late night TV stuff where they film shows in clubs is just doing what we were doing years ago. Chris Evans' *TFI Friday* is basically just a posh, perfectionist version, though it still strives for the atmosphere and unpredictability that we had, naturally. It was *The Hitman and Her* that started that whole trend.

Doing the show was a lot of fun. We started to widen our fan base because whereas the kids had been able to get into the roadshows, they couldn't get into *The Hitman and Her* because of licensing laws. All of a sudden I was reaching a different audience, going from twelve-year-olds to twenty-two-year-olds.

There was no fakery to the show and we weren't going to pretend that things didn't go wrong. Sometimes they did and sometimes the shows were absolutely brilliant, but whatever happened the audience could always be guaranteed full-on fun. I didn't mind looking a prat if it was going to entertain people, and I worked hard making it work. It sometimes used to take me eleven gin and tonics to get through the show, but I still got through it. We took away the sterility of studio-based TV pop shows and took the camera into a real club where we had to adapt to the environment, rather than the other way round. We had cameramen roaming around for two hours in a club with the music at proper club volume and a temperature of about 120°F. It was all completely authentic and the cameramen used to hate lugging the heavy equipment around, stopping only for the commercial breaks, but we felt it was important for the person at home to feel that they were really there with us in a place going wild. Nowadays you see that kind of fly-on-the-wall stuff all the time, but there was nothing like it around back in 1990.

Because filming was like a military manoeuvre, it meant that the cameramen got very fit, very quickly, and that the whole team bonded within weeks of the show starting. Everyone knew what to do and where to go and when we got it right it was exhilarating to be a part of.

The director of the show used to watch the shots from all around the club in the van outside and he communicated with us through our earpieces, so we used to play to him when we spoke. No one else in the club could hear a bloody word we were saying because the music was so loud, but if we could hear him laughing we knew we must have been doing something right.

I had a fantastic relationship with Michaela. There were all these rumours going around that we were a couple, but we weren't. It was much more of a father-daughter or brother-sister relationship. She had a lot of boyfriend problems at the time and so I became a shoulder for her to cry on.

She'd come from mainstream TV and I think she was a bit shocked by a lot of the stuff that was going on. She wasn't used to that whole club world and we were filming in places like Manchester's Hacienda at the height of Acid House, so she was in an unreal environment. She also had problems with a few fans who got obsessed with her. One guy had made death threats to her so when we filmed the show in Liverpool, every single dancer on the stage was a policeman or policewoman. That night, they arrested a guy with a machete who'd been threatening her for eighteen months.

The show ran for six or seven years and probably kept Stock, Aitken and Waterman in the public eye a good few years longer than we would have been otherwise. It was a fantastic place to try out new records that we'd made to get an instant reaction. We were under a constant strain to keep on coming up with better and better records, and the show was a great place to see how successful we had been. It's that pressure that I enjoy most of all and to get an instant reaction just gave me a bigger buzz.

I didn't just play records we'd made ourselves, though, and Matt and Mike absolutely detested a lot of what I featured. I only played records we'd made if I thought they deserved to stand alongside whatever else was on, and invariably those records of ours that I did choose went on to be massive. The audience isn't stupid and if I'd turned the programme into one big plug for PWL they would have seen through it instantly. It was a brutal, fantastic experience doing that programme and while, by the end, it had obviously got past its sell-by date and had lost its spontaneity, it was something I'll always remember with affection. Because we were doing the show just before the whole club scene fragmented and got so ghettoised, we could play great records that appealed simply because they were good records, not because they were the week's hippest new genre. So we had the Prodigy and Snap before anyone else had heard of them simply because I loved the records, and I don't think such diversity would be given that sort of space these days.

I didn't think of myself as a celebrity and thought I was just a doddery old git messing about on the telly, but thanks to the programme, I did become famous among certain sections of the community; people like Indian and Chinese waiters, cabbies and doctors and nurses. *The Hitman and Her* used to be the show they'd always watch when they got home in the middle of the night, or when they were sitting around with nothing else to do, so I've had a lot of free curries and Chinese meals in my life because of that programme!

14 No Limits?

THE COMPANY HAD grown from six or seven people to sixty or seventy people by the middle of 1990. Over the previous two or three years, while we were unarguably more successful than ever before, the whole operation had inexorably changed from a tight-knit family to something far more impersonal. I had realised how it was changing when we held our Christmas party in 1989 at the Savoy because there were 2,000 people there, all allegedly connected with the company, and I knew hardly anybody. It had just become so big and sprawling.

I hadn't started the company to throw a party for thousands of people, including fifteen of Kylie Minogue's dancers and Jason Donovan's make-up artist. I walked out of the party that night and I hated what PWL had become. I absolutely detested it.

That Christmas I'd moved from Winwick to a new place in nearby Daresbury. It was the house that used to belong to Lewis Carroll, the author of the *Alice in Wonderland* books, and I'd invited a load of friends and family including my auntie, who was my oldest living relative. I was really down in the dumps over the whole of that Christmas, thinking about how much I'd hated the company Christmas party, and I seriously considered jacking it all in. It just wasn't what I wanted any more and I wasn't enjoying it in the slightest. My company had become a monster, a corporation full of people who were only there for the money. I went back to work at the beginning of 1990 and things carried on just like before, but somehow the dream just didn't feel the same.

Our sales were going through the roof and there was nothing we couldn't buy. Or at least it seemed like there was nothing we couldn't buy – I certainly saw the accountants rubbing their hands with glee. I'd never sat down and asked anyone just how much I was worth, because I'd originally become involved in the business purely out of a love of music rather than a means to wealth, and maybe finding out just how rich I was would have frightened me too much. It might have made me approach things from a different perspective and I didn't want that.

As I've said, I had never taken a salary and I was living a modest lifestyle. To quantify that, it was a modest lifestyle in terms of the lifestyle that some other people in the company were enjoying. Compared to the average person in the street I was living a luxurious life, but within the world I inhabited I considered myself to be fairly restrained. When people were buying brand new BMWs, I bought a Volvo. And when people bought houses for half a million, I bought one for £70,000. Although I had a fantastic, showbiz life and a theoretically profitable company, maybe subconsciously I'd not wanted to see the actual cash in the bank. Maybe I should have, since right through that period I can't remember a time, even though there was money flying in all over the place, when a bank wasn't involved somewhere along the line. There always seemed to be loans or negotiations with the bank on the go. And because I'd never been in that position before, I thought it was normal. I presumed everything was fantastic and because we had accountants and tax advisors, I thought everything was rosy.

One day I had a conversation with David Howells about my car collection. By then I'd built up a big collection including 18 Ferraris, one of which had admittedly cost me £3.2 million. Talking to David I got the impression that there was a problem about it, which struck me as a bit strange since I'd not paid in cash for the cars, but used bank loans and various forms of hire purchase. Now, though, I got the feeling that there was some resentment about me buying them, even though I'd only got them as an investment since there was no tax on the sale of second-hand cars. It was startling that the cars had even been brought up since I hadn't taken any money out of the company to buy them. I knew that Matt and Mike had earned something in the region of 16 million pounds each since the company started, so you would have thought that I could have bought a two or three million quid Ferrari without it being unreasonable. Don't forget, I owned the company as well, so I would have been making 16 million, plus the money the company was making, plus the publishing. That had to be lot of money, seven or eight million pounds a year at least.

The one thing that I have never done is spend more than I can get back in a fire sale. That's my background, coming from such a poor upbringing. Whatever I do, I always know I can get out without affecting other people financially. I knew that no matter what I'd borrowed in my life, I'd covered. I just had to sell something or move stuff around and I'd be able to pay anything back. I never got myself in more debt than I could cope with. It was managed debt, if you like, and I think that business entrepreneurs manage debt very well, because to me if you're not in any form of debt, you're not focussed. It doesn't matter if you owe the bank five million pounds if you can always realise that five million should you need to repay the money – and I knew that I always could. I had the company, for goodness' sake, which was huge collateral in itself.

As I've mentioned, though, the banks back then simply didn't understand the record industry. They didn't understand royalties, they didn't understand copyright and, most of all, they didn't understand the global economy. So they were completely mystified by something like our company. If I said I was going to drop two million pounds into the account the next day, they couldn't get their heads around the idea that I found the two million but that they didn't know where it came from. They didn't seem to understand that everything we did was interconnected not just with the UK, but with other companies and markets all over the world.

The banking industry lives on the theory that if I've got money in their bank then I'm a good customer. Yet if I deposit money in their bank then I'm only going to get a return of a few per cent above bank rate in interest. If I use the money I'm making to reinvest in another act then, because I know I'm good at what I do, I know I can make thirty or forty per cent. I learned very early on that if you invest a pound in something that gives you a thirty per cent profit in return, you're going to make enough for a bag of crisps. If you invest a million quid, you're going to get enough back to buy a house. It's that simple and that's why I built the company so we could make large investments and therefore get large returns. And if you've earned a million pounds you must know how to earn another million, so you would have thought banks would realise that without you physically leaving your million in an account with them so they can stare at it. It's no use there, you have to keep reinvesting, and that's something that banks never understood with regard to the record industry. By its very nature, the industry relies on constant reinvestment.

As far as I was concerned, at that point in time I was in an entirely manageable situation, but for some reason the bank were still ringing up. I got an inkling that all was not well, but I couldn't imagine that we could be short of money.

I did feel though that the company had become too large, so I went around and asked for three redundancies in every department, closing down all the parts of the firm that I hadn't personally been involved in setting up. I did that off my own back, just to be on the safe side.

We'd got two fabulous new accountants in, one from EMI and one from Polydor, and they suddenly announced to me that we owed 8.9 million pounds. This was a total shock to me! We were Number One in the charts every week, everything we touched was, it seemed, turning to gold and here I was being told that the company was in serious financial trouble. With hindsight I've found that we weren't particularly in debt at all, it was just a cash-flow problem that could possibly have been solved by six months' hard graft and a bit of belt tightening. We didn't know that at the time, though, and it's only in the last year or so that I've actually seen the way that the company back then had swallowed what should have been profitable. Back in 1991, 1992, I was told by the accountants that we had to do something very quickly to get ourselves out of trouble.

I was supposed to be a genius businessman, but like everyone else at the company I didn't have a clue what was going on. I tell you, if this was a genius business then my uncle is a gorilla. In fact a gorilla could have run it better than we were running it, because as far as we could make out it was a disaster area. It didn't make any sense that we could have been so successful and yet still be in so much trouble. And even when I tried to stem the wounds by downsizing, we still seemed to be haemorrhaging money just as fast. We had meeting after meeting and still I just couldn't understand where all the money had gone. The inference was that somehow I'd spent it all myself, but I knew that what 'luxuries' I'd bought had not been financed by company money.

Later on we were to find that the problem was the deals that we'd made concerning the artists we were producing. They'd been absolutely awful deals and had somehow been allowed to go through. It turned out that I'd actually been *paying* to make hits. I'd have the hits and they would cost me money. The Kylie deal was awful, the Pal Productions deal was awful, it was just a shambles. Even when we found out years later about it all we had to give up trying to unravel the complexities of just how bad all the deals had been, because none of them made any common sense. Money had disappeared all over the place, and then there were situations like charity records, where not only had we given the profits to the charity, but all proceeds including the cost of making the records. If it hadn't been so bewildering it would have been laughable. I'm not angry about it and I'm not blaming anyone for it except for myself. I shouldn't have let the company get so big in the first place, and I should never have let the business side get separated from the creative side, but when I saw the sort of sales we were having I'd thought we were untouchable. It was a shock to find out we weren't. So I didn't become a billionaire. Who cares? The preferred option of our accountants was to take all the risk out of the business and meanwhile the banks were petrified that they were somehow going to be left with us owing a huge debt. We had to get rid of part of the record company if we were going to raise money fast. That was the easiest part of it all for me because I hadn't wanted a record company in the first place. We decided to sell.

We were the most successful independent record company around until it came to trying to sell it, and then we became prey overnight. The major record companies started to circle around us and we knew that we weren't going to get any favours. Anyone who saw we were in trouble wasn't going to help out, they were going to kick our head in. We spoke to three or four record companies and, to be honest, the offers were derisory, and it became obvious that I needed a partner to provide some money.

I knew a chap called Dave Munns who had first approached Stock, Aitken and Waterman pre-Rick Astley, when he was managing director at EMI. He'd offered us a joint venture deal for £250,000 which the EMI board had turned down. Afterwards he'd gone to Polydor and approached us in 1991 about a deal worth ten million pounds to us. I'd originally thought it was some joint venture that was being proposed, but it turned out to merely be a distribution deal, so it never came to anything. It did, however, reinitiate interest among other record companies.

Meanwhile EMI had approached us with a most peculiar proposition that seemed to involve them giving us a couple of million pounds and us giving them back whatever work we thought two million pounds would buy them. It was a completely off-the-wall approach, but it didn't seem like a sound business plan, or at least the sort of plan that would get us out of our immediate problems.

Then I got a phone call from the Warner label telling me to meet them before I concluded any negotiations with anyone else. So I went along and was introduced to Stephen Shrimpton and Ramon Lopez from Warner Music in Europe, two guys I liked instantly. I'd always admired the Warner image over the years that I'd seen them from the standpoint of a DJ, a record shop owner and a promotions man. I'd always liked the way that they handled themselves, so I sat down and talked to Stephen and Ramon about a deal. It was a very complicated deal, which I decided to go for, wrongly perhaps, simply because I liked the image of the company. In hindsight it was naive of us to sign, but I didn't have the luxury of thinking level-headedly.

Now, my company could be split into five arms at that time: studios, producers, publishing, production company and record company. They took one of those arms, which was the record company. However, that one arm relies on the other four in order to function properly and vice versa, or at least that was the way that our company had worked in the past. Very quickly the production and publishing side became detached from the record company side, and on top of that I was contracted exclusively to Warner. Matt and Mike could work for who they liked, but I had to work just for Warner. They had paid me a lot of money and the exclusivity went with the territory.

The problem with major record companies is that, by their very size, they can't act quickly enough. They work globally, so they see the industry globally. To use my football analogy, the big companies are watching the game from their elevated super-suites from behind glass, while we were used to being at the side of the pitch where we could shout at the players. We saw the whole business from a very different perspective to them and were able to predict what was going to happen in the match with far more accuracy.

Yet again I found myself in a rarefied world where people seemed more interested in internal politics than in the basic impulse of making great records. I'd been in the business for twenty years and I still couldn't understand why who had the best car was apparently more important than whether a record was any good or not. I thought that Ramon was a great man, but the foot soldiers for the company didn't seem to have a clue about pop music, the one thing that I presumed they'd understood to be my greatest strength.

The problems that the deal was going to cause became obvious from the very beginning. On the day we signed in October 1991, we had a Number Two single with 2 Un- limited's 'Get Ready For This'. When we took 2 Unlimited into the deal we had options on them for territories all over the world, but Warner turned down every single one. It meant that we only had the rights on their record in the UK which was a foolish decision since they went on to sell six or seven million albums. We'd put together the whole project and done all the work, but only ended up with the UK rights, so any money we might have made out of it had already been spent on research and development and stuff. With worldwide sales they could have been a profitable enterprise and we could have made three or four million pounds, but I was barely breaking even due to all the money I'd invested into the project in the first place.

It was so sad to be having problems with Warner, because I'd had tremendous affection for the company in the past, and I really liked Ramon Lopez, but the whole organisation was totally flawed. For example, Rob Dickins ran the UK company, which I had nothing to do with because I was signed to Warner in Europe, but for me to get priority for using the warehouses in Britain, I had to get permission from Rob Dickins. Now why on earth would he give permission for me to get priority over an act of his? So we had to pay through the nose for our own promotion, which cost yet more money.

Of course we got bills paid for by Warner and a partnership, but what ended up happening was that we weren't making records any more because we couldn't get them past Warner, who didn't seem to want anything to do with pop music. It was relentlessly dispiriting to me, like being in a straitjacket.

To be fair to Warner, because they'd done the deal with us, people over here suddenly thought that PWL was a proper record label with the same sort of intentions as Warner itself, so we were suddenly approached by loads of rock groups, and were expected by Warner to sign rock acts. That's just not what I wanted to do, but I felt I should make an effort to go along to see rock bands. Warner were also working in a world where albums were king, another form that we had completely differing opinions on. We knew how to make great singles and saw the singles as equally important as the albums, if not more so. Warner didn't care about singles because when they wanted to get an act rolling they could easily lob three or four million pounds into the project. What I'd been used to was getting an artist's career underway for £30,000 by making a hit single. I never commit to a big budget until I know the public is interested, but the big record companies just liked to hurl the cash at the artist and *then* think about the problems. They would market an album rather than A&R it, which was a fundamental difference between them and us.

I remember sitting in a meeting at Warner about a particular act. Their previous album had sold several million and they were discussing the sales of the next album, mapping out profits and cash-flow for it in different territories. I asked if anyone had actually heard the album and they all looked at me like I'd committed a crime or something. Listening to the music itself didn't seem to play any part in their policy decisions and, as it turned out, that album completely bombed! Warner didn't mind though, because their attitude seemed to be, 'Oh well, there'll be another bus along in a minute.' Whether it was R.E.M. or Alanis Morrissette or Madonna, there'd be another big seller along to replace whatever had flopped.

I began to find myself excluded from my own company. Not long after signing the deal I realised no one was listening to a single word I said. And in the middle of all this, the production side of things was dying because Matt, Mike and I just weren't getting on. Matt was really into motor racing and used to devote a lot of time to that, meaning that he sometimes wouldn't come into work until two or three in the afternoon, which pissed me off and meant we were down to three working days a week. Very quickly it became intolerable and Matt left. After all the years together, suddenly the team had broken up and although Mike and I tried to carry on, and did manage to produce successfully together for a few months – having a hit with a girl called Sybil who released a single called 'When I'm Good And Ready' – it was never really the same. Particularly since Mike himself had begun to strike me as completely set in his ways about what he saw to be good pop records.

The records we were making were not always going to have some divine right to be the most popular, but once Mike decided that the public were buying something that he considered to be rubbish, he became almost evangelical in his disregard for them. My belief has always been that it's not for me to decide what should be in the charts. By definition, it's the public who make up their minds for themselves. Mike had previously agreed and had been fully prepared to give the public their due, while using someone else's success to spur us on to make us do what we did even better. But he had a serious problem with Ace Of Base's 'All That She Wants'. He thought it was a bad record and I thought it was a bad record, but the public liked it enough to buy it in copious amounts. Mike, however, couldn't stand it and seemed to see its popularity as a personal public affront. Things went from bad to worse and, inevitably, Mike left too, to form his own production company called Love This. Knowing what I do now, I can see that what I thought was a genuine friendship was far more businesslike on their side than I'd ever imagined, but I still think that as a team we worked incredibly well. Matt and Mike remain two of the most talented people I've ever known.

There was another shock to come. I got into the office one day in 1993 and found a solicitor's letter from Mike and Matt saying that I had no right selling part of the company because they each owned a third of it. This was news to me, because there was no way I would have just given away a third of the company that I'd put all the money into to anyone else. A few solicitors' letters flew back and forth and the friendship between us was suddenly blown out of the water.

For a while I heard no more about their complaint, until I was informed that they were taking me to court about my right to sell 50 per cent of the record company to Warner. It would take until 1999 before the case finally came to court. It was horrible that a relationship I'd believed to be so strong had come to an end, but in fact I'd felt the first body blow to my perception of our friendship at the end of 1992. Matt and Mike wanted to get their copyrights back from publishing. The only way I could help them was to lease the catalogue to somebody and then the copyright could return to them, so I did a publishing deal with BMG that was the biggest publishing deal in British history for three writers. We signed the deal in front of loads of lawyers just before Christmas and it was enormous, but afterwards we only went for half a pint in a pub, then the two of them went off to a restaurant. I went back to my flat with cod, chips, peas, a Diet Pepsi and a cheque with more noughts than you can imagine. And it felt tragic.

I sat there on my own, and I burned the cheque.

All I could think was that for the best part of a decade we'd been three guys taking on the world and now it had gone so sour that we couldn't even go out and have a meal together to celebrate the enormous publishing deal we'd just done and which had helped them out enormously. I was thinking that if I'd given a £50 note to a tramp in the street, he would at least have said thank you, but this just seemed to show that something had gone horribly wrong with a relationship that had been important to me.

I felt as if over the past ten years I'd lived in a fairy story. We'd had made more hit records than the Beatles, and had dominated the industry beyond our wildest dreams, and we weren't even civil enough to each other to go out for a meal. It was horrible.

The financial situation of the company being what it was, I later got the money back for the cheque I burned, but that night had shown me that I'd been horribly misguided about my friendship with Matt and Mike. It was bitterly disappointing to realise that they hadn't enjoyed being part of the fairy story as much as I had.

I'd taken the money from Warner to take the strain off the company, keep the employees in a job and take PWL back to doing what we did best, making great pop records. It may have been a naive belief, but it was genuine. If Warner had permitted me to do what I wanted to do I could have turned the company round and made a profit, but it wasn't going to happen.

In 1995 David Howells resigned, and Warners brought in Peter Price, the guy I'd worked with on Musical Youth all those years earlier. They asked him to do his own A&R, which seemed a ridiculous decision since my track record had proved that I was patently the most successful A&R man in the past twenty-five years of the record industry. They might as well have just told me to get lost altogether, since by giving A&R policymaking to someone else they were effectively excluding me from running my own record company. I was perplexed about what role they actually saw for me in the company.

The thing was that, since Warner had been involved and despite the brick walls that constantly seemed to be built in front of me, I had continued to have hits with acts like Opus III, Urban Shakedown and Salt'n'Pepa. They had never been able to entirely shackle my motivation and ability to make hit records. And one of the biggest successes, although one of the least proportionately profitable, was 2 Unlimited. While the Warner years were overshadowed for me by frustration, I'm proud at least of what I did with 2 Unlimited.

In 1991 I'd been doing *The Hitman And Her* at a club called Liberty's in Sale, near Manchester. The place was absolutely rammed and the DJ was a guy I'd known years earlier from my roadshow days in Liverpool. He was announcing me to the crowd and the music he used to introduce me was a mad techno fanfare. I was straight over to the decks asking him what it was and he said it was a track by a band called 2 Unlimited called 'Get Ready For This' on Bite Records, a Dutch label. I was straight on the phone to a friend of mine in Holland called Tony, asking him to track the band down, talking away on the phone as the DJ was still introducing me. Tony knew already that I had to contact Ton Van De Leer, the guy who ran the label. Within hours I was on the phone to Tony who told me that 'Get Ready For This' was actually a B-side. He played me the A-side and it was the most awful rap record I'd heard in my life, so I just bought the B-side and told him he could sell the A-side to anyone he wanted, but it certainly wasn't going to be me.

It only cost us £1,000 to buy the track and the whole deal was done within four hours of me hearing it for the first time. I loved it, but when I took it into the office on the Monday morning, everybody in the office told me they thought it was rubbish. I wasn't going to be dissuaded so we put it out and even formed our own little company called Black Diamond (a nod to the black diamond on the PWL logo) to promote it. It caught the public's imagination instantly and suddenly everyone was playing it.

There was no such group as 2 Unlimited in terms of anything to present visually to the public, but the Dutch got a duo in to front the track, Ray and Anita. They looked really good and I knew that this wasn't just going to be a novelty record. These guys were going to be pop stars, and I knew we were going to take it further. The journalists started calling them 2 Untalented, and berating them for not making some serious socially aware music, which just inspired me to make them even more successful. 2 Unlimited weren't supposed to be deep, they were just two kids dancing and as two kids dancing went, it was fantastic.

Come the second single, 'Twilight Zone', the musicians behind the group sent me another rap record, so yet again I just took the rap off and put out the instrumental version. It was another big success. The same thing kept on happening for the next three singles of theirs that we put out during 1992, climaxing in their biggest hit 'No Limit'. They'd keep sending me rap records and I'd take the rap off and release the instrumental. No one said anything, that's just what I did and they were selling so many records they weren't about to complain. Ray did send me a clog once with 'Now you'll let me rap on the next record, yes?' written on it, but I just sent him a bottle of champagne back with 'No I won't' on it. The 2 Unlimited records soundtracked the world that year and wherever you went, even if it was a beach in Australia or the top of a mountain, you'd hear their records.

Of course, when the whole craze had faded, suddenly Warner were inundating me with requests to come up with 'something like 2 Unlimited', even though it was they who'd turned down the option to license them all over the world in the first place. That was so typical of how slowly a big company could respond to pop cultural trends. Ton Van De Leer got all his rights back and made enough money from the band to set himself up for life, which I'm the first to congratulate him for. He should be celebrated for being open-minded enough to realise that pop music isn't brain surgery, it's a piece of fun.

The Warner period, 2 Unlimited excepted, was an un-creative part of my life. For the first year or so we still had the last vestiges of the old PWL, but gradually other people from the company stopped asking my opinion about any-thing. The general opinion seemed to be that the company was no longer mine, it belonged to Warner. And in many ways that was true. I remember having a conversation with people at the company about an album that we were supposed to put out, warning against certain marketing decisions. Then I went away for a week and when I came back I found that everything I'd told them not to do, they'd done. It was hard to stay motivated when that sort of thing was going on, so I retreated into my office and played with my trains for the next two years. It just wasn't fun any more.

Eventually in March 1996, the day I'd been expecting came and I was politely told that I should resign. I was to sell the remaining 50 per cent of the record company to Warner and they would take PWL Records in house to their offices in Kensington. Pretty soon they changed the PWL name to Coalition Recordings International, which I was perfectly happy about since they'd signed some very ordinary acts, and at least I didn't have to have my name associated with them. Coalition Recordings lost an awful lot of money before it finally folded a year later.

I didn't care about walking away from PWL Records, because I'd never wanted a record company in the first place, but what I did care about was that this was the only time in my career that I'd lost anybody money. I felt utterly embarrassed about letting down Ramon Lopez because while I didn't particularly care about the money, I do care about my reputation and I'd been trusted to do a job by Ramon which I hadn't been able to do. It was the first time that I had ever done any sort of a deal with a record company where I hadn't been able to deliver what I wanted. The whole of the Warner experience should have been the best opportunity I'd ever had in my life, but it became creatively suffocating. There was no point in carrying on.

I remember the day I resigned. I was angry with myself for letting Ramon down, but I knew that I wasn't just going to come to a shuddering halt in the industry. I came back to my offices and rounded up the people that had really stood by me and told them that I wouldn't blame them for going off and taking any jobs that had been offered to them at Warner because I knew that at that moment I couldn't better any of those job offers. A core of people told me that they appreciated that I'd looked after them over the past few years and said that they would stick by me. They asked me what I was going to do.

'I don't know yet,' I said, 'but I'll think of something.' I went off to another room, came back a few minutes later and said, 'Right, I've got an idea.'

I'd heard from Brian Scholfield, who'd vouched for me to the leasing company when PWL had first started. He'd been working in America and had returned to the UK to become Financial Director at VCI, a distribution company. He was looking to build up the pop copyright side of the company and was interested in doing a joint venture. His company were also doing the merchandising for Manchester United Football Club, and knowing that I knew people at the club he'd asked if I'd be interested in making the official single for the club to celebrate their getting to the FA Cup Final.

That day I decided to do it and so, while my contract with Warner ended on 1 April 1996, a few weeks later I recorded a single with Manchester United and contributed to rebranding an entire football club. A month later the single had sold 400,000 records and was Number Six in the charts.

I was back.

15 The Locomotion

O NE OF THE few good things to come out of my exclusion
from my own company during the Warner period was
that I got to spend more time devoted to trains.
Trains, as everyone knows, have been, along with music, the
real passion of my life, as exciting to me as drugs are to
others. Whereas many people in the music industry get their
kicks from cocaine, I only have to go off and look at a train I
haven't seen before to make me excited. I've collected model
railways from about 1960 and in the early seventies I had a
desire to expand into the real thing and preserve what I saw
as a disappearing lifestyle. I could see even then that people
were perceiving rail travel completely differently from how it
had been in the fifties. The advent of the motorways had
completely changed the way we viewed the infrastructure of
transport in this country, which struck me as a shame. I've
always believed that unless you understand your past, there's
no way you can ever go forward properly, and unless you
acknowledge the social and economic order of the past,
you're just going to spiral off into a world where tradition
counts for nothing. And in my opinion that makes for a world
where people forget about the importance of their fellow
man. That might sound overblown, but I genuinely feel that
the world I grew up in had a lot going for it. The railways,
particularly the integrity and the honour of the men who
worked on them, have always been something I've looked up
to.

I'd been a trustee of Pendon Museum in Oxfordshire for
some time. The museum had preserved, in the Vale of the

White Horse, what Britain had been like in the thirties, and I thought what they had done was fantastic. I decided that I wanted to be involved in something similar, but with rather more breadth. I'd already had experience with model railways of creating a snapshot from time, in the form of a 214-foot-long replica of Acton railway junction in the 1890s, a pivotal location for the development of industry in this country. I'd set that up in a barn behind my house and was very proud of it. But I knew that I wanted something more.

The model trains available in the past were simply too small for kids to appreciate just how wonderful they were as miracles of engineering, so in the late seventies, with the money I'd earned from working with John Travolta, I'd started a company called Models and Leisure with two people, Ron Cadman and Barry Jones. We used a brand new technique called photo-etching and married it to white-metal casting, a process that only railway modellers are interested in, but suffice to say we took the hobby forward by twenty years overnight. It created a revolution within the modelling trade and took the quality of the market up by at least 75 per cent. Suddenly the average modeller could look like a really great modeller because of what we'd done – which I suppose you could say is what I later went and did with the record industry. There were certainly parallels in that we bought all our own equipment to ensure that what we did was of the highest quality and we did bring a 'pop' element in terms of packaging to what had been a relatively staid pastime.

All this was being developed at the same time as I was working my way up through the record industry, but I've always been prepared to work seven days a week so for a couple of years I managed to juggle the two enterprises. Eventually records started to take up all my time so I had to give up the modelling company, but I was glad that I'd played my part.

I was still passionate about trains though, and as I got more successful, I realised that I wanted to be involved in something bigger and came up with the idea of opening a museum dedicated to 100 years of rail travel from 1890 using larger-scale model trains that take up to three years each to build. This was in 1985 and I was thinking about opening up the museum in the year 2000, so you can see that it was very much a long-term project.

In the early nineties I got a chance to devote a lot more time to trains. I was on *Start The Week* on Radio 4 and one of my fellow guests was Sir Peter Parker, the Chairman of British Rail, and we got talking about my interest in railway preservation, something I'd been committed to for thirty years. Most of those railways had been concerned with preserving steam engines, but by the end of the eighties and the beginning of the nineties, there were no steam trains left for people to buy, unless they were prepared to devote years and years to restoring them. I was actually more interested in diesel engines on an aesthetic and engineering level. I don't know why, but I've always found them to be even more beautiful than steam engines, perhaps because when I was growing up it was the diesels that I used to see going past the back of my house.

Hearing of my interest in diesels I got a phone call from the East Lancashire Railway organisation in Bury, who were looking for someone to help with running a diesel on a length of restored track running out of Bury. I was interested in playing a part so I rang around trying to see where I could buy a loco, eventually getting help from a friend of mine. He took me down to Derby to the Stores Officer who sold redundant stock and I found out that I could buy a railway engine for ten thousand quid! I'd thought it would be at least ten times that much, so I came away determined not just to buy one, but to buy loads. I was all ready to buy, but then the deal fell through, so I asked Sir Peter Parker for his help. To his credit he came through for me and he put me in touch with another guy at Derby who told me he had a train I might be interested in. Funnily enough, it was one that had been mentioned to me by someone else a few days earlier, and which I was trying to track down, a train with the grand name of 25-909 – which just happened to be the last engine ever built in Manchester. It had been offered to the Science Museum, but they'd turned it down, so I managed to get it for £15,000 plus VAT and it was promptly delivered to the East Lancs Railway. I caused a commotion by telling them I wanted it painted in two-tone green, as it had originally been, rather than in British Rail blue.

At the time I'd been too busy to ever go and see it more than a couple of times, but by '94 I had a lot more time to think about buying additional trains. I was aware that for some reason everyone wanted pre-war trains and that those from the fifties and sixties were just being left to rot, which was a tragedy. It was up to those of us from the rock'n'roll generation to ensure that our memories of what the railways had been like when we were growing up would be preserved. The National Railway Museum in York weren't interested in that part of Britain's history at the time, but the way I saw it, if it hadn't been for the electrification of the railway line between Crewe and London I could never have become a millionaire because I could never have commuted. Electrification had pushed the commuter belt into the Midlands, so I owed a lot to those engines and now they were being scrapped. I had to do something about it, particularly since the technology involved seemed, and still seems to me today, a thing we should be championing as a nation. Trains basically started as glorified kettles and we've managed to make them aesthetically beautiful. Surely that's something to be proud of?

The rail industry has also been at the heart of making people's working lives better, in terms of it being at the forefront of safety issues and the establishment of a decent working wage. It was on the railways that all those things were first introduced.

So I decided to collect everything that the National Railway Museum didn't want – which meant diesels and electrics and just about everything that British Rail was scrapping from the fifties and sixties. By the mid-nineties I must have had 35 engines and coaches, and thanks to my collection we've preserved one of every first generation of electrics produced in this country, an archive that would have just been left to rust otherwise. People thought I was a crackpot at the time, but I hope now they can see what a mistake it would have been to have just abandoned a vital part of our national heritage.

In about 1993 I was approached by Tony Moseley of the Crewe Heritage Centre, a railway museum, who asked me if I would take my locos there. I was only too happy to do so, since they had workshops, and it was costing me an arm and a leg just to keep the trains in any sort of nick. Plus Crewe, along with Swindon, is arguably the railway capital of the world.

When I went down to visit the museum, though, it didn't take me long to realise that the place was in real trouble. It was run down, the council had withdrawn their support and the whole place was in total chaos. As a result I got involved with the place and became chairman of the Crewe Heritage Trust.

At the same time, the government announced the privatisation of British Rail and I got interested in the idea of running my trains back on the main lines as a kind of heritage excursion service. This meant that I became very involved in the mechanics of how British Rail worked. I'd originally been opposed to privatisation, but as I began to understand how the company worked I started to think that the quicker they privatised the whole thing, the better. There were some fantastic managers around, but there was also so much money being wasted and so much political intriguing going on. I soon became aware that some people would help me, people who understood how important an institution the railway industry was and who really wanted it to work. And then there were others who were determined to stop me at all costs, people who didn't want anyone coming along trying to change the nice little earners that they'd set up for themselves. I went in there like a bull in a china shop and it must have terrified them, because they couldn't bully me. There were certain basic engineering standards that had to be adhered to and I had the money to make sure everything about my trains was in order, even if they tried to break me by redefining standards just to put me off. We accepted that railway standards would be constantly changing as soon as Railtrack was formed after privatisation, and agreed to abide by the rules of what would basically be an ever-moving set of goalposts. But I naively expected that the rules would always be there primarily to avoid any problems with safety rather than simply to put up barriers against people like me. I was wrong.

I remember an occasion when I was taken to task because the brakes on one of my locos wouldn't self-adjust, this despite the fact that we'd had the whole braking system rebuilt by British Rail engineers in Crewe. We had to get one of the engineers in to prove that the brakes on the engine had never self-adjusted in the first place when it was running for British Rail. The rules were being used as ammunition for victimisation, and we came across that sort of thing time and time again, even though we'd put huge amounts of money into our trains, sometimes up to £150,000 on each loco, and they were in better condition than anything currently in service. They tried to wear us down, but we weren't going to be beaten and eventually they had to concede that we had a right to run the trains.

By now I'd become involved with Sir William McAlpine. He was involved with the Steam Loco Owners' Association, the organisation in charge of running all the steam trains on the railways along with the British Rail Special Trains Unit. Because I was running diesel trains, I was invited to liaise with him as part of a tripartite organisation. It was like the old school tie network of the railways. Bill McAlpine wanted to sell the Flying Scotsman which to any train fan would be a dream, although I didn't much like it myself, but I agreed to invest in half of it because I admired all the work that he'd done for steam trains. Being part of that deal put me in a position where not only was I seen as something of a player in the privatisation of the network, but I was also privy to all the deals that were going on.

One day I got a phone call from Chris Green, who was the Managing Director of InterCity at that point, asking me if I would be interested in buying the Special Trains Unit, the company in charge of chartering trains for things like football specials, royal trains and all other trains that weren't on the official timetable. He offered to sell me the STU for a pound.

In the past I'd found Chris to be one of the finest executives I'd ever met. He was straight talking and never tried to hide anything or pull the wool over your eyes, and you knew when you were dealing with him that you could trust him. Most importantly he seemed to be a railwayman in the old sense of the word, in that his prime concern was to get the passengers from A to B and make their journey as safe and comfortable as possible. These days it's a rarity to find many people with that as their highest priority.

Chris wanted to see the Special Trains Unit protected, and he realised that in the privatisation that might not happen. That's why he'd come to me, and that's why I bought it.

You'd think that if you bought something from the government no one would try and swindle you, but I soon found out that the government and the civil service are sneakier than second-hand car salesmen. And it became clear that there were people within the industry who had begun to carve up the lucrative elements of the STU for themselves. That was why when the 1995 Railway Act was drawn up, the Special Trains Unit had not been protected by law, something that you would have thought would have been imperative for such an important branch of the operation.

In my view, the skulduggery that went on at the time was absolutely unbelievable. I'd seen things in the record business that took my breath away but the privatisation of the railways really shocked me. I just couldn't believe some of the things that went down. I tried to highlight what at best could be described as sharp practices to the people who I thought would care about what, after all, was a nationalised industry. I went to meetings where people were obviously being deceitful and witnessed first-hand the victory of greed over everything else when it came to breaking up the railways. When I was trying to borrow money from banks for investment in the railway privatisation, I was told that railways were a bad investment because they didn't make any money. Then, once all the major parts had been sold off, the banks swooped in to pick up the scraps, made an awful lot of money in two years and all sold at exactly the same time. When you love the railways as much as I do, and you see people making serious amounts of money by using information that no one else was supposed to know about, it's heartbreaking.

We've seen accidents at Paddington and Ladbroke Grove and my only surprise is that they have taken so long to happen. You can't take an industry where it takes a man fifteen years to become a train driver and then replace it with one where it only takes him fifteen months. You can't condense that much responsibility and knowledge; an accident is inevitable. And you can't run the railways as if they are just another branch of road travel. Different safety standards have to apply and you have to realise that railways were always run by people who understood the culture and the workings of their business with all the knowledge that that entails.

These days when people talk about what we call SPADS, Signals Passed At Danger, they talk of them as if they are traffic lights. SPADS are not like traffic lights, they're like precipices, and because the government is treating the industry like just another branch of road transport, they are incapable of seeing that vital difference.

I have no problem with the safety element when private companies are running the network because I know that the person at the head of each company is personally liable for any accidents that might happen, something that never happened under British Rail where all the managers were protected from liability by the government. That personal liability is as good an incentive as any to make sure standards are met. The thing that has to be understood is that you have to run each company with the same integrity and care as in the fifties and sixties. Competition is the only way that fares can be made cheaper, but people have to understand just how much money has to be invested into the infrastructure to make the railway network here as good as it is in, say, France. Over there they put three times the amount of our national debt into the railways every year.

After working with the Special Trains Unit I started my own company called London North Western, based in Crewe, which is in charge of overhauling and carrying out mainten- ance on coaches for other networks, and we have even stricter maintenance criteria than British Rail ever had. I bought the company because it was the biggest company in the world in 1929 and it was up for sale for fifty quid. I liked the idea of being chairman of a company which was once the biggest in the world and I'm pleased that it plays an important part in an industry that still remains closer to my heart than any other. It's only that private care for the railways that is ever going to make them great again in Britain.

There's far too little pragmatism around in the industry. People talk about new trains with swish carriages and then they raise the fares. No one asks if you would mind sitting in a refurbished seat for less money, if the company could then vow not to compromise on safety. I'm sure if fares came down then the general public would be only too pleased to stop using their cars and re-establish the railways as a vital, profitable service. The privateers have to look to what is acceptable as a profit, and every private company has to think about the wider picture in terms of the viable future of rail travel. It's entirely possible that with enough thought behind it all we could be about to re-enter a golden age of rail travel and I'd like to be a part of that. I know that by 2005, London North Western will be one of the most important companies in the railway network, which the multi-nationals will hate because when we started they just thought we were a bunch of trainspotters.

On top of that, the model train museum covering the history of the industry over the last hundred years that I planned back in 1985 is finally coming to fruition. We're looking for a couple of million pounds' Lottery funding to match the money we've invested, and by Easter 2001 it will be established on a very sound financial basis. We'll have over 300 model coaches – thirty complete trains over 17 feet long each – on exhibition, which will make it one of the largest exhibitions of its sort in the world, certainly the biggest in Britain.

When I was young and I used to sit behind my house watching the trains go by I never dreamt that I would end up owning some of them, nor that I would play such a part in the railway industry. I've achieved all the things I've ever wanted in music, and maybe in the future I can take my involvement with trains that little bit further, so I will be able to say I'll have achieved all the things I wanted with them too. I don't think I'll ever be remembered as a railwayman and I have no right to claim that, but I'd like to be remembered as a rail enthusiast who made some sort of positive contribution to the most fantastic industry, alongside music, that this country has ever had.

Maybe all that time spent playing with model trains won't be wasted after all.

16 Move, Move, Move

I 'VE HAD A CLOSE RELATIONSHIP WITH BOTH LIVERPOOL and Manchester United Football Clubs for a number of years. I know that fans of both teams would find it hard to believe that they both could have played such an important part in my life, because the two have a traditional rivalry, but I support Coventry *and* Walsall which, I think they'd agree, allows me to view them both with detached admiration.

My relationship with Liverpool Football Club began when I was doing my radio show in the city. Like so many people, I was shocked and saddened by the Hillsborough disaster in 1989 when 96 Liverpool fans died at an FA Cup semi-final in Sheffield. We decided to put together a charity record for the families of the bereaved, a cover version of 'Ferry Cross The Mersey', and got a lot of famous names in to contribute vocals. One of them was Paul McCartney, a man who remains a hero of mine all those years after the Beatles first got me excited about music. We got him into the studio and, of course, Mike and Matt were equally excited about him being there, although I have to confess that I might not have been at my most diplomatic during the recording session.

We were rushing to get all the vocals done and he seemed to be taking an awful long time preparing to sing. I shouted, 'Tell him to hurry up, we've got Holly Johnson coming in at six', trying to convince everyone that the ex-singer from Frankie Goes To Hollywood was as important as one of the Beatles to the whole process. To his credit, McCartney didn't take offence and did his vocals absolutely superbly. It was a performance that just made you tingle to hear it. He wasn't completely happy with it, because he reckoned that there was a bit in the middle where he was singing out of tune, but I've always valued pure emotion over technical perfection so I insisted we stick with the original take.

The next day I got a phone call from Paul's wife Linda, and she said that she'd heard the tape and loved his vocal on it, especially the bit where it went out of tune. And, like me, she thought the strength of the performance was in its raw emotion. She thanked me for being the first person in twenty years to stand up to Paul McCartney about his vocals, and that call from her is something I'll treasure for the rest of my life. As much as the fact that the record went straight to Number One.

The most important thing, of course, was that the record raised a lot of money and allowed me to show my support for the people who'd lost their loved ones in such a tragic way.

I went down to Anfield, Liverpool's ground, on the last day that the fans were allowed in to pay their respects and there was an enormous queue outside. When the fans saw who I was they picked me up and passed me along the queue, lifted me through the turnstiles and into the ground. There were thousands and thousands of flowers and the crowd were all hugging me and singing 'Ferry Cross The Mersey'. I cry just thinking about it now, and if anyone asked me what was the greatest moment of my life, I'd say that was it. Forget the money, the millions of record sales or anything else. It was those people hugging me that day and making me feel I'd been able to do something that helped ease some of their pain. It will always be the greatest moment of my life, whatever else I do.

There's obviously a strong bond with Liverpool, but I'm also close to a lot of people at Manchester United, particularly the directors and the manager, Alex Ferguson. Through my rail company, we always used to run the official train for the team bringing the FA Cup back after finals, so there'd been contact with the club for some time. When they wanted to record a single for the FA Cup Final in 1996, and my mate at VCI put my name up for it, they were happy to agree.

That record, called 'Move, Move, Move (The Red Tribe)', was actually to provide an impetus for what went on to be a very clever piece of identity-branding by United. When I'd thought about what sort of record to do in the first place, I'd decided that the very worst approach would be to fall back on that old-fashioned, woolly jumper sort of song that constituted so many football records. I wanted to do something dynamic, something fitting for a club of United's stature and I wanted to acknowledge that the club, while an institution, was forward-looking. The brief was basically to make a corporate record for a corporate club, which is where the idea for using the phrase 'Red Tribe' came from. And far cleverer people than me, people connected with the club's marketing and advertising departments, picked up on that by making things like Red Tribe beer and using the phrase on all sorts of merchandise.

I was also aware of that usual scenario with football records, where you get the team looking vaguely embarrassed as they mumble into a microphone and I decided that the only way to deal with the problem was to make a virtue of their awkwardness, so I made the single a techno record. You watched it and knew that it was absolutely the last thing that any of those players would normally consider singing, which made it all the more enjoyable. I remember one of the players, Steve Bruce, coming up to me and saying, 'I haven't a clue what all this is about, but I'm sure my kids will love it.' And that was exactly the reaction I wanted to achieve.

The most important thing the project gave me was a chance to re-establish myself, and the money that I could have accrued from holding the copyright to the phrase 'Red Tribe' was less important than the fact that I had rediscovered my enthusiasm.

United have done me favours in return, though, and perhaps their finest was when I flew back from a fishing trip in India to watch Walsall play United at Old Trafford in the FA Cup. Finding out that they'd won in the round before against Peterborough had involved bribing an Indian kid with a bottle of whisky to cycle miles out of the jungle to find out the result, and I had no way of rearranging my flight – which was due into England on the day of the match. I flew back from Bangalore to Heathrow and got the shuttle up to Manchester, leaving me twenty minutes to get to the ground before the match started, so I decided to call in some favours and put a phone call through to a well-known person at the club. I told him to hold the kick-off up for five minutes, and to their credit he did! I got to the ground, sat in my seat and gave him a wave. He gave the nod to the referee, the teams kicked off and I hadn't missed a second. Walsall got walloped of course, but it was worth doing the record if only to get the kick-off delayed just for me.

And so it was that in May 1996 I was suddenly taken from the despair of being ousted by my own record company to being given a new sense of focus. I decided to build a new team around me, starting with my old mate Steve Jenkins from Walsall, whose company, Impulse, had done the promotion to the record shops for all the Stock, Aitken and Waterman records. Impulse had been bought by Zomba Records and Steve had become MD there. I'd done Big Fun and Samantha Fox for him in the eighties, so our careers had been locked together for many years. I brought Impulse in to work on anything I made, but insisted that Steve came as part of the package. I'd regenerated my interest in making records and was expecting money from the Manchester United record that would be the first step of rolling my involvement with them into something bigger.

That was until I realised that the money I'd invoiced them for didn't seem to be being paid. I was eventually told that Brian Scholfield, who'd given me the job in the first place, had left the company, but that there was no need for me to worry. I believed them, but weeks went by and no cheque arrived, so we finally realised that we weren't going to get paid. And to cap it all the bank, who had extended me quite a few facilities, suddenly got a new manager who announced that he hated all my records and didn't think I'd ever sell another one again. You'd think I'd be about to give up after all that, but the thought never entered my head. I had total conviction that things would turn out well and that something would come along to excite me. It sounds arrogant, but I knew I still had great things to do.

I was talking with Steve one day and he asked me why I hadn't thought about just retiring and enjoying the money I'd earned over my life. It was a concept that I found completely incomprehensible, since what I enjoy doing is working and to stop doing what I enjoy wouldn't make any sense. He asked me what I wanted to do.

'I want hits,' I said. 'And if you think I was successful before, just wait and see what I'm capable of next.'

So Steve suggested we work together and that I do a joint deal with Zomba. It was amazing that we hadn't thought of doing it before, but now the idea had been proposed it seemed increasingly exciting. I asked Steve to agree to just one condition, which was that if I told him black was green or that water flowed upwards, he had to trust me. I'd delivered in the past when people thought I was mad, and all I was asking was a total trust in my ideas. I wanted him to back me 100 per cent, even when everyone else thought I was wrong. It was important for me to know that I had the protection of his support and we'd had such a good relationship over the years that I knew I could ask him. He agreed. The Manchester United record had shown that when people just let me get on with what I was doing, I could come up with good records very easily, but when people started shoving their oars in, I just didn't feel like I was doing my job properly. I knew that it would take me a while to focus properly and I was thinking in terms of eighteen months from the summer of '96 for everything to come together, but I also knew that it would only work if I was given total control over my ideas. If that made me a dictator, then so be it, but I knew that it was the only way the future was going to work. Throughout my career, the best things I've done have come from being the person who had the final say.

I don't think of myself as dictatorial, because I do take on board other people's ideas, it's just that before I do so I like to have a shouting match with people just to see if they're able to stand their ground. If they can't then there's no point in even considering their ideas in the first place. It's those arguments that make relationships stronger and make people really think hard about what they're suggesting, and while it might sound brutal, experience has shown me that it's the only way to work effectively. When someone comes to me with an idea and knows we're going to have a shouting match, they come along having already prepared in their head what I'm going to object to and how they'll respond. So they think a little bit more to try and counter the argument that hasn't even started yet, and that results in any suggestions being properly thought out. From there on the arguments over a record are nailed down to very precise points, and without realising it, they've done most of the hard work for you. I get accused of bullying people, but it's not out of any mean-spiritedness, it's to see just what kind of integrity and self-belief they have. I want to see if they are as honest and as open as I am, because I've learned over the years that if you lie to yourself when you make a record, you are lying to the audience and the kids pick that up immediately. That's why throughout my career I have maintained that I'm not making the records I want, I'm making the records the public wants. It's as simple as that.

So many records in the charts these days sell a certain amount through marketing and promotion, but then, after the hype, they bomb. That is because the kids can recognise dishonesty more astutely than anyone else. People think that pop records are about 'moon' and 'June' and 'croon' and 'soon'. They're not. They're about real feelings, about passion and anxiety and hope and hard work. You don't put in those ingredients, you don't sell millions. We've got to say 'I love you' or 'I hate you' or 'come back' or 'go away', and we have to do that day in and day out. If you don't communicate that with honesty then you are betraying the kids who have bought the songs, because they mean something to them and they'll punish you for it by losing faith in what you do. I know that if I've made an honest record, it's invincible. Integrity sells and it sells a lot. I knew that while I'd made some great pop records in the past I was capable of doing even better in the future, so right from the off the idea of the partnership with Zomba for a new label, which we had decided to call Ebul, was very exciting. And I was sure that there were talented people out there who we could make into stars.

The first act we signed was Tina Cousins. She'd sent a demo tape to me and became the first person in the whole of my career that I've signed just from a demo tape. She'd sent her photo in too and, if the truth be told, I think the rest of the team wanted to sign her because, basically, they fancied her. She had a great voice and when she came into the office we got on really well and I could see she had real potential. Other commitments, however, meant that we had to keep her on the back burner for a while.

A band called Kaleef who were just about to leave London Records also approached me. They were an Asian rap act and they had an idea for a track using the Stranglers' song 'Golden Brown', but they couldn't get it to work. As soon as I heard it I knew exactly how to combine the rap and the rolling riff from 'Golden Brown', so I got them in the studio and we put the record together without any trouble. It went into the Top Twenty, and was a big hit in Europe.

I had got my excitement back about making records, and we picked up several new acts. The soap star Will Mellor was a short-term project, and I also did some consultancy work with the Backstreet Boys, coming up with many ideas about mixing pop with rock riffs that they later went on to use. I was itching to make records, but it seemed that as soon as I came up with an idea it would be cloned by major labels before we could even get the records out. I was beginning to detect a ruthlessness that I'd never experienced to date, and realised that the majors who'd shunned us before were now trying to compete at last, albeit with watered-down versions of our ideas.

I knew that there was only one way for us to go, and that was to wholeheartedly celebrate making great commercial records. For the last year I'd been telling everyone I met that while I had been successful in the past, that would be nothing compared to what I would do in the future. Now was the time to stop messing around and start proving it.

Steve Jenkins came to me one day in early 1997 and told me about a band that a mutual friend of ours, Tim Byrne, was managing, called Steps. They'd arranged for an audition at Zomba Records and wanted me to go along and have a look at them. I asked him what sort of music they were making and he told me they were line-dancers, which is just about the last thing to tell me if you want to pitch me an idea. I've never understood the appeal of Country and Western, and line-dancing didn't seem to me like the way forward for my renewed desire to make commercial records.

Anyway, since Tim was a mate, I agreed to check them out and went along to the audition. And what I saw blew me away.

Steps looked nothing like they do now. There was absolutely no thought of having an image or anything, so they just looked like a bunch of dancers, which is basically what they were. But they did this song called '5,6,7,8' which sounded to me like 'I Should Be So Lucky', but speeded up. Nevertheless, they were quite engaging, with a nifty little dance routine, and I immediately understood exactly what they were – they were Abba on speed.

The song itself didn't sound much good, but you could see that there was something there that was worth working on. I immediately thought they were great, because they had a vitality and enthusiasm that I'd found missing from the pop world at the time. And I had to admit that they were very accomplished at the choreography they were doing. After they'd finished I immediately went off on one, organising for them to come to the studio the following Saturday and saying I knew exactly what I wanted to do with them. As happens so often when I get excited about something, I'd just stopped listening to what anyone else was saying and so I hadn't really picked up on the story behind the song that they'd just played me. It wasn't just a demo as I'd thought, it was actually a finished record. And I later found out that they hadn't come straight to me with it, but had also been to see lots of other people in the industry, too.

I went back to the office and played it to Karl and Mark, two incredibly talented jazz-funk musicians who had become part of my regular team after I worked with them on the Man-U single, and they thought I'd taken leave of my senses. They told me they thought it was rubbish, but I insisted that, with a bit of work, it was a hit record. I was sick of people being afraid to make straightforward commercial records and I knew that this was a smash. I told Mark and Karl to modernise it, first by taking out the obvious Stock, Aitken and Waterman sound, because that was now a sound from the past. We discussed how to give it more of a contemporary production and they did it, having come up with the fantastic idea of getting a banjo player and a fiddle player on it.

However, they refused to even have their name on it, as if it was something they didn't want to admit to. I disagreed; I thought it was something to be proud of, because more than anything I wanted a hit. It was all very well for me to be getting accolades for records I'd made ten years earlier, but the bottom line was that I was The Hitman and I wanted to start selling records again.

I had complete faith in the song being a smash, but still everyone I played it to thought it was terrible. They were just being so snobbish! I knew that my mother-in-law, who was into line-dancing, would love it and I knew that my kids who were aged eight and six would love it. No matter what anyone else thought I was going to put it out.

When it was released, it got just about the strangest reaction I've ever experienced. People loved it, but seemed to think that it was nothing more than a novelty record. We had a launch party at the Atlantic Bar in London and everyone from the radio and TV stations had a great time, told me how much they liked the song and then added that of course there was no way they could feature it on their programmes because it was just a throwaway novelty.

To be honest, it might have all fallen apart there, had it not been for a phone call I received from Anthony H. Wilson, the TV presenter and ex-boss of Factory Records. Tony and I go back many years and he's always known that if he wants someone to spout off some opinion that will get up people's noses, he can rely on me. He was hosting a late night TV discussion programme where the topic was line-dancing and he knew that the only way to make the show controversial would be to have me on it. He knew that there was a massive craze for line-dancing, but had to find a new angle on discussing it, so we agreed that I'd go on and he'd accuse me of raping and pillaging the movement with my Steps record. That sounded like manna from heaven to me.

I appeared on the show and the audience was packed with Country and Western fans. Tony had really chucked me into the fray; I think the first half of the programme was about child molesting, the second half about line-dancing. I was only too happy to play the part of the evil record producer cashing in on the craze for line-dancing, especially since we managed to get Steps to play twice on the same show. They came on at the beginning and did the song, then later on someone in the audience said, just to be controversial, that the dance Steps did for the song was far too energetic for the over-fifties who made up most of the line-dancing aficionados. Now that turned the whole thing around and the crowd wanted to prove that while they may not have been in their first flush of youth, they were more than capable of dancing to '5,6,7,8'. So we got Steps on again and they all danced to it. Suddenly I had gone from being the villain of the piece to the hero who was going to take their cult pastime overground.

From then on we got loads of TV exposure for the band, but the radio stations were still really snobby and wouldn't touch it. It got to Number Fourteen in the charts, but was our biggest selling song never to make the Top Ten. We even got them on *Blue Peter* and when they'd done it, my girls, Toni and Charlie, came to me and said they'd seen it and started copying the dance. When they did that, I knew Steps were going to be big, although I have to say that even I didn't realise just how huge they would become.

17 Steptacular

STEPS' GREATEST STRENGTH WAS THAT THEY came across as lovely people who looked like they were enjoying themselves, and that fitted perfectly with my notion of them as Abba on speed. Tim Byrne used to describe them as Mixed Spice, which was his take on their image, but the idea of a techno Abba seemed far more appropriate to me. It was obvious that they were a lot more than just a bunch of line-dancers, but without my contribution I don't think they would have become the phenomenon that they are. It was the combination of my ideas, plus the manager's ideas, plus the songs that we had up our sleeve for them and also the dynamism of Zomba that launched Steps into the public consciousness.

Steps were my vision. Tim had the plan for what he wanted from them stage-wise and in the videos, but that side of things is something I've never involved myself in. Musically, nobody else except me and my team had any input into Steps.

I ran Steps ruthlessly right from the start. I wanted to make sure that no ideas got leaked, that everything was documented and that only Karl, Mark and I knew what we were doing with the band. This time I wanted everything done my way and it was.

I've always been a fan of Abba from right when they started in the early seventies and had tried to bring together a project with Bananarama called 'Abba Banana', which should have come to something for the title alone. It was going to involve Bananarama singing Abba-type songs, and

Matt, Mike and I had written the lyrics for 'Last Thing On My Mind' and 'Movin' On' for it, but for various reasons it all fell through. This was way before everyone started to get into Abba; in fact that whole fashion for them came out of me playing Abba records on *The Hitman and Her*, especially a gay disco Abba medley. Within two years everyone was back into Abba again, but only on a retro level, and I could see by 1997 that the time was right for someone to do a new version of the band.

We'd worked earlier that year with a group of girls from Sweden called Solid Harmonie who went on to make up part of the Honeyz, and maybe that had refocused my mind onto Abba, but whatever the case, when Steps came along I knew exactly what I wanted them to be.

I got Mark and Karl to come up with a tune for 'One For Sorrow' and when I heard what they'd made of it, I knew that Steps were going to be massive. It had these great little hooks in it and, once Tim Byrne and I heard it for the first time, we both knew we'd got the song that would push Steps through the roof. When I saw the dance that went with it, I couldn't imagine it not being a big hit. Funnily enough no one else I played it to seemed to be able to get it, but I knew the public would, because it was such a great, honest pop record. When we released it in April 1998, it went to Number Two in the charts and launched Steps towards where they are now.

Seven months later I went to Manchester Apollo and saw 3,000 kids jumping up and down and dancing to it, doing the whole routine along with the band. That was exactly how I'd pictured it the first time I ever heard the song. A year later the same thing happened at the Manchester Evening News Arena, only this time there were 10,000 people dancing along, reacting to the record just like I'd done when I'd first heard the Four Tops thirty years earlier. It was a fantastic vindication of what I'd known Steps could be.

The band always get a fantastic reaction in the North West of England and that's because the sound and the spirit that I'd brought to the Steps records was consciously influenced by my own interaction with the pop music that had been popular in the North West for the past thirty years. It was a celebratory sound that was supposed to make you feel like letting your hair down and jumping on the tables and dancing, and throughout my career I've found that Northern audiences are far more responsive to that kind of carefree impulse. Of course, Steps are incredibly popular in the South as well, and have done more gigs at Wembley than any other band, but up North the audience's reaction is indisputably more abandoned.

Steps were making music for everyone's party and what they were bringing to the party was a combination of Abba and Motown by way of Northern Soul. They were part of a definite lineage and that was why I knew they would work. Despite having one of my favourite pop songs of all time, 'Wannabe', the Spice Girls seem to me to be nothing more than a brilliant demonstration of marketing. This is how they differ from Steps, who are a group of people, not a brand. Nobody can deny the Spice Girls' enormity, but I wonder how successful they would have been if their record company hadn't made them into quite such high-profile media figures. And while I'm in the business of hype myself, I think the way that the Spice Girls have been hyped has been just a little too excessive. Maybe if more faith had been put in the songs themselves they could have gone on to be even bigger than they were, and lasted for longer. They obviously copied the Stock, Aitken and Waterman formula, but just spent millions more doing it than we ever did, and because they used so many different writers and producers they just came up with a watered-down version.

I always wanted Steps to be perceived as a cohesive group rather than a collection of individuals, and there was always the danger of them going down the road of being just a load of caricatures, like the Spice Girls. We all did our best to resist that and I'm sure that because they're seen as a group above all else, that has contributed to their success. It doesn't stop them all having different personalities, but they don't ram those different personalities down the audience's throats. Of all the big pop bands around, I think Steps seem the most genuine. The audience knows that the band are honest about what they are doing and it's that honesty that gives them their credibility, something that marketing alone can never achieve.

For instance, when Bruce Springsteen's record company were marketing *Born In The USA* with all sorts of posters proclaiming him the 'saviour of rock'n'roll', it seemed so over-the-top that for two whole years it put me off realising what a genius he actually is.

Everything I've done with Steps since I first saw them has been done to make them as successful as they can possibly be. And, as with my whole career, if that means that someone else comes along with a song that is better than mine I have absolutely no problem with that. We've never advertised for songwriters to pitch their songs, because, like I say, the vision behind the band mustn't be diluted. If I hear a song that fits into the vision of where Steps are going, then I'll use it, but if someone comes along to me and tells me what *they* want Steps to be, I'm not interested.

Although I personally only wrote four songs on the first Steps album, every single moment on the record came from the initial vision of what they were about. No Steps song gets past me unless it gives me goosebumps and, most importantly, it has to tell a story, it can't just be a collection of words that rhyme. I could write a song for, for example, Christina Aguilera in thirty seconds because, for me at least, there's nothing there, it's just ether. I know full well that she's not going to be able to make twenty great singles. As a songwriter I'm in the business of making the listener smile or heartbroken, all in the space of two or three minutes, like a pop version of Catherine Cookson; so there has to be something real at the heart of the song.

Steps' 'Better, Best Forgotten' is a good example of this way of thinking. The inspiration for the song came when I was walking across the office and someone used the phrase 'better best forgotten' which I immediately thought would make a great title. Then I had to think about what the story behind it would be and I imagined someone coming back from being away and their partner asking them what had happened while they were gone. The other person would be telling them that they didn't want to know because if they did they would be heartbroken. So there was the story, and the payoff, and from then it was easy to build the whole song.

I get people coming along to me with songs that they've written and when I ask them what the song is about, they're surprised that the song has to be 'about' anything at all. They think they can just throw in a few rhymes and have a hit, but of course it's far harder than that.

When writing pop songs, I've always had one hundred per cent faith in the audience's intelligence, their ability to cut through the hype and discriminate, but it doesn't seem like that faith is shared by many other people in the industry any more. There are more quick-buck merchants around now than I've known in all the years I've been working in the business, people who are only interested in ripping the heart out of any idea that comes along and then running off with the cash. And it's that attitude which destroys creativity.

Steps should be proud of what they've achieved. There's a lot of competition, but they do what they do so much better than anyone else. In H, they've got one of the friendliest guys I've ever met, a kid who still says hello to every single person in the studio or office when he comes in. He's never forgotten how he felt when he came into the studio in the first place, and on stage he communicates that loveable personality, like Buttons in a pantomime. He has always been something of a focus for the group, but throughout the past three years there has never been one member who you would call the leader. Or, rather, there has been a different leader every week. Claire, for example, was very quiet when she started, but she's blossomed as the group has gone on and now has one of the greatest character-filled pop voices around. I've always looked for voices with character, because that's what can make a good song a great one and she's definitely got it.

There have been rumours flying around that we paid the band a weekly wage, but the truth is that they have their own company and pay themselves salaries from it. Certain members of the group may spend their money rather more freely than others, but at the end of the day they each take an equal slice of the pie.

Financially they are just about the most successful act I've ever worked with. I'm glad that they've vindicated that vision I had for them when I first saw them doing their line-dance song at their audition for me.

18 Better The Devil You Know

I 'VE BEEN ON THE BOARD OF THE BPI, the body that polices and regulates the record industry, for many years. And although I've had my run-ins with the majors over the years, I've always respected the financial contribution they make to the industry which helps enforce anti-piracy legislation and the like. I've also done my best as a songwriter member of the organisation to stand up for and promote the rights of songwriters everywhere.

Songwriters in Britain get a terrible deal and it's a myth that you can write a hit and be set up for life. When Steps play in Britain, for example, the songwriters of 'One For Sorrow' get a pound a night each, a fifth of what they'd get in Europe and America. The guy who sells the whistles outside the venue gets £400, so live performances don't rake in the millions. And even if you write a song that gets played on the radio all the time, you still don't make enough for a life of luxury. I'm lucky in that I've written hits for so many years, but some people might only write one or two and then it's back to the job at the factory.

On top of that, the role of the songwriter has been treated with increasingly less respect. For example, we were recently approached to write a song for one of the major American divas, but refused when we learned that just for singing on the track she wanted fifty per cent of the credits. It's a scandalous state of affairs and I've always done my best to stick up for writers.

The BPI are also responsible for organising the Brit Awards, and in 1999 they approached me to come up with a finale for their televised awards show. I thought of paying tribute to Abba and put together a track called 'Thank Abba For The Music' to feature a whole host of stars including Steps, Tina Cousins, B*Witched, Cleopatra and Billie. It was done in a real rush and the whole thing was finished only an hour before the rehearsals for the show, but it turned out to be a real success. From that day to this, though, I haven't heard a word of thanks from anyone, or received a gold disc, despite the fact that the accompanying single went to Number Four in the charts.

At those same awards, Steps were confidently expected to pick up the gong for Best British Newcomer voted for by Radio One listeners. In fact, on the morning of the show I'd actually been told that Steps had won. However, come the evening and the award went to the indie band, Belle and Sebastian. I'm still convinced that Steps were robbed. I kicked up a fuss publicly because that award belonged to them for the phenomenon that they'd become. They deserved to receive it.

Later on in 1999, I was approached by LWT to expand on the Abba thing I'd done at the Brits and put together an hour-long peak time Abba spectacular. It was perfect timing, what with the popularity of Steps and the show *Mamma Mia* having opened in the West End, but you wouldn't believe how difficult it was to get acts to perform. Everyone I approached at first turned it down and I kept on getting told that it was 'old hat'. It wasn't old hat at all, rather it was populist and it seemed irresponsible that major record companies were betraying their shareholders by not encouraging a project that would go on to be a huge success and raise over a million pounds for charity. On the night of the show itself I went along with Rob Dickins, the BPI chairman, one of the only people who'd actually showed any belief in the project, and we both pointed out how it was one of the best things we'd ever been to, especially since there was hardly anyone there from the record industry. It was a good night out with real people enjoying themselves, but apparently that kind of populism isn't fashionable enough for the rest of the music industry. The fact that the accompanying album was such a huge hit shows just how out of touch much of the industry is with its public.

The experience of doing something for television after all those years on *The Hitman and Her* reminded me how much I love the medium. Indeed, in the future I can see myself being involved in it again in some capacity. I certainly think that while everyone talks about the revolution starting with the Internet, it's only going to work if it's incorporated into TV. The Internet's real strength as regards the pop industry will come when you can watch a track being performed on the telly, then click a button on the screen and order it. Television and the Internet combined seem to me like the most viable way forward.

One of the great things that came out of the Abba programme was that I got to work with Westlife on 'I Have A Dream', one of my favourite Abba songs and one that seemed perfectly suited to them. Louis Walsh, who manages Boyzone and co-manages Westlife, had offered me the chance to work with Westlife before they had even put a record out. I loved the story he told me about how he'd got them together by going up to guys he'd seen singing in karaoke bars and asking them if they wanted to be in a band. Whatever the story behind their formation, the first time I heard them, I knew they'd have a lot of Number Ones.

Karl, Mark and I worked on a couple of tracks for their debut album, but it was decided that, because we'd worked with the Backstreet Boys (who were seen as Westlife's competitors), it would be best for us to take a step back.

We got a chance to work on a single with them, though, when the Abba project came along. Simon Cowell, who'd signed them to BMG, told me that he wanted them to do 'I Have A Dream' because he'd just been to see *Mamma Mia* and had been inspired by the song. I made sure not to tell him that 'I Have A Dream' was the song I'd wanted to be involved in them doing all along.

The best thing about Westlife was that they sang like angels and it was obvious they were going to be huge. Somehow I knew that 1999 was going to be Steps' year and 2000 was going to be Westlife's, so I knew that I'd have my bases covered for the Millennium Number One. It was Westlife, as it happened, but I was pleased that I'd been involved in both of the artists.

That Westlife single was the one that kicked them into a whole new record-breaking dimension, but if I was in charge of Westlife now, I'd be concerned about what step they should take next. As far as I'm concerned, it's time for them to stop doing ballads and start finding a twist that will give them longevity, a challenge for their future that I wish I could have been involved in, especially since the boys in the band are such great guys. Brian is particularly entertaining and whenever he comes round to hang out, his impersonation of a Dublin karaoke singer gets funnier and funnier.

It was great to be involved in another wave of exciting pop, but it was all the better when I could finally get the court case settled.

In November 1999, the legal wranglings between Matt and Mike and me which had been dragging on for seven years finally came to court. Because I knew it was a case that I wasn't going to lose, I didn't feel any fear. If anything, it would finally let me get away from the past and start concentrating on the future.

Way back when I'd sold half of PWL Records to Warner, I had been sitting in the office one day when I got a solicitor's letter informing me that Matt and Mike were claiming that I had no right to sell their share and that they owned two-thirds of the company. It seemed such a ludicrous claim that I fell about laughing at the time and sent a cease-and-desist letter back to their solicitors. I really didn't take it seriously and it all went away for a while, then the letters started going back and forth again and I realised that they really meant it.

Their original claim was that I had given them a third each of the company, something that they weren't backing up with any sort of documents. Now, Mike is a highly intelligent man and he never lies. But in court his case revolved around a conversation that we'd allegedly had on the way back from the pub one night where I'd apparently promised Mike and Matt a third of the company each. I couldn't deny that we'd had a conversation, except that during that conversation I had only agreed that we split the *publishing* equally. I had no problem with that, because it cost me nothing and it would mean we could each hand something down to our children.

I'd invested an enormous amount of money in the company and I obviously wouldn't have just given it away.

As it happened, I'd kept every bit of paper for the last twenty years; every bill, every receipt, the whole lot. There were fourteen boxes full of evidence of how I'd paid all the bills from before I met Matt and Mike until the present day. I'd even paid a lot of their bills to help them, to the extent that I was actually losing money, whereas they were making 100 per cent of royalties. If we earned three pounds then we all had a pound each and if it cost me two pounds to get that three pounds then they *still* had a pound each. That was the way that the company worked and I never complained about it. My financial and personal commitment to those guys had been greater than anyone else had shown them in their lives, and I genuinely believed we were creating something special together. I didn't mind paying for everything, because I knew we could all be successful. I'd sold half the record company to Warner because I wanted to keep the people who worked for it in employment, but in hindsight maybe I would have been better just closing the whole thing down. We were generating so much money at the time that the debts would have been paid off in four months.

When the case finally came to court, it was obvious that Mike and Matt didn't have a leg to stand on. We'd all submitted affidavits that were like encyclopaedias and the judge had had to plough through them all, so right from the beginning I knew that, having read the evidence, he'd realise I was in the right.

I didn't feel any sort of emotion really when I saw Mike and Matt in court, although I did feel sorry for Matt by the end. The case had started on a Wednesday and Mike had capitulated on the Friday after court had finished, but because Matt was still officially in the witness box at the time, Mike couldn't legally talk to him until he had finished his testimony. Neither could we tell him that Mike had walked away and so we had to keep on questioning Matt on the Monday, with the case costing £45,000 a day.

The judge said on the Monday that there was no case to answer and even remarked on Mike's litiginousness. Mike and Matt lost, and had to pay massive costs in the end, all because of a claim they were never going to prove. I won the case, but the worst thing is that I have to look back at the time the three of us were working together, taking on the world, and I can't help knowing that they didn't believe in me like I believed in them. I will never deny their extraordinary talents, but I wish they had been more honest with me.

Now that the court case is out of the way, it feels like one chapter of my life is finally closed and I can move forward to the next stage. The new studios are finished and open in the building opposite our old ones and I feel like I can embark on the ten years that I think will mark the last decade of my career in pop music.

I'll be working on a third of the next Steps album, but that will be the end of my involvement with them. They, like all the bands who have gone before them, have decided it's time to move on. Their new direction will be different and it is up to them to find out on their own if it works for them. I just hope they continue to make good use of the unique appeal they have, and carry on playing to their considerable strengths. They put on tremendous stage shows and really come across as the audience's best mates, an audience that encompasses everybody from grandmothers to grandchildren.

This business has been very good to me and I've led a life that I could never have even dreamed about when I was growing up. Because of what I've done over the past thirty years, including my work with charities, I've met people from every walk of life and have travelled all over the world. My grandfather would have called me a liar if I told him that his grandson from Coventry had helped arrange Prince Philip's seventieth tribute birthday party for the Duke Of Edinburgh awards scheme, but it was something I did without thinking it was out of the ordinary. I knew Princess Diana through her work with Help A London Child and because she was a big Stock, Aitken and Waterman fan, we got on really well. When I meet royalty and lords and ladies in general, I find them fascinating to talk to just as people. I don't stand there doffing my cap to them, I find them genuinely interesting and love listening to their stories. For instance, my neighbour in

Daresbury is the Duke Of Westminster and I've been to his house for dinner on several occasions. One time I was there, Prince Charles was a fellow guest and he talked to me about his divorce from Diana. He knew he could tell me because he knew I wasn't going to sell the story to the papers. I'm actually more interested in talking to him about history or the countryside, and I find him a fascinating person to have conversations with.

I'm sure Prince Charles meets thousands of people and I've never presumed to think that I'm anything more than an acquaintance but, whenever I meet him, I'm reminded what a likeable man he is. A few years ago I was at a function at which he was the guest of honour. I'd met him a few weeks earlier, but I made sure I stood as far away from him as possible in the line of people he was shaking hands with because, knowing he meets so many people, I didn't want to go through the awkwardness of him not recognising me.

I'd entered some of my Koi carp in a competition in Japan a few months earlier and had actually won, which was almost unheard of for a westerner. The Emperor of Japan had been presenting the prizes and had taken great interest in a foreigner picking up a top prize. Coincidentally, Prince Charles had also been in Japan and had met the Emperor too so, when he saw me in the line of people, he came straight up to me, and the first thing he said was, 'The Emperor of Japan asked me to ask you something. How are your fish?' Prince Charles was passing on a message from the Emperor of Japan to Pete Waterman, a scruffy little kid from Coventry who loved pop music and trains and spent his life doing things that he knew he could do well.

As a child I knew I wasn't going to be a great footballer or a champion racing driver, so I ditched those dreams before they even started. I've spent my life fully believing that I can do anything if I set my mind to it, but the important thing is that the 'anything' is realistic. And my 'anything' has meant I've met kings, queens, princes and pop stars and been places and done things that most people can't even imagine.

People who say I've just been lucky have to remember that I've been 'lucky' time and time again. And the more I've learned, the 'luckier' I've got. But by being so single-minded about what I've done, I've also created one of the loneliest jobs imaginable for myself. And just about the only person I've ever seen experience that same degree of loneliness is Michael Levy, my old mentor at Magnet Records.

A few months before the last general election I got a phone call from one of the broadsheet newspapers about Michael Levy, with the journalist asking me what I thought of 'The man behind the Labour Party'. At first I thought it must be a different Michael Levy from the one I knew, but the journalist explained that it was indeed the Michael Levy I'd known for almost thirty years. I hadn't seen Michael in months, but after the article was published he rang me up and explained that ex-Labour leader John Smith had asked him to help organise the modernisation of the party and that he was going to concentrate on getting Tony Blair elected. He asked me to help out in the running of his company, while he took time out to focus on the election, which I was happy to do since Michael had been so good to me over the years. A week or so before the election itself he confessed that he had some doubts about whether Labour would win, but we talked about it all and I gave him advice about what I would do if I were him.

I'd met Tony Blair at the House of Commons a few weeks earlier and he'd come up to me and confessed to being a Stock, Aitken and Waterman fan, reeling off the names of his favourite songs, but I really didn't take much notice of the fact that there was an election. It was only when I woke up and put the TV on to find that Labour had won by a landslide that I thought about Michael's involvement and went up to see him in his North London offices.

I stood next to him as he watched Tony Blair on the television, and just for a moment Michael seemed the loneliest man in the world. Here was someone I'd known half my life who'd been heavily involved in getting Tony Blair elected and he was standing in a room miles away, watching all the glory from a distance. I'm sure he was congratulated later on (and he was later rewarded with a peerage, making him Lord Levy) but just for that moment, I saw him observing the revolution he'd been a part of creating, from the sidelines. I understood his loneliness, because it's the loneliness I've felt in the past, having made so many people successful and had to view it all from afar.

It may be a lonely business, but it's still something I couldn't live without. If I didn't have an outlet for creativity I think I'd just die. Which is why I still work eighteen hours a day and still believe that the greatest record ever made might be released next week. I still love music and that includes a broad spectrum from classical to rock bands like Travis and the Verve. And, of course, great pop records. I must be the only 53-year-old father who's never shocked by the music his young kids play.

Thirty years ago the record business was treated like a novelty side show full of pimps, prostitutes, gays and circus acts. Nowadays it's the second biggest industry in Britain and run by people with MBAs from Harvard. But how do you do a course in thirty years' experience? I've got that experience and that's why I'll always remain a maverick. Any youngster thinking about going into the music business now might believe, seeing the way that the industry is going, that the way to be successful is to sell your soul to marketing, but that's exactly the attitude that will kill the whole record business. If you want to be successful, you have to have respect for what has gone before, and in my opinion that means never forgetting the importance of making great records.

Over the past thirty years I've seen the 7-inch, the 12-inch, the cassette and the CD all come and go, so technologically it's not just been a case of men getting to the moon, but getting all the way to Mars. The bottom line is that we're still here making catchy little pop songs. We're still playing with the eight notes to get the kids to go out and spend their money on a record on a Saturday morning. And if I've got any kind of secret, it really is as simple as that.

A record label like Zomba has proved that there are kindred spirits out there. In four years it has gone from nothing to being the biggest record label in the world thanks to acts like Britney Spears, N Sync, Backstreet Boys and, of course, Steps. The dream is still possible and I for one will keep fighting the battle to keep the dream alive, letting people know that if they have regard for a few fundamental beliefs, they can do what I've done.

I will admit that it's harder than ever before to make a living in this business. You used to be able to buy equipment for fifteen grand and you got three years' use out of it. Nowadays you pay your fifteen grand and you only get three weeks' use, because technology is moving so fast. And whereas we're the exception in being able to make a record for Steps for £15,000, their videos cost £290,000. To keep up with it all and to be able to afford to compete, you have to ensure that you're consistently successful, and if you want to do that you have to always remember why you wanted to make records in the first place.

When I started, my ambition was to make the new Motown and to an extent I've achieved that, but I know I can still do more. The new studios are finished and I'm also thinking of setting up a studio in Paris, because I think there is going to be some great music coming out of France in the future. I'm looking at some new artists with lots of potential and in the years ahead I hope I can make something that's even more successful than what went before. I'm still as driven and I've learned from my mistakes, knowing that the only way is forward. I don't make excuses, I make hits.

That said, I think I'm going to be more selective in what I choose to work on over the next decade. I think I've earned the luxury of being able to pick and choose and I don't want to die over a mixing desk. I'd much rather die in my workshop making model railway engines.

When that day comes, and I get to the Pearly Gates and the guy who's standing there says, 'You've been a bastard', I won't be able to disagree. You see, if I regret anything, it's that I've hurt people along the way. I walked out on two young families, which caused many people pain. I also know that I've caused pain to people around me, but the people who matter will know that it has never been malicious. And I'm so proud to have four of the most sensible, smart, well-adjusted children you could imagine.

* * *

I always used to think that I wanted my gravestone to read, 'Here Lies Pete Waterman – He Had A Go'. Now I think it might just say, 'He Had A Bloody Good Go. *And He Won*'.

The next ten years start here and I know that I'll either fail magnificently or make the best records of my career. My apprenticeship is over. And I'm ready for anything.